Kenotic Ecclesiology

Kenotic Ecclesiology

Select Writings of Donald M. MacKinnon

John C. McDowell, Scott A. Kirkland, and
Ashley John Moyse, editors

Fortress Press
Minneapolis

KENOTIC ECCLESIOLOGY
Select Writings of Donald M. MacKinnon

Cover image: Medieval and Gothic Arch. Photo by Luca Daviddi. Used with permission granted by Thinkstock, item number 469711986

Cover design: Tory Hermann

Library of Congress Cataloging-in-Publication Data
Print ISBN: 978-1-4514-9628-4
eBook ISBN: 978-1-5064-1898-8

The paper used in this publication meets the minimum requirements of American National Standard for Information Sciences — Permanence of Paper for Printed Library Materials, ANSI Z329.48-1984.

Manufactured in the U.S.A.

This book was produced using Pressbooks.com, and PDF rendering was done by PrinceXML.

To the Reverend Dr. Fergus King

Contents

Foreword

Rowan Williams

Donald MacKinnon's reputation remains both powerful and controversial. In recent years, he has begun to receive some of the attention he deserves from younger researchers, and we have seen a more balanced and three-dimensional picture emerging—rather than what was earlier the conventional focus on his supposedly "near-Manichaean" view of tragedy (and on his undoubtedly manifold personal eccentricities). There have been detailed intellectual biographies, anthologies of his mature work, and dissertations on his very complex philosophical sensibility.

All this is most welcome. But perhaps one area that still has to be fully examined is his passionate engagement with the life and integrity of the church. One of the things he most abhorred was what he called "ecclesiological fundamentalism"—the mindset that happily relegated central Christian doctrines (notably the substantial divinity of Christ) to museum status while accepting the church's ritual and (in the broadest sense) political status quo. It was the ethos he identified—not always justly—in writers like the American New Testament scholar John Knox or his Cambridge colleague Dennis Nineham. For MacKinnon, this mixture of doctrinal indifferentism and practical ecclesial conservatism left the believer with no solid critical foundation: if traditional Catholic doctrine is true, we have something that makes it supremely and urgently worthwhile to engage with, and battle against, the church's manifold corruptions, so that the church will in turn be an effective critical presence in a corrupt and violent world. This was the impulse he recognized, in his younger days, in Karl Barth, and it was one of the things that made him so consistently uncomfortable a presence in the Church of England.

And of course this immediately relates to that deep concern not to soften or underplay the element of the tragic in human—including Christian—life. The church exists so that there may be that "life in abundance" promised by Jesus; yet the human world is such that the church itself may become an enemy of life in a number of ways—by collusion with tyranny, by promoting institutional dishonesty, by subtly reinforcing unaccountable and abusive power in its own ranks. MacKinnon speaks as someone who cannot live with the church as it historically is but cannot live outside the church as it theologically must be. The texts in this collection help us to see the roots in MacKinnon's early work of this inescapable and insoluble dilemma—what Charles Williams (well known to MacKinnon), writing about Evelyn Underhill's long struggle with whether or not to become a Roman Catholic, called living with the impossibility. The church is necessary, not as an aid to personal piety, but as the specific and given way in which the mystery of the incarnation is made visible; and so it is surrounded by all the ambivalence that incarnation involves in the life of Jesus himself, and all the further ambivalence that comes from ignorant, self-deluded human psyches.

To see MacKinnon whole is to see him as a "man of the church" in this typically paradoxical sense. His later collection of short pieces *The Stripping of the Altars* has an importance disproportionate to its length because of the centrality of these conflicts and impossibilities. It is not hard to imagine how MacKinnon might have seen the shadows recently cast on the name of George Bell—charges that there is now no way of fully investigating or substantiating, but which leave a deeply painful question—as reinforcing the point that being in the church is no guarantee that we shall not be in the company of the most conflicted moral agents, and that being in the church gives us some grace to look more honestly into our own conflicted and compromised souls, loving our crooked neighbor from our crooked heart, to paraphrase Auden.

These texts will be a very significant resource for all students of this utterly remarkable figure, but also a stimulus for thinking about how we do our theology of the church. Theologians like Ephraim Radner have written recently of the theological importance of the church's constant failure to be itself. MacKinnon would have understood and agreed that this is the reason for inhabiting the church more deeply, prayerfully, and critically, not for more doomed efforts to find the perfect community or the satisfyingly invisible church that will not hurt or compromise anyone. And if this is in many ways a hard saying, he would have reminded us of the maxim of St. John of the Cross that the disciple cannot claim exemption from what the Master's incarnate presence entails in terms both of uncontrollable cost and unimaginable transfiguration.

Editors' Acknowledgements

The collection marks a further step along the path to reissuing writing that continues to be both inspiring and provocative. We therefore wish to acknowledge the exemplary theological impact of Nicholas Lash and Rowan Williams, in both of whom we find an appealing sensibility that has attracted us to MacKinnon's work. To Fergus King, a biblical scholar of the highest order, we are indebted for his grace and encouragement in our attempts to continue to come to terms with MacKinnon's legacy. And we wish to thank Fortress Press for their interest in publishing this collection of MacKinnon's writings. We have been impressed with the energy, enthusiasm, and professionalism of those with whom we have worked in the publishing house. Finally, allow us to express our gratitude to those at our respective institutions, Trinity College Theological School at the University of Divinity and Vancouver School of Theology at the University of British Columbia, who have been supportive of this, and other projects.

Volume Introduction: Donald MacKinnon, Speaking Honestly to Ecclesial Power

John C. McDowell

> If we are interrogated by Christ across the centuries: 'Who do you say that I am?', in our answer it is our conceptions at once of the actuality of divine existence and of the possibilities of human that are brought to the bar of a questioning more devastating, more searching, and (must we not say?) more intellectually demanding than the Socratic. . . . One should not attempt to iron out the inconsistencies, but rather to see their presence as an invitation to more searching enquiry: finding in that presence evidence that the reality of Jesus defied any sort of easy, and indeed most sorts of comparatively painful, assimilation. This strangeness may be judged rooted in, and expressive of, the way in which he lives uniquely as the frontier of the familiar and the transcendent, the relative and the absolute, and by so standing, demands that our every conception of both alike be revised.[1]

A Fragmentary Style

Introducing the moral philosopher and philosophical theologian

1. D. M. MacKinnon, "Prolegomena to Christology," *Journal of Theological Studies* 33 (Apr. 1982): 154.

Donald Mackenzie MacKinnon (1913–1994) is not an easy business. Of course, those who are already familiar with the work of the Scottish Episcopalian from Oban in the Highlands will know this but regard it as a necessary difficulty. It is *necessary* for two main reasons. Firstly, despite the fact that he is arguably the most influential and important postwar British philosophical theologian, (although many would want to place T. F. Torrance in this category), he remains relatively unknown to theological scholarship outside of those who have in some way had connections with the Universities of Aberdeen and Cambridge, at which MacKinnon had occupied Chairs. Secondly, the intellectual labors of this former Cambridge Norris-Hulse Professor of Divinity are proving to be fruitful for a new generation of theologians (the three scholars involved in this project are examples of this) in a way that saves MacKinnon, at least for a little longer, from being relegated to the fleeting memory of a historical footnote in British intellectual life. What makes the introductory project difficult (and here the term is being used in a rather glib sense, especially with reference to a thinker so deeply immersed in refusing to evade the difficulty emerging from the intractable problems of the surd by offering premature resolutions) is that MacKinnon's work is so resistant to the quick summary, the pithy statement, or the reductive sound bite. The style of his writing is often allusive and therefore particularly demanding of his audience.

The difficulty for the reader is not, however, one of elusive and opaque purple prose, the kind of rhetorical obscurity that sometimes serves to mask intellectually tenuous and substantively vacuous work, or that makes academic writing into a rhetorical *cultus* solely for the initiated. In contrast, MacKinnon rarely hides behind the tortured phrase. He always asks questions of the quality of commitment to good argument, which refuse to conceal the weak and disordered behind bluff and assertion; his writing style is rather compellingly lucid instead. The difficulty is more one of being left behind by his fertile imagination and erudition. In his massive tour de force entitled *Theology and Social Theory*, John Milbank explains that secularity has "positioned" theology.[2] The immobile and rather lifeless metaphor of positioning works badly certainly in relation to MacKinnon's work, given the beautiful fluidity of his intellectual performance and the rich imagination that could skilfully float with seamless ease in "the borderlands of theology" between the Gospels, Plato, Shakespeare, high Attic drama, Leninism, Ernst Bloch, Arnold Schoenberg, Teilhard de Chardin, Hans Urs von Balthasar, Karl Barth, and P.T. Forsyth, to name but a few of the evident expressions of his erudition. This is not merely a somewhat old-fashioned, cultured don performing John Henry Newman's post-Humboldtian vision of what a university is good for. It is an express refusal to theologically curtail the hearing of God through a stingy gospel, a gospel that spells bad news for the makings of persons, that precludes them from the transformative action of the redemptive God. As Fergus Kerr notes, "In 1951 MacKinnon was lecturing on utilitarianism and Kant, citing the New Testament, Sophocles and Shakespeare, as well as Dostoyevsky, George Eliot and Joseph Conrad. . . . As he says somewhere, the moralist's 'theorizing is impoverished if he ignores the dimensions of human experience to which such writers admit him.'"[3] MacKinnon's dealings with a host of writers was frequently generous, and even when he critically pushed them to their limit, the argument was passionately conducted in and through a conversational wrestling that attempts to achieve as much aid in understanding his own mind as he could. This appreciation of the complexity of the theological task as a conversational task enables MacKinnon to positively judge the place of literature within theological and philosophical reflection as explorations of "living discourse."[4] Speaking of the moralist, for instance, MacKinnon argues that "his theorizing is impoverished if he ignores the dimensions of human experience to which such writers [as Tolstoy, Dostoyevsky,

2. John Milbank, *Theology and Social Theory: Beyond Secular Reason*, 2nd ed. (Malden, MA: Blackwell, 2006), 1.
3. Fergus Kerr, "Remembering Donald MacKinnon," *New Blackfriars* 85 (2004): 267.
4. MacKinnon, *The Problem of Metaphysics* (Cambridge: Cambridge University Press, 1974), 79. While he refers here to parables, his descriptions are applicable to his use of drama. A parallel between parables and drama is made when arguing that one can "receive what is offered to us as tragedy as parable." D. M. MacKinnon and G. W. H. Lampe, *The Resurrection: A Dialogue Arising from Broadcasts*, ed. William Purcell (London: A. R. Mowbray, 1966), 109.

George Eliot and Joseph Conrad] admit him."[5] Fiction's possibilities are no less "'true," and therefore theologically significant, for being fictive. According to Paul Ricoeur, for example, fiction "refigures time," and thus reaches beyond simple *mimesis* (imitation) to *poesis* (invention).[6] "It purposes change" by enabling a redirecting of our horizons for "reading" the world, expanding the capacity of language through the new reality of metaphor, suspending and redirecting literal description of actuality by performing the possibility of metaphor. So MacKinnon suggests, with reference to *Hamlet*, that

> It can hardly be denied that our understanding of such notions as responsibility, free-will, decision are enlarged, even transformed (or should be enlarged and transformed) by the dramatist's most subtle exploration of the Prince's personal history. And this enlargement the dramatist achieves not by the enunciation of some general principle, but by laying bare, in the subject of his hero, the deepest recesses of the human spirit, the half-acknowledged emotional overtones and undertones which belong to any processes of decision, and which can so easily be overlooked.[7]

Of course, Milbank's use of the spatial marker refers more specifically to the way modern theology adopted directions that had redirected its imagination as much as its energies. MacKinnon was, in contrast, fascinated by the specificities of the materials he was working with. In relation to the Christian faith, as will be explained below, his commitment to refusing to evade the demands of particularities was deeply rooted in a generative sense of responsibility to honesty and truthfulness.

In an introduction to another collection of MacKinnon's writings, it was mentioned that in this regard the very allusive style of MacKinnon's oeuvre is itself theologically revealing and suggestive.[8]

5. MacKinnon, *Borderlands of Theology and Other Essays*, ed. G. W. Roberts and D. E. Smucker (London: Lutterworth Press, 1968), 215.
6. Paul Ricoeur, *Time and Narrative*, trans. K. McLaughlin and D. Pellauer, vol. 2 (Chicago: University of Chicago Press, 1985), 27. *Poesis* is not here to be conceived as a *creatio ex nihilo*, but as always is ontologically charged and disclosing of what is the case in order to make and remake it. Being is not exhausted in *mimesis* or actuality, but more is always possible.
7. MacKinnon, *Borderlands*, 50.
8. John C. McDowell, introduction to *Philosophy and the Burden of Theological Honesty: A Donald MacKinnon Reader*, ed. John C. McDowell (London: T&T Clark, 2011).

Undoubtedly it expresses his personality, an eccentricity of which anecdotal oral materials are legend among those who met him. But for the editors of this present collection who were unable to meet him in person, there is something more theologically interesting and significant here than simply the strange quirks of a highly unconventional academic. They gesture towards being "stylistic expressions of MacKinnon's refusal to engage in providing simplistic systems . . . [or] to 'take the broad road' of easy solutions, premature resolutions, and trivialising abstraction from concreteness."[9]

While his fragmentary theological writing does not allow for a focused set of interests (his thinking was scattered and diffuse, un-Apollonian), it could be legitimately argued that one can detect a pervasive theological mood in his writings (while they may be scattered and unsystematic, they are not intellectually chaotic or Dionysian). That mood has been defined as "profoundly interrogative" by Kenneth Surin and others.[10] The essay style works well as a way of depicting the restless energy for the question, for the subversive moment of MacKinnon's theological imagination, his compellingly intense fascination with the particular, and his refusal to take the broad road of premature resolution, which is borne of a deep moral sense of responsibility towards the uncontrollable and incomprehensible. It is in this way, and only in this intrinsic pressure for a theological honesty rooted in a deep sense of moral responsibility, that Surin's assessment of MacKinnon's profound interrogative style makes sense:

> In theological matters, he refuses to take up substantive positions, and prefers instead to 'map' the ramifications of the espousal of such positions. This task is invariably undertaken with great subtlety and a deep respect for the complexities of the subject matter treated. The reader is always left with the impression that what matters for MacKinnon is precisely what is left unsaid, though, typically, this too is somehow indicated in his texts. A thinker who prefers to create an agenda (as opposed to dealing with one that has been pre-set), to articulate

9. Ibid., viii.
10. Kenneth Surin, "Donald MacKinnon," in *Christ, Ethics and Tragedy: Essays in Honour of Donald MacKinnon*, ed. Kenneth Surin (Cambridge: Cambridge University Press, 1989), ix. Cf. Kerr, 269.

problems (as opposed to resolving them), to use speech to register (rather than to subdue) the complexity of 'realia', is very likely to produce a body of work that demands further exploration and elaboration.[11]

The Honesty of the Theologian

Telling stories of God's ways with this world is always a hazardous enterprise in itself, risking what Nicholas Lash terms "bondage to . . . unacknowledged narrative[s]".[12] Precariousness and vulnerability, or living "an exposed life," are part of the price paid for being honest, MacKinnon argues, a necessary disease that refuge in tradition, Christian culture, or claims to a finality in metaphysical explanation tempers the sense and tranquilizes the pain of.[13]

It is a desire for honesty that results in his exposure of the dishonesty in theological work. So his little known 1966 paper, "Can a Theologian Be Honest?" indicates a deeply disturbing question lying at the heart of MacKinnon's churchmanship.[14] What he most personally struggles with is how to be true to his academic "calling," whose integrity is in "follow[ing] the argument whithersoever it leads," as one churched.[15] This particular paper certainly displays little explicit sense of responsibility to the struggle of knowing how to appreciate epistemic mediation and contextualization, and of being indebted to those contexts. For instance, a question has to be asked about the statement that the theologian is "particularly alert to the clerical bias which almost inevitably on occasion threatens objectivity of judgment."[16] Nevertheless, that questions of ecclesial contextualization were not too far from his mind at this time is suggested not only by the reflection on ecclesial practice provided in his other works of the period, but by his advice to church members on

11. Surin, ix.
12. Nicholas Lash, *Easter in Ordinary: Reflections on Human Experience and the Knowledge of God* (London: SCM, 1988), 144.
13. MacKinnon, *The Stripping of the Altars: The Gore Memorial Lecture Delivered on 5 November 1968 in Westminster Abbey, and Other Papers and Essays on Related Topics* (London: Collins, 1969), 34.
14. MacKinnon, "Can a Divinity Professor Be Honest?," *Cambridge Review* 89 (Nov. 12, 1966): 94–96.
15. MacKinnon, "Divinity Professor," 95.
16. Ibid., 94.

this question, and both are visible in the collection *The Stripping of the Altars*.[17]

If one was to press the sense implied by MacKinnon's reflections here one could say with Barth's *Church Dogmatics* IV.3 (hereafter cited in text as *CD*) and the fragments of the uncompleted IV.4 (and this suggests something important about Barth's own conception of the nature of limitations of the theological task) that falsehood, or lack of truthfulness and consequently also integrity, is subtler than any simple giving of a false impression—the externality that is lying. Falsehood, in this simple sense, is the mask worn to hide one's motives (expressible primarily in the active voice, the deliberate activity of a deceiving agent). Rather, lack of integrity constitutes a *being false*—the delusion of those themselves lied to. This sense of falsehood expresses the creation of one's being in untruthfulness (expressible primarily in the passive voice, of being made), the untruth that "possesses," shapes, and determines the particular motives, consciousness, and active deliberations one has and is involved in.[18] This sense of what is false is hidden from one's awareness as something gathered, learned, obtained, fallen into, a determinant of one's consciousness and presumed "natural" to its believer.[19]

What characterizes the politics of certain kinds of power-relations (propaganda, totalitarian coercion and manipulation, even certain apologetic strategies) through which these falsehoods are predominantly expressed is their incapacity for conversation, as Rowan Williams, a former student of MacKinnon, suggests.[20] One steps back from the risk of conversation into a position of (imagined) invulnerability by displaying the "control" over the real subject matter. Williams targets "the tyranny of a total perspective," that

17. MacKinnon, *Stripping of the Altars*. MacKinnon argues that theology "must always reflect the unacknowledged personal prejudices and the inherited moral assumptions of the theologian." *Borderlands*, 97.
18. Karl Barth, *The Christian Life: Church Dogmatics IV.4 Lecture Fragments*, trans. George W. Bromiley (Edinburgh: T&T Clark, 1981), 224f.
19. Terry Eagleton, *Ideology: An Introduction* (New York: Verso, 1991), 184.
20. Rowan Williams, *On Christian Theology* (Oxford: Blackwell, 2000), 3.

which subsumes all-knowing into a framework laying claims to comprehensiveness and finality.

This can make ideology sound more a matter of rationalization, of ideas imagined to be infallible, which consequently evade self-critical testing of their genetics, interests, and exclusions of the interests of others, than a matter of the very constitution of social subjects themselves. While suggesting something important about his own conception of the nature of limitations of the theological task, Barth's description of ideology is similarly ideas-oriented. He calls it "a distinctive numbness, hardening, and rigidity, and therefore an inertia in which he will cease to be a free spirit."[21] Herein, one's presuppositions achieve "not just a provisional and transitory but a permanent normativity, not just one that is relative but one that is absolute, not just one that is human but one that is quasi-divine." Simply, one no longer questions or learns from elsewhere since one's formulations have achieved a normative and definitively binding status. Barth bluntly asserts: one's "ideal becomes an idol," possessing and dictating. However, there is something ethically significant in Williams's and Barth's descriptions. So Barth continues: "What they [viz., ideologies] have to push systematically is their own excellence and usefulness, and by way of background they must show how utterly valueless and harmful their rivals and opponents are."

There are shades of *CD* I.1 in which Barth speaks in a more eschatologically nuanced way than does MacKinnon of theology as a "penultimate" discipline, "a work of critical revision and investigation of the Church's proclamation in view of the divine verdict," yielding all too human fallible and uncertain results.[22] As such, theology is necessarily fallible, fragile, broken, penultimate, decolorized by sin, and resistant to all conceptual foreclosures or "systematization."[23] Embracing this recognition of one's proper eschatological location will render to theology's broken words the proper service of a humble

21. Barth, *The Christian Life*, 224. Eagleton rightly warns, however, that one person's bondage and rigidity is another's freedom and open-mindedness. Eagleton, 4.
22. Barth, *Church Dogmatics*, 14 vols (Edinburgh: T&T Clark, 1956–75), *CD* I.1, 83.
23. See, e.g., Barth's *CD*, I.1, 83; I.2, 483; III.3, 294.

witness, and remind any *theologia gloriae* of its prematurity. In other words, theology cannot escape the risk of bondage to unacknowledged narratives. And yet an ethics that includes self-testing through doubt does not have to assent to the belief that all discourse is necessarily as ideologically regulated, and therefore as free as any other from the constraints of seeking the best forms of ideolo-clasm.

The form of "closure" proper to a concept of ideology needs to be carefully handled. The notion of fixing an otherwise inexhaustible process of signification around certain dominant signifiers with which the subject can identify, artificially arresting linguistic productivity into the "closure" of a sealed world of stability, is, Terry Eagleton contends, "a latently libertarian theory of the subject, which tends to 'demonize' the very act of semiotic closure and uncritically celebrate the euphoric release of the forces of linguistic production. . . . But [w]hether such closure is politically positive or negative depends on the discursive and ideological context."[24]

As mentioned above, precariousness and vulnerability, or living "an exposed life," are part of the price paid for being honest, MacKinnon argues. It is a sense of a necessary disease that takes refuge in tradition, Christian culture, or claims finality of metaphysical explanation and therein tempers the sense and tranquilizes the pain of the exposure.[25] Instead MacKinnon advocates a "deliberate cultivation of an interrogative . . . mentality," a way of being true that attends to the multiple complexities that resist neat resolutions and evacuate particularities of their concreteness in generalities, and to the substantial limitations involved in our knowing.[26] Certainly he does engage in certain speculative constructions and even reengages in a certain type of metaphysics. But these are carefully disciplined by a deeply challenging and discomforting interrogative style of doing theology in "the borderlands." This he otherwise names his "untidy

24. Eagleton, 197.
25. MacKinnon, *Stripping of the Altars*, 34.
26. MacKinnon, "Divinity Professor," 94. In a statement pregnant with implications for any theodicy project, MacKinnon describes an anxiety of "official Churches . . . always to secure apologetic victories' that therein constitutes a loss of integrity." Ibid., 95.

and inconclusive exploration," so that his assessment of R. G. Collingwood could almost have been a self-depiction: "In the end he raised more questions than he answered; but here certainly he reminds his readers of Socrates, who made his associates face the difficult truth of their own deep ignorance."[27]

This way of couching MacKinnon's work might suggest that his ongoing worth is as a negative theologian, as an iconoclast who casts a careful eye over the masking of idolatrous tendencies even in, with, and under the pretext of theological performance. In this vein, Surin depicts MacKinnon's work as "profoundly interrogative . . . *rather* than affirmative."[28] In his discussion of Arnold Schoenberg's *Moses und Aron*, MacKinnon contends for "an agnosticism which continually insists that where God is concerned, we may only confidently affirm that we do not know what we mean when we speak [or conceive] of him."[29] In this vein he speaks of the primacy of the apophatic, and suggests that "we continually swing between . . . anthropomorphism . . . and . . . agnosticism."[30] According to Williams, for example, "the theologian's job may be less the speaking of truth . . . than the patient diagnosis of untruths, and the reminding of the community where its attention begins."[31] However, firstly, this would be to do MacKinnon a disservice, and secondly it could lead to a perspective that would be a theological mistake in its own right.

To take the second suggestion first, the so-called negative way, if that be grounded in the event of unspeakably determining one's own subjectivity or in reaching the limits of human reason, can be construed as equally a reflection (albeit a negative reflection) of personal subjectivity of the God-imagist. Yet for MacKinnon, not any kind of theological silence will do, and his reflections conducted in apophatic mood enable a differentiation of silences. He is clear that the claim regarding God's incomprehensible otherness is not a projected

27. MacKinnon, *Borderlands*, 167, 174.
28. Surin, ix, (my emphasis).
29. MacKinnon, *Themes in Theology: The Three-Fold Cord. Essays in Philosophy, Politics and Theology* (Edinburgh: T&T Clark, 1987), 12.
30. Ibid.
31. Williams, *On Christian Theology*, 196.

note immanent to reason. Unlike a kind of "bowdlerized apophaticism" in which God "is but vaguely glimpsed through the clouds of metaphysical [and linguistic] distance,"[32] apophasis functions very much in terms of the theological purification or therapy of theological speech, and thus has a determining context, or set of conditions, that shape our ability to properly perform theological *askesis*. The negation of our "gods" is not a given of the projections of interiority, whether through the movement of "reason" or the even more nebulous "experience." After all, Williams recognizes, "searching for a single concealed agenda that can be unmasked by the triumphant modern interpreter is to remain . . . in thrall to crude models of power."[33] Critique is never an acontextual moment, but is rather an examination driven by an irreducibly particular history. As Denys Turner claims, "That we cannot form any 'concept' of God is due not to the divine vacuousness," or, we could add, of the predicable limitations of reason reached its boundary-position, "but, on the contrary, to the excessiveness of divine plenitude."[34] That means that the ways of negation and affirmation cannot be seen as sequential or independent. Thus when MacKinnon concludes with the comment that "it is therefore only within the context of the most rigorous discipline of silence that we dare think of such a reality [of divine love]," the kind of silence he has in mind already moves beyond the kind of empty silence Turner has complained of. MacKinnon has in this context already mentioned "the strange and perhaps hardly explored silence of Christ in his passion." Likewise, he argues elsewhere that Christian commitment requires one "to focus an always questioning faith in the figure of a man" since "here is the point at which faith must seek to mature itself by the effort of understanding."[35] This talk does not offer a release from the constraints of a proper sense of the divine

32. Robert W. Jenson, "The Hidden and Triune God," *International Journal of Systematic Theology* 2, no.1 (2000): 6.
33. Williams, *Wrestling with Angels: Conversations in Modern Theology*, ed. Mike Higton (London: SCM, 2007), xvi.
34. Denys Turner, "On Denying the Right God: Aquinas on Atheism and Idolatry," *Modern Theology* 20 (2004): 148.
35. MacKinnon, "Prolegomena to Christology," 156.

inexpressibility, but provides the very site of, or rule for, its learning. MacKinnon's reading, in other words, begins to implicitly contest the possibility of an indeterminate reading.

While his interrogative mood does tend to dominate matters, MacKinnon's pronounced sense of fascination with reflexivity is not of a piece with a deconstruction that self-ironisingly erases ethical responsibility. Christians may be encouraged to be the most suspicious people around for iconoclastic reasons, and yet they are also suspicious of any unreconstructed suspicion. The God we approach in this way too easily becomes "a God whose infinity renders him indifferent to the very distinction between good and evil on which Moses lays such weight."[36] This God becomes a morally absent space, an emptiness or void at the heart of human performance, a conceiving of divine difference that results in moral indifference. MacKinnon asks whether Moses must "not also accept for himself the discipline of silence, [and] even admit with a smile that the Aarons of this world help administer such discipline?"[37] The issue is not simply one of speech and silence, but one of the nature of human existence, and thus one of ontology with an ethical significance. "[W]hat sort of silence," he asks, "what sort of repudiation of every image best conveys the ultimacy not of judgement but of love?"[38] In fact, the abandonment of the God of the commandments results in moral disintegration, as the people negate the proper shape of their being-as-responsible-agents. MacKinnon's Aaron is in error not in the attempt at public communication, but, despite his pastoral concerns for servicing the religious needs of the people, his mistake is in yielding to the pressure of the demand for a visible and comprehensible form of the restoration of "the old gods."[39] Aaron's is "comforting, indulgent worship." MacKinnon does not suggest that the truth is not comforting (Matt 5:4), but his target is a disposition that preeminently requires comfort, since this is a self-

36. MacKinnon, *Themes in Theology* (1996), 17.
37. Ibid., 18.
38. Ibid., 19.
39. Ibid., 11. The phrase in Exod 32:6 "and rose up to play" suggests sexual orgiastic behaviour of the type important to Canaanite fertility cults.

indulgence that instrumentalizes the faith. Aaron's is a "conforming, consoling, too humanly human idol" that "trivializes the worship of God to the level of devotion to a godling who will condone every human weakness and indulgence."[40]

On the other hand, there are types of Christian faith that forget how to doubt, of Christian joy that are afraid to weep, of Christian preaching that are afraid to listen, but MacKinnon's deeply and uncomfortably interrogative theological mood resists such shortcuts to resurrection faith. Our time has not yet known the revealed glory of resurrection. MacKinnon's theology, then, can encourage schooling in new ways of resisting the paralyzing introspectiveness of a therapy culture by learning how to hope beyond any refusal to face the darkness of the cross or any pessimism that cannot see the cross in the light of the resurrection.

The first suggestion mentioned above gestures towards another note in MacKinnon's writing—even if it is sometimes offered only on the margins, at other times only as directive of his critical voice from well under the rhetorical surface, and on others even distinctly audibly subdued even if never domesticated. This note is MacKinnon's testimonial voice, a voice that "seeks to illuminate things as they are,"[41] a voice that attempts to offer guidance to understanding the infinite mysteriousness of the God whose ways are healing for creatures. That call to life takes its shape in and through the compelling witness to the depths of divine embodiment in the life of God's world. This is where the critical mood is in the business of servicing the celebratory, for disciplining Christian conviction against the spirits that are not responsibly reflective of the iconization of the Spirit of the divine.

If MacKinnon appears hesitant to allow full reign to the celebratory mood, to the urgency of confessional testimony, it is because he is struck by the antikenotic tendency to leap over the unstanched wound inflicted on the Christian imagination by the cross, the stubborn messiness of the tragic. Kerr argues that "For MacKinnon, the *locus*

40. Ibid., 18.
41. MacKinnon, *Explorations in Theology* (London: SCM, 1979), 9.

theologicus, the 'place' to begin and end Christian theology, was Gethsemane, the 'agony' in the garden."[42] Recognizing this is crucial, for it is not only this refusal of the dishonest slip into the glib and facile modes of the imagination that eminently attracts MacKinnon to von Balthasar, but it is from here that his self-reflexivity takes its rise. His interrogative theological disposition, or as in George Steiner's description of Kierkegaard, the prevention of "the frozen certitudes of the dogmatic, the inertia of the canonic," is irreducibly informed by the cross[43]—this necessitates a refusal to absent thought from the pressure of the surd. As Williams suggests, "The final control and measure and irritant in Christian speech remains the cross."[44] It is in this context that MacKinnon finds the dramatic imagination of tragic drama an eminently fruitful resource for the theological imagination.

The Tragic Gospel?

It is in refusal to capitulate to the self-indulgent temptations of imagining that the way one tells one's story is free from articulated falsehoods and that humble dialogue with other perspectives and disciplines begins. Barth's famous assertion concerning the possibility of hearing God in strange places conceptually belongs here[45]; it is a way of, as he later describes it, "eavesdropping on the world." Thus while alien categories are not brought in, theology of this sort is "willing to learn from non-theological sources something about the mechanisms of deceit and control in language."[46] Jürgen Moltmann's claim is that "Ideological and political criticism from outside can force theology and the church to reveal their true identity and no longer hide behind an alien mask drawn from history and the present time."[47] What one senses in MacKinnon, however, is the very fact that there is a certain

42. Kerr, 269.
43. George Steiner, introduction to *Fear and Trembling and the Book on Adler*, by Søren Kierkegaard, trans. Walter Lowrie (London: Random House, 1994), xi.
44. Rowan Williams, *Christ on Trial: How the Gospel Unsettles our Judgement* (Grand Rapids: Eerdmans, 2000), 3.
45. Barth, *CD* I.1, 60f.
46. Williams, *Christ on Trial*, 14.
47. Jürgen Moltmann, *The Crucified God: The Cross as the Foundation and Criticism of Christian Theology*, trans. R. A. Wilson and John Bowden (London: SCM, 1974), 3.

problem with sloppy talk of "outside"—there is no "outside" to grace other than sin, and sin pervades the church as well. Putting this into a little more practice, MacKinnon cites a broad range of dialogue partners: "A radical Christian should be among the first to insist that many existing religious beliefs, institutions and *performances* . . . are fair target not only for disciplined academic criticism but for the kind of merciless satire on TV and radio which has caused so much indignation among the *bien-pensants*"[48]

In other words, Christian theology, for the sake of its own health (hearing the world's judgment upon itself) and that of God's world (the environment of the now fallen-but-still-graced-creation), has to be in the business of conversing widely. "God," Williams declares, "is to be sought and listened for in all occasions."[49] This perspective, of course, requires qualification, since while one ought to be enabled to make reference to God differently, there are severe dangers, and thus one's address to God must heed and follow (albeit not slavishly) Jesus's address to God. What it is that serves to control the reading, as Barth suggests with his talk of the little lights of creation receiving their radiance through participation in the light, is what David Tracy calls "an interpretation of Christian fact."[50] And as is the case in MacKinnon's theological sensibility, a far more radical notion (and various forms of ideological and political criticism seem to have led him to this recognition) "is the crucified Christ himself," as Moltmann is surely right to argue.[51]

Characteristic of his theological alertness to the power systems operative in understanding is his attention to the multiple

48. MacKinnon, "Divinity Professor," 96.
49. Williams, *On Christian Theology*, 6f. Matthew C. Bagger's claim that "To rule out the possibility of self-deception, we must test our appreciation of our situation by at least opening ourselves to alternative appreciations" is unclear as to whether this is only a matter of a *principle* of honesty. "The Ethics of Belief: Descartes and the Augustianian Tradition," *Journal of Religion* 82 (2002): 223. In practice one can never consider all the options, would frequently have to act before even many of the options are considered, and would only be able to read the options in any other way than though one's own dispositions.
50. David Tracy, "The Foundations of Practical Theology," in *Practical Theology*, ed. Don S. Browning (San Francisco: Harper & Row, 1983), 62. To miss this is to not be able to converse at all. It would be to forget who one is in some neutral space where all can freely dialogue on an equal footing.
51. Moltmann, 2.

complexities and contingencies that resist neat resolutions and oppose the evacuation of particularities' concreteness in generalities, and to the substantial limitations involved in our knowing. Being attentive to the potential for discourse distortion by reference to all discourses' inescapable cultural embeddedness does not entail that one can ever know that one has wriggled free from the grip of distortion and illusion. But it is at least a good start to maintain discourse in constant self-interrogation—or better yet, to acknowledge self-interrogation as a constant travelling companion (a discomforting one at that) that reminds us not to prematurely halt our journeying, since this commencement talk may unwittingly suggest a philosophical foundation to our discourse or that this interrogatory mood can be left behind once the journey is underway.

What this version of interrogation, and its description by mobile metaphors ("journeying"), can do is register the sense in which, in an era when relations are describable in terms of market economics of exchange, MacKinnon's theologically regulated interrogation announces his particularity. The market, on the one hand, speaks of the consumer's situation (there are no world-transcendent reasons for who we are), and yet on the other implies a kind of Docetism (one can choose freely from competing options), as if one's culture plays no part in the process of self-determination. But yet if Michel de Certeau can insist that Christians must have a sense of their communities' boundaries so as to register the alterity of those experiences that are not Christian rather than to exclude, MacKinnon could remind that those boundaries are necessarily fluid and unstable,[52] necessarily so by the nature of the gospel itself. In other words, this interrogative mood is theologically located, and that, among many other things, it resists any suggestion of "absolute suspicion," which is logically like the proverbial snake devouring its own tale but cannot, more importantly, be hope inducing.

That this is so may be detected in a particular series of conversations

52. Frederick Christian Bauerschmidt, "Michel de Certeau (1925-1986): Introduction," in *The Postmodern God: A Theological Reader*, ed. Graham Ward (Oxford: Blackwell, 1997), 135–42.

that MacKinnon had regarding tragic drama. One of the theologically significant features suggested by MacKinnon's eclectic use of tragic dramas as enablers of more appropriate scriptural reasoning is the type of broad ranging conversation that is enacted and the potential for theological therapy that that can generate. Theological "integrity can be recovered . . . from any crass ideological bondage," Williams announces, to the extent that it can show itself "capable of conversation."[53] It is in MacKinnon's resistance to any premature foreclosure of the theological task—his refusal to capitulate to self-indulgent temptation to imagine that the way he tells the story is necessarily the way in which it has and always will be told, while rooted in seeking to better comprehend what is identified as the regulating primal story of faith—that his concrete and humble (but yet not uncritical) conversations with other perspectives and disciplines are shaped.

Sophocles and Shakespeare, or at least Shakespeare as author of *Hamlet* and *King Lear*, stand alongside the likes of Aristotle, Kant, von Balthasar, and Barth in MacKinnon's list of important educators and thinkers on the nature of human knowing and living. His concern, unlike Balthasar's worry about the banishment of the actor,[54] is more particularly that of what has been lost to theology by having uncritically followed Plato's exiling of the tragedians as presenters and explorers of "ultimate issues."[55] He expresses disappointment that religious people tend to speak and act as if there were no revelations concerning the human situation to be obtained from writers such as Sophocles and Shakespeare. These people then lack the courage to read the gospels in the light of tragedy (and indeed also to read God in a modified kenotic *theopaschian* sense), and ultimately anesthetize any sensitivity to the tragic by converting history into a dance of ideas, a process that MacKinnon detects in theodicies that unwarrantedly attempt to resolve the problem of evil through facile optimisms or

53. Williams, *On Christian Theology*, 4.
54. See, Hans Urs von Balthasar, *Theo-Drama: Theological Dramatic Theory: Volume 1: Prolegomena*, trans., Graham Harrison (San Francisco: Ignatius Press, 1988), 10.
55. MacKinnon, *Borderlands*, 50.

teleologies. Plato's repudiation was of a piece of his rejecting "the sense that from tragedy we continually renew our sense of the sheerly intractable in human life," a "flight from the tragic as an ultimate, irreducible form of representation of the relation of the transcendent to the familiar . . . a prolegomenon . . . to establish a world without ambiguity, a world from which the kind of darkness that Sophocles, for instance, had profoundly understood was expelled. For Plato it was demonstrably blasphemous to query the certainty of a 'happy ending.'"[56]

MacKinnon's perspective on the tragic is more complex and subtler than that of either Reinhold Niebuhr's or P. T. Forsyth's readings, controlled as they are by the *Divina Commedia*, although MacKinnon has publicized his appreciation of Forsyth.[57] If Forsyth neglects "the manifold issues raised by the surd element in the created universe," the same, if the brilliant intellectual George Steiner's comments are anything to go by, cannot be said of MacKinnon.[58] In a tribute, Steiner speaks of "Donald's genius" particularly in terms of his deep post-Auschwitz fascination "by pain." "Fascination" can, of course, take the form of something trivialising, an aloofness akin to a voyeurism that evades responsibility for witnessing to sites of healing and reconciliation. Steiner's description has a markedly different function, however, offering a MacKinnon, "haunted by the . . . mystery of the crucifixion" as he was, who even assumes "that there is incarnate evil." Steiner's reading is of a positive rendering of wickedness, as not only that which perversely distorts the conditions that shape human relations, but which is categorically manifest as a destructive reality in its own right. Consequently, for Steiner, "he [*viz.*, MacKinnon] had Kierkegaardian doubts about our ability to conceive of a resurrection.

56. MacKinnon, *Stripping of the Altars*, 38. Echoes of MacKinnon's disdain for the manner of the politically cultured post-Constantinian state church resound here. It is little wonder, then, that Nietzsche set up the Socratic man (referring primarily to the philosophical style of Socrates/Plato) as the antithesis of his own dramatic spirit, and that a tragic one, in the *Birth of Tragedy*.

57. MacKinnon, "Teleology and Redemption," in *Justice the True and Only Mercy: Essays on the Life and Theology of Peter Taylor Forsyth*, ed. T. A. Hart (Edinburgh: T&T Clark, 1995), 105–9; cf. P. T. Forsyth, *The Justification of God: Lectures for War-Time on a Christian Theodicy* (London: Latimer House, 1917), 76; cf. 30.

58. MacKinnon, "Teleology and Redemption," 109.

It was a fascination so vehement that it suggests, at least to me, a, certain Manichaean centre."[59] In the Scottish theologian, Steiner discovered a voice though which Auschwitz puts in question "the resurrection itself." And significantly this tribute comes from one who had earlier asserted that "Christianity is an anti-tragic vision of the world."[60]

Here, however, is the point at which the assessment of MacKinnon often takes an odd turn, seeing in him an indulgent delight in a theological agonism and therefore of providing a "tragic theology."[61] A Manichaean center! The question would be whether this relates to a darkened character temperament, a theological sensibility, or both, since they are not necessarily equivalent. In Steiner's hands, the terms provide a reference not to some theological masochism, but to MacKinnon's refusal to evade the painfully interrogative dimensions of the tragic.[62] A number of commentators have, however, followed the line of associating both, tackling MacKinnon's use of tragic drama in terms resonant with a Schopenhauerian representation of the texture of the real. Is there not something strange in appealing to the tragic for a faith that takes its rise from an eschatological event of resurrection, a faith that, according to Niebuhr, must transcend tragedy and swallow tears up in victory through the cross as "the resolution of tragedy"?[63] No little importance must be attached to MacKinnon's comment that the "belief that Jesus was raised from the dead . . . is a *prius* of my whole argument" on the resurrection.[64] Nevertheless, in a particularly telling comment on "theology beyond tragedy" rhetoric, he remarks that only "apologetic eagerness" can lead theologians "to suppose they had reached solutions [to the so-called 'problem of evil'], when in fact they had hardly begun effectively to articulate their problems."[65]

59. George Steiner, "Tribute to Donald MacKinnon," *Theology* 98 (1995): 2–9.
60. Steiner, *The Death of Tragedy* (Oxford: Oxford University Press, 1961), 331.
61. David Bentley Hart, *The Beauty of the Infinite: The Aesthetics of Christian Truth* (Grand Rapids, MI: Eerdmans, 2003), 380f. This term is used by Hart in conjunction with his reading of MacKinnon's use of the tragic.
62. Steiner, "Tribute to Donald MacKinnon," 6.
63. Reinhold Niebuhr, *Beyond Tragedy: Essays on the Christian Interpretation of History* (London: Nisbet, 1938), 155f.
64. MacKinnon, *Borderlands*, 95.

Instead, according to MacKinnon, there is an irreducibly tragic element in the Christian faith, as is particularly evidenced in the cross, and is not silenced by the gospels' "extremely complex and elusive resurrection narratives."[66] Indeed, he goes so far as to acclaim it as "of central importance."[67] So, if it appears that he is asking inappropriate questions that are alien in mood to Christianity's self-understanding, he provides several series of brief, impressionistically sweeping, but no less profound or disruptive, meditative readings of Jesus's ministry as illuminated by tragic drama: that, as far as the realization of Jesus's eschatological hopes for Israel were concerned, language of (a purposive) failure is not inappropriate; that Judas went his damnable way; that the open-ended horror of anti-Semitism is "the terrible sequel to the story of the cross"; that victories are not free from the tragic qualities of waste and destruction; and that moral planning exhibits a tragic texture. In that regard, it is the very texture of the gospels themselves that press to be read, in some sense, in terms of "the tragic" rather than some predefined tragedy that can be seen "as in an important sense paradigmatic for theology."[68]

In chastising MacKinnon for promoting a Manichaean ultimate dualism of forces, Brian Hebblethwaite misconceives the nature of MacKinnon's appeal to tragic drama, as does another commentator when claiming that the Scot uses the categories of "cross" and "tragic" purely interpretatively (which thereby reinforce social and political status quos by imagining the inevitability of evil).[69] MacKinnon's recognition of the existential relevance, and theological chastening, of tragedy is not the same as fatalism. He rejects as trivial and simplistic any talk of "the tragic sense of life" (a phrase used by de Unamuno), and disdains anything that sounds like a cult, or celebration, of

65. MacKinnon, *Problem of Metaphysics*, 124.
66. MacKinnon, *Explorations in Theology* 5 (London: SCM, 1979), 195.
67. MacKinnon, *Borderlands*, 94.
68. The claim is made by Giles Waller, "Freedom, Fate and Sin in Donald MacKinnon's Use of Tragedy," in *Christian Theology and Tragedy: Theologians, Tragic Literature and Tragic Theory*, ed. Kevin Taylor and Giles Waller (Farnham: Ashgate, 2011), 103.
69. Brian Hebblethwaite, "MacKinnon and the Problem of Evil," in *Christ, Ethics and Tragedy: Essays in Honour of Donald MacKinnon*, ed. Kenneth Surin (Cambridge: Cambridge University Press, 1989), 131–45; Philip West, "Christology as 'Ideology,'" *Theology* 88 (1985): 434.

powerlessness or despair; although he does acknowledge, but more as a warning against hubris, that "our greatest achievements bear within them the seeds of tragic disorder as well as the promise of a new heaven and a new earth."[70] What is more appropriate is "a certain reverent agnosticism."[71] Indeed, not read by critics is his tentative manner, his plea for caution in reading the gospels tragically.[72] MacKinnon's is no totalising form of "metaphysical solace . . . [that] assures the spectator that this is how things are . . . [and thus] the wisdom of resignation and tragic consent, a wisdom that is too prudent to rebel against what is fixed in the fabric of being."[73]

What he does with "tragic drama," that umbrella term for a complex and multifarious set of only very generally thematically overlapping plays with an "open-textured quality," is quite different from what is usually done in talk of "tragic existence."[74] MacKinnon was no Schopenhauer, and hence any appeal to the ambiguities in life, with sorrow and joy, tragic and comic, judgment and grace, and so on, is only a superficial response to his interrogative spirit. What lies beyond human competence, however, is to see where the lines of "tragedy" and "comedy" intersect. Hence, for MacKinnon, there is a real sense in which tragic dramas live beyond any simplistic optimism-pessimism dualism.

Tragic drama, then, for MacKinnon involves an indeterminacy of "endings" and a multiplicity and diversity of expression whose depth narratively testifies (like theology) to what cannot be transcribed into theory without loss of meaning, and resists undisciplined abstractions that fail to attend to the particularities and ambiguities of concrete

70. MacKinnon, *Explorations in Theology* 5, 4.
71. MacKinnon, *Borderlands*, 186.
72. MacKinnon, *Stripping of the Altars*, 51.
73. Hart, *Beauty of the Infinite*, 380, 386.
74. MacKinnon, *Stripping of the Altars*, 50. MacKinnon speaks, in Wittgensteinian mood, of being able to "at best . . . discern a family resemblance between" tragic dramas, provided one avoids "a blind indifference to the multiple complexity of those works which we class together as tragedies." *Stripping of the Altars*, 42. "It would be a grave mistake to generalize about tragedy as if there were an 'essence' of the tragic that we could extract and capture in a manageable formula. The world of Racine is very different from that of Shakespeare, and both alike from the worlds explored by the ancient Greek tragedians." *Explorations in Theology* 5, 186. Recognizing this is vital for understanding how MacKinnon uses the notion of the tragic in his theological work. Cf. Taylor and Waller, introduction to *Christian Theology and Tragedy*, 1ff.

conditions, events, and contexts.[75] It thereby disrupts easy coherence of thinking about the whole of reality, such as Steiner is prone to do in reflecting on the universe's ultimately tragic condition in an Archimedean perspective denied by his hermeneutics.[76] Instead of answering any philosophical or theological questions, tragic dramas raise them in acute fashion, particularly over any created securities of meaning and value. Tragedies teach, then, less by didactic or conceptual means, but, as Ricoeur argues, by "more closely resembling a conversion of the manner of looking" through destabilizing interrogation, which therein reorients action.[77] As such, in their ethical responsibility, they can particularly inform and critique Christian hope's mood, reminding it of its long Saturday in which the hope for Sunday's dawning regulates and shapes its fragile agency for the sake of the humanization and dedemonization of the world. This is not so much a case of a theology aware of its own blindness, as a theology that gropes its way in the dark, stumbling certainly, and yet fragilely enacting the drama of redemption.

Hebblethwaite overlooks the nature of MacKinnon's more hopeful mood, which nevertheless refuses eschatological prediction or premature talk of "ultimates." While Christian hope is reticent in the details of the shape of the future, it is nothing less than "a message of which our world is in direst need," a world which swings from various forms of facile optimism to debilitating despair.[78] MacKinnon cites Barth here as an example of this reminder of this joyous hope. The otherwise sympathetic David F. Ford appears not to notice this voice in MacKinnon, albeit a barely audible one, when he contrasts the latter's emphasis on the darkness inherent within tragedy with both

75. See Ricoeur, *The Symbolism of Evil* (New York: Harper & Row, 1967), 212.

76. See McDowell, "Silenus' Wisdom and the 'Crime of Being': The Problem of Hope in George Steiner's Tragic Vision," *Literature and Theology* 14 (2000): 385–411.

77. Ricoeur, *Oneself as Another*, trans. Kathleen Blamey (Chicago: University of Chicago Press, 1992), 245ff. Philip West's analysis appears to be shaped by a Cartesian-type disjunction of the aesthetic (body) and logic and ethics (mind), which MacKinnon undermines. This loss of the ethics and logic of aesthetics is concurrent with the loss of the ontological sense of beauty and its eventual reduction to a product to be consumed.

78. MacKinnon, *Borderlands*, 120.

Paul's "sorrowful yet always rejoicing," and Gardener's explication of the "redemptive" quality and joy in Shakespeare's *King Lear.*[79]

And yet Ford's contrast is pertinent to the effect that the celebratory mood, the note of excessively creative trinitarian overflow (albeit a creativity whose way endures a scaffold death), which reaches its crescendo in the enraptured celebration of human doxological response, is somewhat muted in MacKinnon. Nevertheless, MacKinnon himself reminds us of the theological complexity of a hope without the secure enclaves of even pious talk of triumph. Indeed, "all our hopes," MacKinnon articulated in 1946, "are set" in "the descent of Christ into the tomb."[80] MacKinnon's interrogative mood would entail theologians sensing the eschatological provision and hubristic brokenness of thought and action, culminating in the almost tortuous, tentative, and stammering bringing of Christ's reconciling action to speech and practice. The redeeming action of God in Christ has not yet been resolved, and of its successes within our times, there can be no guarantee.[81] But of one's responsibility to act in hope, there is the firmest call not to stand still.

Kenosis and Power

In the introduction to a volume of papers from the remarkably perceptive twentieth-century English Dominican theologian Herbert McCabe, the following claim is made: "McCabe held that there is a sense in which the philosophy of God leaves everything as it is since God makes no difference to anything: not because God is impotent, but because God is the reason why there is anything at all. Yet McCabe was very much concerned with the difference people can make. So he always had strong interests in moral philosophy."[82] It is in this

79. David F. Ford, "Tragedy and Atonement," in *Christ, Ethics and Tragedy: Essays in Honour of Donald MacKinnon*, ed. Kenneth Surin (Cambridge: Cambridge University Press, 1989), 123.
80. MacKinnon, "The Tomb Was Empty," *The Christian Newsletter* 258 (Apr. 17, 1946): 12. Language of "descending," however, suggests an activity whereas, as Alan E. Lewis reminds us, the grave was a void, a place of desolation and the inactivity of the dead. *Between Cross and Resurrection: A Theology of Holy Saturday* (Grand Rapids, MI: Eerdmans, 2001), 3; cf. Moltmann, 73.
81. Moltmann claims that the place of the cross in Christian faith "offers no recipe for success." Moltmann, 39.
82. Brian Davies, introduction to *God Still Matters*, by Herbert McCabe (London: Continuum, 2002), xiii.

interface between what might be called "theology proper" and the shaping of lives that MacKinnon's writings on ecclesial matters are formed. Church has to do with the people of God, and that has to do with a people being disciplined by the grace of the new life to living as those who are claimed by God. In Stanley Hauerwas's terms, these are "communities of character," although the character that MacKinnon detects is invariably one distorted by a failure to be renewed by the salvific action of God in Christ.[83] This is not a series of communities or the gathering of interest groups, or for the taste of sublimity, and so on. Instead, MacKinnon's work calls church back to the exposure of all human desire and its reordering in the ontological depth that the kenotic form of God in Christ expresses.

In MacKinnon's hands, then, kenōsis is not construed as an emptying out, a negation, or giving up, if by that there comes to be in the performance of Jesus Christ something other than the display (even if complexly hidden) of God's grace. MacKinnon is familiar with the different understandings provided by the metaphysical rendering of the term. He considers this form of the language deeply theologically inappropriate and indeed perversely tamed by the approach that characterizes the dominant German kenotic tradition of the late nineteenth century associated with Tübingen and Giessen. Considerably more aid is provided by the likes of P. T. Forsyth, H. R. Mackintosh, and Hans Urs von Balthasar, for instance, from whom MacKinnon learns that the form of self-emptying that God takes in the incarnate event is not a theological moment, as such, that can be locked away from its necessary disciplining of the Christian imagination and its resultant performance. Consequently, the concept of kenōsis, being bound up with the passion of the Son of God, operates as an uncompromising measure of the adequacy of any and all attempts to witness to the God of Jesus Christ. "The Cross reveals the final secret of the relation of man and God," MacKinnon claims in a paper on "Revelation and Social Justice." "Apart from the darkness of

83. See Stanley Hauerwas, A *Community of Character: Toward a Constructive Christian Social Ethic* (South Bend, IN: University of Notre Dame Press, 1991).

Golgotha, we know neither what we do, nor what we are. Its bitterness, its pain, its sheer questionability are the condition without which we are neither bound to God nor to ourselves."[84] Kenōsis, then, operates not as a Christological category as such but one of theological ontology, refusing to hide what is meant by "God" from the self-donating, self-limiting perils and pain of a life that is confessed to be the incarnation of Triune God's own Logos, the paradigmatic act of God, a historical performance that is the very *Anknüpfungspunkt* between the substance of the Godhead and God's creatures.[85] MacKinnon argues in a paper on Donald Baillie, "In Christ God is revealed as submitting himself to the very substance of human life, in its inexorable finitude, in its precarious ambiguity, in its movement to despair."[86] Accordingly, what is meant by God and the qualities predicated of God, such as omnipotence, are transformed. The political consequences of such an account of theological discipline are pronounced. The Henrician envisaging of divine potency is subverted in favor of understanding the truth of power itself to demand keeping company with the Crucified. It is his life that shapes what is meant not only by divine power, but its proper reflection in human performance. "The theological reading of the history of the Church is inevitably a *theologia crucis*."[87] MacKinnon flips the sense around and reveals one of the disturbing ethical performances that exhibits keeping company elsewhere, with Pilate, therein deconstructing one of the most common qualities cited as a Christian virtue, obedience. MacKinnon reveals the dark side in a paper reflecting on the work of Oliver Chase Quick:

> The fourth evangelist has seemingly some sympathy with Pilate's unwillingness to risk Tiberius' displeasure; the first three evangelists seem to agree in acquitting the centurion who supervised the execution of the three condemned men of doing more than carrying out an inevitable duty involved in his military office. . . . Yet crucifixion was an obscene

84. MacKinnon, *Burden of Theological Honesty*, 159.
85. See MacKinnon, introduction to *Engagement with God*, by Hans Urs von Balthasar, ed. E. L. Mascall, trans. J. Halliburton (London: SPCK, 1975), 1–16.
86. MacKinnon, "Reflections on Donald Baillie's Treatment of the Atonement," in *Christ, Church, and Society: Essays on John Baillie and Donald Baillie*, ed. D. Fergusson (Edinburgh: T&T Clark, 1993), 115–21.
87. MacKinnon, *Burden of Theological Honesty*, 149.

> and horrible business, and although such an attitude may properly be regarded as self-indulgent anachronism, members of a society which has learned to regard the 'defence of superior orders' offered by many defendants at Nuremberg in 1945-6 and the years that followed, as at best an excuse that may sometimes be allowed partially to diminish the culpability of the man who has obeyed nefarious orders, find it psychologically impossible to dismiss as impersonal executants of a grisly judicial procedure those who would supervise such torture as matter of routine. Obedience as such is not a virtue.[88]

Passionately refusing to temper the scandalously radical demands of such a kenotic vision, MacKinnon uncompromisingly continues by admitting that "only an obstinate flight from the deep imposition of a Christological discipline on their theological thinking has enabled people to see it otherwise." It is precisely such a flight, in evasion of the path that follows Christ's role in the temptation narratives, that MacKinnon perceives as being evidenced in the performance of the church, the body that is theologically characterised as the "the place wherein the scandal of the Cross is forever actual."[89] Consideration of Christian origins in relation to the question of the temporal location of identity has, in significant ways, to be traced back to a very particular dark night. "On the night he was betrayed," begins Paul's liturgical remembrance. As MacKinnon observes, "in time there has been accomplished not simply the eternalization of a particular biography but the constitution of that biography as the way for the insertion of all human circumstance into the tapestry of the eternal."[90] While his ecclesiastical critique takes assorted forms in his various talks and writings, MacKinnon is often particularly attached to what descriptive possibilities are made available through the image of another night. It is here, in what he broadly names "Constantinianism," that the church is portrayed being led into further betrayal in a way that has reshaped and plagued its ongoing history, self-understanding, and enacted witness. The story is a familiar one and needs little detailed recounting here: A Damascene, road-like experience only now located on the eve

88. MacKinnon, 'Oliver Chase Quick as a Theologian', *Theology* 96 (1993), 101–17, 104–5.
89. MacKinnon, *Burden of Theological Honesty*, 159.
90. MacKinnon, "Prolegomena to Christology," 160.

of battle. Prayer is offered to the mighty Lord who brings victory. However the accuracy of the two witnesses, Lactantius and Eusebius, remains questionable. Very soon after the climatic imperial confrontation near Rome, there was clamor for depicting the victor at Milvian Bridge as God's politician, the "revelation of the hand of God in history," the agent in God's eschatological reordering of the world.[91] Schismatic Christian groups even early in his reign appealed to Constantine's imperial judgment for favor in their particular ecclesial conflict, and the Emperor's involvement took his role as *pontifex maximus* considerably further than was traditional.

Rather sweepingly, MacKinnon declares that "Constantine's so-called conversion in all its consequences . . . [is] arguably the greatest single disaster in the history of the Christian Church."[92] His particular concern lies less with worries over Constantine's temperament or even with his religious motivations for professing conversion and Christian commitment. While these questions have indeed long exercised the scholarly imagination, the more interesting theological matter has to do with the nature of the reordering of Christian identity that comes in with what is frequently broadly referred to as the "Constantinian settlement." The recognition of the lack of historical specificity is important here, since while the category of "Constantinianism" is historically imprecise, it functions well as a figural delineation of tendencies for understanding and the practice of power, and their transformative impact on Christian identification.

The issues, then, are deeper and more theologically significant than the matter of the intensity of Constantine's religious affiliations. Of course, one must recognize that the nature of the issues of power, authority, and their abuse common to critiques of Constantinianism are usually not so much the pressures of current conditions, which have considerably more to do with the very intensification of the presentness of momentary temporality itself—the secularization and so-called privatization of religious commitment, and the forms of

91. Gillian R. Evans, introduction to *The City of God*, by Augustine of Hippo, trans. Henry Bettenson (London: Penguin Classics, 2003), xiv.
92. MacKinnon, *Themes in Theology*, 142.

spiritual interest that have developed over the past four decades or so are largely consumerist in spirit, fluid or liquid in substance. Nonetheless, the way MacKinnon redevelops the politically charged critical category of Constantinianism is with regard to the failure to exist in a countercultural witness. The "Constantinian Church," he declares, is "the Church whose status is guaranteed and which allows the manner of that guarantee (i.e., the State) . . . to invade the substance of her life."[93] This, he maintains, is the church requiring the legitimating existence of state establishment.

In a broad parallel, one of the criticisms of the Barmen Declaration has been that it delegitimizes the German Church's struggle for a flourishing German nation in favor of the accommodationist succumbing to the Confessing Church's concern for the churches' own survival. At root, this remains every bit as qualitatively self-aggrandizing and as agonistic a sensibility as the seemingly different German Christian Movement in certain crucial ways. In other words, it is an ecclesial performance not grounded in the sheer precariousness of Christ's own existence. The church, MacKinnon argues, has "necessarily to live *an exposed life*; it is to be stripped of the kind of security that tradition, whether ecclesiological or institutional, easily bestows."[94] Fear of death and its attendant desire for self-securing are the theological order of the day here, so that the resistant action takes the form of an unfaithfulness to the gospel by opposing the enemy who would imperil this existence. It was Lactantius, sounding like an American exceptionalist, who wrote that the enemies of the imperial family are the enemies of God. If it is in God that Lactantius trusts, then the supplementary confession is: "and in his earthly political representative, the Emperor."[95] Paul Valley, therefore, complains that "since the Emperor Constantine had placed the institutions of Rome at the service of Christianity, and vice versa, the church, despite the lifestyle of its itinerant founder, had almost always intuitively taken

93. MacKinnon, *The Stripping of the Altars* (London: Fontana, 1969), 25.
94. MacKinnon, *Stripping of the Altars*, 34.
95. Lactantius, "The Divine Institutes," in *The Ante-Nicene Fathers* vol. 7, ed. Alexander Roberts and James Donaldson, 2nd ed. (Peabody, MA: Hendricksons, 1995), 10.

the side of authority and the rich."[96] In this regard, the theological imagination would do well to reflect on matters of the political in the context of developing a theologically well-ordered hermeneutics of God's time for providential action for the flourishing of the creature, and therefore provide a theologically informed perspective on how judgments are made about governance and service and the proper end they are ordered towards. It is God who delegitimizes these false construals of power, power that mitigates the realization of good relations. And God does not do this as the Being of the Other who stands as competitively related to all that is not God, lording it over beings in servitude as a self-aggrandizing power. As MacKinnon complains in his critique of the practice of a certain kind of power practiced by a triumphalist church, "the Christian God [has been] endowed imaginatively with the attributes of a human Caesar."[97] The image the church embodies is the image of "a transcendent Caesar" rather than the disruptive image of God embodied in the "vulnerable Nazarene."[98]

> From Christ there issues a continually repeated question, and his Church is his authentic servant only in so far as it allows that interrogation to continue. It is always easier to escape its remorseless probing: to take refuge in the security of a sharply defined orthodoxy, or to blur the riddling quality of its disturbing challenge by conformity to the standards of the age.[99]

Conclusion

According to McCabe, "the norms of traditional morality, like those of grammar, are never stable, and never quite adequate to deal with new forms of human behaviour. So we need some way of determining what is a growth in our understanding and what is merely a decay, what, in

96. Paul Valley, introduction to *The New Politics: Catholic Social Teaching for the Twenty-First Century* (London: SCM, 1998), 4.
97. MacKinnon, *Burden of Theological Honesty*, 266.
98. Ibid.
99. Ibid., 264. "In order to maintain a social advantage, it is often necessary to tell the truth about God in false ways, because the 'really real,' that is, the gospel truth about God in revolutionary, subversive, and disruptive." Walter Brueggemann, *Truth-Telling as Subversive Obedience*, ed. K. C. Hanson (Eugene, OR: Cascade, 2011), 75.

the case of grammar, is a new and linguistic form, and what is mere slovenliness."[100] That means that "rules" are never simply a given, even if we want to maintain that it is only as we can make sense of things through sensitivity to continuities and convergences that we can be freed from the tyranny of the individuated self thrown continually upon their own constructive potentialities for self-disposal. Suffering, then, is not a problem to be solved, nor endured, if talk of endurance is not very carefully qualified. Rather, it is to be acted against as that which God in the Son resisted the temptations to take an easier path.[101] And this is all done without being able to make any grand claims about what the end of the story looks like; Jesus Christ, Barth observes in *CD*, IV.3, is still on his way with us, and of his asking questions of us there is no end. Faith in the Crucified, MacKinnon argues, cannot have set for it any "limits or frontiers to the forms of that interrogation."[102]

> Jesus, in the reality of his self-giving, in the mystery of God's self-giving in him, in his movement from Galilee to Jerusalem to Galilee, in his life, death, and resurrection, remains the only valid *raison d'être* of his Church. . . . But we crave security: we flee from the reality of crucifixion-resurrection, impatient of the indirection of Christ's resurrection, wishing that he had come down from the Cross that so we might have believed by a faith finally corrupted by its object's betrayal of his mission. . . . [Instead] it is to Jesus, author and finisher of our faith, that we must look and look again.[103]

John C. McDowell
University of Newcastle, NSW
February 2016

100. McCabe, *The Good Life: Ethics and the Pursuit of Happiness* (London: Continuum, 2005), 4.
101. MacKinnon, in this mood, would be able to broadly agree with Sobrino's complaint that those who stand within the Enlightenment tradition tend to interpret suffering and disorder as a "crises of meaning" by which they seek to explain and accommodate alienating experiences within preconceived model of reality, whereas this search is a luxury denied to those who can barely hold to existence itself that is a "crisis of reality." Their question is less with how to understand evil than with how to withstand it, to overcome suffering or at least mitigate its destructive effects. Jon Sobrino, *The Church and the Poor* (London: SCM, 1985), 17.
102. MacKinnon, *Explorations in Theology 5*, 28.
103. MacKinnon, *Burden of Theological Honesty*, 274f.

Part 1: Signposts

Part 1 Introduction: The Terrible Occasion and Particular Paradox of the Gospel

Ashley John Moyse

The 1940 Signposts series, for which the following two texts of part 1 were written, offered its readers twelve small books released monthly that intended to illuminate the vital questions of human life, answerable by way of Thomist philosophy and of the Anglo-Catholic theology representative of the series contributors. Rather, as the publisher's note reads in the front matter of each volume, this series is one "dealing with the relevance of the Christian Faith to the contemporary crisis of civilisation."[1] Although intended to provide such answers as part of the series, MacKinnon's particular contributions, some have declared, failed to have any historical effect

1. See, for example, the front matter from the inaugural volume: J. V. L. Casserley, *The Fate of Modern Culture*, Signposts 1 (Westminster: Dacre Press, 1940), 4.

upon the culture.[2] Even though this might be the case,[3] it is not due to the potent significance of MacKinnon's claims.

The texts following must continue to be read, as the argument is as vital to recognizing the failure of humanity to acknowledge our hope rightly now as it was then. That is, the apologetic importance of MacKinnon's Signposts might help us to proclaim rightly the world we are taught to see by (and with) Jesus Christ, the Lord of the world, whom we have hung to a tree. Accordingly, MacKinnon's two contributions to the series might be thought to revolve about the following thesis aimed at those, including the church, enamoured by and complicit in the modern cultural milieu and its preoccupation with the promise of progress and human achievement: Apart from Jesus Christ, we cannot know who it is we are (and before whom we are gathered). With the coming of Christ, however, we can know in his *illic et tunc* as well as in his *hic et nunc* that we are sinners reconciled to God, Father, Son, and Holy Spirit. More appropriately to the two texts, we come to distress of "that terrible tale of Christ's coming and rejection"[4] as with the paradox of the church (the gathering by Christ of those who have crucified him), which "is only resolved when we have grasped . . . the primacy of the divine initiative."[5]

Although the thesis of MacKinnon's Signposts contributions may be as such, his two texts sit as the second and seventh in the series after J. V. L. Casserley's *The Fate of Modern Culture*, which labors to diagnose the pathology of the modern world, argued to have abandoned

2. See Richard Roberts, "Theological rhetoric and moral passion in the light of MacKinnon's Barth" in *Christ, Ethics and Tragedy: Essays in honour of Donald MacKinnon*, ed. Kenneth Surin (Cambridge: Cambridge University Press, 1989), 3.

3. The challenge to reading MacKinnon is to work through his fertile imagination and erudition, as John C. McDowell introduced, while remaining open to the challenges presented. Indeed, his writing is not overtly technical or opaque. Rather, his writing, and these volumes specifically, offers an incriminating challenge to its readers that might preclude a settled reading and a reasoned acceptance of the claims argued. This might be why it has failed, among the many, to find its voice in the church and culture.

4. D. M. MacKinnon, "God the Living and the True," in *Kenotic Ecclesiology* (Minneapolis: Fortress, 2016), 45; Originally published as *God the Living and the True* (Westminster: Dacre Press, 1940). Hereafter, cited in text as GLT.

5. D. M. MacKinnon, "The Church of God," in *Kenotic Ecclesiology* (Minneapolis: Fortress, 2016), 112; Originally published as *The Church of God* (London: Dacre Press, 1940). Hereafter, cited in text as COG.

metaphysics for epistemology, and, specifically, epistemology as power. That is, the failures of modern philosophy and the victories of modern science have reinforced a recession from metaphysics (from those fundamental questions of being) while emphasizing the merits of the mechanics of knowing, thereby turning *knowing* towards positivist and pragmatic ends—"towards its culmination in the Kingdom of Man"[6]—rather than the vital aspect of human being and becoming.[7] Moreover, the pursuit of knowing as a means to further means, as a means for acquiring power to overcome nature, highlights the mechanisms of a technocracy that Casserley laments as the malady of modern scientific discourse, which cannot discover that remarkable beauty that will save the world. Rather, if left to exhaust itself again (and again) between the tensions of human sin and destiny, the fate of modern culture groomed by "confused thought and invalid aspiration" is a reciprocal rebellion collapsing into an abyss of "shapeless ruin"[8]—bewildered, disillusioned, and despairing. However, for Casserely, as with his series colleague, such ruin can only be avoided by a belief in the riches of religious and intellectual orthodoxy (viz. "belief in God, belief in man, and belief in reason"[9]).

There is a general continuity with Casserley in MacKinnon's work—even though MacKinnon makes little mention of his argument or rhetorical construction. The critical assessment of the modern culture (including that of the Church of England[10]), preoccupied with an intellectual history wrought by idealism, pragmatism, and positivism, looms large in MacKinnon's two volumes. That is to say, as with Casserley, who has labored to elaborate the modern mind and its religion, which is "powerless either to challenge, humble, or guide the world [because] it tends to confirm at every point the baseless modern notion that 'we are the people' and that 'wisdom was born

6. Casserley, *Modern Culture*, 76.
7. Ibid., 9–14, 49–61.
8. Ibid., 76, 111.
9. Ibid.; See also pp. 41–42.
10. MacKinnon, GLT, 47; MacKinnon has elsewhere grieved the collapse of the church, which has "shown a distressing tendency to reflect, rather than redeem, the standards of secular society." MacKinnon, "The Task of the Christendom Group in Time of War," *Christendom* 9 (1939): 141.

with us,'"[11] MacKinnon has sought to show that we can only come to know of ourselves as we give ourselves unto death,[12] while resisting, under the authority of the church, the "tug of the world."[13] Unto death, therefore, we are gathered to bear witness to Jesus Christ, who, by the event of his life, death, and resurrection, constitutes our being (and hope) while authorizing, albeit paradoxically, our participation as his mystical body, the church, proclaiming the achievement of his work.[14]

This position in tow with Casserley, however, follows the trajectory set out in 1922 by Charles Gore and his fellows in the Christendom Group. That is to say, as Timothy Connor has noted, MacKinnon's thesis, from which his two volumes follow, adheres to and expounds upon Gore's description of the program taken up by the group—the church is the body of Christ, visible as "his organ and instrumental for action in the world.[15] Yet, for MacKinnon, what we see embodied before our eyes is both irruptive and disturbing—the interrogative particularity of Christ, who is most distressing.

Nevertheless, as introduced above, MacKinnon leads his reader to consider that our distress brought by Christ's incarnation and crucifixion impels us to see that the "tragedy of our situation is that God can speak no other language to us, and that is the language we find it hardest to understand. For that sets over against human achievement divine failure. It is not a transvaluation, but an inversion of human failure."[16] It may be such as this that prompts MacKinnon to declare in his introduction to *God the Living and the True*, "We do well to remember how terrible a book the New Testament is."[17] Moreover, MacKinnon includes in his first volume a discussion of the church,

11. Casserley, *Modern Culture*, 102–3.
12. MacKinnon, GLT, 88.
13. MacKinnon, COG, 136; Timothy Connor reminds his reader accordingly, for MacKinnon, "the authority of the church directs us continually to that centre point where in the Eucharistic oblation we are thrust back on the perfect obedience of Christ displayed in his cross." Timothy G. Connor, *Kenotic Trajectory of the Church in Donald MacKinnon's Theology: From Galilee to Jerusalem to Galilee* (London: T&T Clark, 2011), 63.
14. MacKinnon, COG, 105, 109–10.
15. Connor, *Kenotic Trajectory of the Church*, 49n21. For the complete introduction, see Charles Gore, introduction to *The Return of Christendom*, by a Group of Churchmen (London: Forgotten Books, 2013), xv–xx.
16. MacKinnon, GLT, 60.
17. Ibid., 45.

which serves, in some ways, as a prelude to his work in *Church of God* (i.e., those who once gathered in a great betrayal at the cross are now gathered, paradoxically, to become, as the mystical body of Christ, "the extension of that irruptive and disruptive activity that was [the incarnation]"[18]).

The New Testament (NT) is terrible for MacKinnon, as it compels us to admit, at once, the futility of "human life and achievement," which is also the "occasion of God's mightiest act."[19] Accordingly, as advertised in the journal *Theology*, that principal claim of the series, as an exercise of theological speech, is to serve as "a signpost warning *Homo sapiens* of the precipice that lies ahead and directing him back to the high road of human fulfilment."[20] The precipice is marked by the hubris of humanity, who attend to the exercise of achievement and of solitary, self-sufficient rationality over against God's self-givenness. Yet we are not forsaken. Rather the precipice is where God gives of himself and "becomes the object not of intellectual scrutiny but of contempt and rejection."[21] And in the NT, where we are reminded of our contempt and rejection of God, condemning Christ to a criminal's death with a cacophony a murderous cheers, we also discover God's agency, descending to the depths of death such that we might ascend to the fullness of life in resurrection: "Man is brought face to face with God, not through his effort, but through his failure. That is the paradox that lies at the very heart of the New Testament—indeed, of the whole Biblical theology."[22] In this, the terribleness of the NT directs our gaze towards the unique event of incarnation—"apart from the coming of Christ, [therefore] we can never know ourselves."[23] That is,

18. Ibid., 67–88.
19. Ibid., 45.
20. *Theology*, 40 (1940): ii; See also "New Tracts for the Times," *The Tablet* (Mar. 1940): 12.
21. MacKinnon, GLT, 74.
22. Ibid., 81.
23. Ibid., 59. André Muller has also written of this theme in MacKinnon's GLT, stating: "The crisis of modernity is only intelligible, MacKinnon is claiming, in the light of the cross, and in that light, such a crisis is revealed as the crisis of humanity before God. The 'tragedy of our predicament' is that we cannot see our predicament 'apart from being brought first to an admission of the historic intersection of history and meta-history in the cross. Only through the grace of God can we come to see that we are sinners; and that perception is contingent upon our being brought face to face with his revelation' [GLT, 64]. It is to the exigencies of this 'journey to the court-room of Golgotha' that 'all our philosophising must, for the time being, be subordinate' [GLT, 64],

as Nicholas Lash has so eloquently stated, our ruin can only be avoided (viz., our fulfillment known) as we are taught to see that reconciliation "springs—according to the Christian story—from what we count as failure, for it is through blood spilt in rejection of love's invitation that, and in spite of which, love's promised peace is made." Lash continues, quoting MacKinnon, "Beyond illusion, and the noise of war, we . . . need to see God as he is. But, 'When we so see him, we are at first shocked that his face is marred above the sons of men. But as he confronts us, we are enabled to see of what stuff we ourselves are. Then no longer does it surprise us that there is no beauty that *we* should *desire him*'."[24]

As our gaze, therefore, is reoriented by the one who stands before our eyes (in the mystery of his body and by his spirit), we do not come to know of ourselves after the direction offered by general principles, the occasion to garner knowledge by way of a theoretical *a priori*, or the achievement of a self-sufficient will. Rather, as we learn from MacKinnon's *Church of God*, we come only to know of ourselves, and of each other, as we are brought to see within the *corpus mysticum*, the church, that city of God, where "grace continually struggles with nature."[25] That is, where GLT was written to emphasize the event of God's own self-giving, which illumines the very nature of God's being, thereby delimiting our speech about it, COG was written so as to make intelligible that particular, albeit paradoxical city of God that gathers around (and is gathered by) God the Living and the True. Rather, as with GLT, COG aims to locate the way towards understanding both God and humanity from within the particularity and passion of Christ, which disciplines our own ideas of the church, a transcendent society not to be achieved by the promise of human intellect, ingenuity, and industry (or by way of a "Christian rationalism"[26]), but inaugurated, impelled, and intelligible by way of Jesus Christ, who alone is the

and it is in this court-room that our religious, intellectual, and political endeavours are brought to judgment." Muller, *Donald MacKinnon: The True Service of the Particular, 1913-1959* (PhD thesis, University of Otago, 2010), 169.

24. Nicholas Lash, *The Beginning and End of Religion* (Cambridge: Cambridge University Press, 1996), 47. See the original quotation MacKinnon, GLT, 66.
25. MacKinnon, COG, 92.
26. MacKinnon, COG, 122–28.

question and the answer to the disciples' query, "Lord to whom shall we go? Thou hast the words of eternal life."[27] That the Word became flesh, for MacKinnon, is the concrete and particular occasion of revelation that cannot be reduced to ordered form, as other objects of modern inquiry have been reduced. Rather, the concrete and particular occasion of revelation, who is Jesus Christ, conforms us—conforming our understanding of the nature and work of the church and of ourselves.[28] Therefore, we do not come to see the world rightly as we apply abstract categories and principles and ideologies upon that which we observe, as though each object, including God as it were, is waiting to be discovered by some exercise of intellectual assent and achievement. Yet MacKinnon further has shown such an exercise, initially developed in Casserley's series introduction, to be impotent and left to the abyss of nihilism and unreason (of ruin). Instead, we come to see the world rightly as we consider and are transformed by Golgotha—as MacKinnon maintains, one cannot see the world the same again once one admits (viz. acknowledges the disruption and redemption brought by) the terrible entry of God into it.[29]

In summary, MacKinnon's Signposts illuminate the gospel of Jesus Christ. That is, these two brief volumes labor to express the tension between the summons and judgment of God, which became known in the death and resurrection of Christ. It is a tension that challenges modern sentimentality to the self-sufficiency of human reason and the techniques sought to placate such summoning and judgment. It is a tension that expounds upon the ontology of the church, which is summoned to be the subject of divine action in and for the world, and therefore vulnerable to the hate of those for whom the church bears

27. John 6:68; See also, MacKinnon, COG, 91. Accordingly, Muller argues the themes taken up by MacKinnon in COG are not to be understood as "fundamental shifts of direction, but as intensifications, and to some extent, clarifications and adjustments, of lines of thought already present in GLT." Muller, *MacKinnon: The True Service*, 177.

28. As I hear it, this rings of a similar tone to Karl Barth, who, responding to a question regarding which is the 'right tradition [church]', states, "Insofar as a church has Jesus Christ it has God the Truth. Churches participate in the Truth, but the Truth is only Jesus Christ. Jesus Christ interprets Himself in the Church. [Jesus Christ] churches us; we cannot be our own churches. . . . What we have in our hands is relative, but we are in the [body] of the eternal Truth of God." Karl Barth, *Table Talks*, ed. John D. Godsey (Richmond: John Knox Press, 1962), 97.

29. MacKinnon, GLT, 62–68.

witness. Yet, in their stead, the church, which is the mystical body of Christ, is also the object of divine judgment and mercy—crucified unto death for the resurrection to life.

Therefore, the interrogation performed in the following two texts, which attends to the interruptive event of Christ, is one that labors to disturb the human with the transformative power of grace. In this, MacKinnon directs his reader towards the interrogation of humanity brought by Christ, himself. Thus, MacKinnon's *theologia crucis,* extending across these two texts, instructs the reader to acknowledge the event of Christ as that one event of judgement and grace that is both terrible and conciliating. They petition us, again and again, to attend not to the exercise of human will preoccupied with our own hubris, which is sinful, futile, and ruinous (to the milieu of this world, which is insignificant in itself), but to the unity of the church (to the reality of God's own self-giving and gathering), which is a unity of those marshalled by and before Christ, who calls us towards death and resurrection.

Ashley John Moyse
Vancouver School of Theology
December 2015

God the Living and True

Donald M. MacKinnon

Preface

This work claims to be no more than an introduction to the study of the subject with which it deals. It seeks to exhibit some characteristic emphases of Christian theology, and to suggest some of the consequences involved in admitting it to be an autonomous science. If it stimulates further thought concerning the fundamental problems it raises, it will have served its purpose.

I should like to thank many friends with whom I have discussed these matters for the light they have thrown on them. But specially I must acknowledge my debt to the Rev. T. F. Torrance of New College, Edinburgh, to the Rev. Fr. Gervase Mathew, OP, of Blackfriars, Oxford, and to my pupils, Mr. R. J. Cumming, of Harvard University, US, and New College, Oxford, and Miss A. H. M. Cree, of the Oxford Society of Home Students. My colleague here, the Rev. J. D. M. Stuart, has read part of the book in manuscript, and the Rev. Dr. F. L. Cross the whole in proof; it has, I know, benefited from their comments.

D. M. M., *Keble College, Oxford*, January 1940

Introduction

The first volume of this series[1] indicated the power of human reason to establish not only the existence of God, but also the possibility, though not the fact, of divine revelation; in other words, it outlined the scope and justified the task of what is known as natural theology.[2]

In the present book, the omission of any discussion of natural theology is intentional. This is not to be taken as implying a denial of either its validity or its importance. Indeed, the author's own professional interests incline him, if anything, to overemphasize the importance of metaphysics for divinity. But this book is concerned primarily with the character of God, Creator and Redeemer, as he is presented in the Christian gospel.

Behind all that is here written lies the conviction that natural reason can establish the existence of God, and that the so-called "cosmological proof"[3] is demonstrably valid. But the exhibition of its validity would involve a treatment of highly technical problems in analytic and speculative philosophy that are not precisely relevant to the theme of this book.

What the present writer has attempted to do is to present the God who is the subject of the Christian gospel. And that God is not primarily the object of a speculative quest. Though in all ages there are Greeks who "would see Jesus," it is not always to such that the burden of that revelation, of which he was the bearer, is made most plain. Often, indeed, the mood in which speculation is conducted effectively precludes any response to the challenge of the Son of God.

In the Catholic scheme, "faith is not contrary to reason." That we grant readily enough, but when we have granted it, we have but said

1. See J. V. L. Casserley, *The Fate of Modern Culture*, Signposts 1 (Westminster: Dacre Press, 1940); The present volume, the second in the series, was published originally as D. M. MacKinnon, *God the Living and the True*, Signposts, ed. J. V. L. Casserley and E. L. Mascall, no. 2 (Westminster: Dacre Press, 1940).
2. As opposed to theology that is based upon the data of revelation.
3. i.e., the metaphysical argument from effects to causes and so to God as the First and Uncaused Cause. For the distinction between contingent and necessary being and for the argument from the fact of the world's existence to the necessity of God's existence, see Casserley, *Fate of Modern Culture*, chap. 1 (15–32).

the first word. We do less than justice to the subtlety and exactitude of the characteristically Catholic appreciation of man's condition if we use that phrase to suggest that the task of faith is always mainly one of supplementation. Grace does not simply perfect nature; rather, its fruit is the restoration of a nature often so wounded that we can only say of it that there is no wholeness in it.

We are not to suppose that the relationship of faith and reason can simply be defined as the supplementation and fulfillment of the latter by the former. Rather, here as always, grace is the necessary safeguard of the naturalness of nature. Apart from faith, reason finds it impossible to remain true to itself.

We are today living at a moment in history in which perhaps the most terrible and alarming fact that confronts us is the triumph of the forces of nihilism and unreason around us and within. Against these forces, the rationalism of our immediate forbears is powerless. For the uprising of such forces is beyond the compass of its understanding. It cannot comprehend, and therefore it can point to no road whereby man can come again to himself.

In this impotence of reason in the face of unreason, we see revealed the bankruptcy of the former, as such rationalists understood it. We are made conscious, almost against our will, of the inadequacy of the concept of man's rational nature, in terms of which our fathers had been thinking. Their appreciation of man's capacities was based on a false estimate of both his inner constitution and his place in the scheme of things, and indeed of that whole scheme of things in which he was placed.

Now, it is through the gift of faith that we assent to those truths that are beyond the scope of natural reason, and it is in and through that assent that we safeguard our understanding of all our natural capacities. For us today, the way back to a proper estimate of man's nature, and of the character of his rational faculty, may well lie through a previous recovery of supernatural faith.

Quem Deus vult salvare, prius dementat. Thus a modern Dominican writer,[4] who is a loyal champion of the rationalism of St. Thomas

Aquinas, describes at least one aspect of God's dealings with his people. The present writer would venture a gloss on that sentence as follows: whom God wills to save, he first drives mad. Salvation is the fruit of grace, and its primary content is forgiveness of sin and the attainment of the vision of God in the fellowship of his saints. But, though those goods are supernatural, their fruit is revealed in the healing of the disabled natural life of man. In that natural life, the proper functioning of reason plays a highly important part. Now, if that is so, what conclusion can we draw but the following? To achieve a proper estimation of our rationality, we must first know the mercy of God in redemption. The acknowledgment of the reality of that mercy may involve us in what we can perhaps ourselves only account as madness. Are we therefore to say that the road back to a proper appreciation of our reason lies through a confession of our present derangement?

That thus and thus alone can we pass to such an appreciation is the message of the gospel. For the gospel speaks of life that is won through death. At its heart is a universal proposition that omits nothing from the scope of its reference, "Then were *all* dead."[5] In this book, we are concerned with the character of the dementia that leads to salvation, and with the manner in which God induces it.

Much will be said of the impact upon history of what we call "meta-history," and perhaps a comment here and now on the precise significance of these words will not be out of place. The narrative of the Gospels is historical in form. It describes events which were the objects of perception. In no sense are the Gospels metaphysical treatises (this is true even of the Gospel of St. John). Yet the character of their central Figure, and the nature of his achievement, is incapable of description in language that completely eschews the metaphysical. The question of who he is can only be answered in terms that refer to the place whence he came.

Such language is of necessity metaphysical in character. If he is the eternal Son of the Father, there is a sense in which we must say that

4. Fr. Victor White, OP, "Kierkegaard's Journals," *Blackfriars* 20, no. 236 (Nov. 1939): 797–810.
5. 2 Cor 5:14.

he has no history. For God, who is the Lord of history, is in himself not subject of change. The use of temporal categories with reference to him is invalidated by his eternity. He is beyond history. If, therefore, we are right to say that Christ is God incarnate, then in him we must admit that meta-history has invaded the historical series. If as the Eternal Word of God he has no history, none the less as Jesus of Nazareth, the tale of his life and death may be told to children.

We are concerned in this book with God, the highest theme of all theology. To the Christian, God is made known first and foremost in the life, death, and resurrection of Jesus of Nazareth. Therefore, a book that is concerned with the All Highest will inevitably find itself compelled to spend much time on the exposition of that terrible tale of Christ's coming and rejection. We do well to remember how terrible a book is the New Testament. But if first it bids us admit the sinfulness and (therefore) the frustration of human life and achievement, it also recalls us to a remembrance that this very wickedness is the occasion of God's mightiest act. *O felix culpa, quae talem ac tantum meruit habere redemptorem!* That remembrance alone is the ground of our hope.

We are not wise to belittle the greatness of the intellectual achievement of Christian theology. To some readers of this book it may seem that the author has surrendered himself to the contemporary mood of anti-rationalism. Evidence of this will be adduced against him from the chapters that follow, and not least from his preoccupations and omissions.

But a great gulf divides the rationalism, whose bankruptcy this book assumes, from the classical Christian tradition. Not the least difference is in respect of the limitations, that the former derides, and the latter willingly admits. We need do no more than take two representatives of scholastic theology at its profoundest, the late Père Gardeil, OP, and the Abbé M.T.-L. Penido, to recognize its steadfast combination of rationalism in method with respect for the incapacity of human reason unaided to scan the interior mysteries of the Godhead. The indictment of "Barthianism" is one in face of which the author believes he can honestly plead, "Not guilty."

But he has throughout written under a profound sense of constraint. There is a respect in which the Christian thinker is circumscribed, in which those who reject the Christian name are not. There is indeed that in the Christian message which does seem a harsh challenge to our recent habitudes of thought. The "givenness" of the gospel is an uneasy bedfellow with any philosophical idealism that would detect the character of the real in the operations of the human intelligence.

This book is occupied first and foremost with stressing all that is involved in that givenness. For in the opinion of the author it is precisely that to which we must recall ourselves. We are not concerned to sit in judgment on that gospel. For he who is the burden of its message is himself our Judge. The weakness of a great deal of modern theology is its refusal to recognize its very relativity, as an independent science, to the admission of divine revelation. If theology does indeed consist in the application of reason to the understanding of the truths of revelation, then, before reason can operate, the reality of that revelation must be admitted. We have got to face the fact that the revelation of Almighty God may indeed fail to cohere with many of our most cherished beliefs. If this is so, we dare not first suppose that we have failed to gauge the import of his word before we have ourselves challenged the assumptions that it seems to contradict.

If this is irrationalism, the author is glad to plead guilty to the accusation. But he would ask the reader to define clearly the irrationalism of which he is guilty. He does not deny the validity of natural theology. All that he is concerned to stress is the primacy for the Christian of revelation, and of the fact that such is the character of the relation of nature and grace that the recovery of an adequate appreciation of the character of the human reason may be contingent on the acquisition of the theological virtue of supernatural faith.

This essay is not concerned primarily with the doctrine of the Trinity. Rather, the author would suggest, the doctrine is implied by its whole direction. Before all else, it is concerned with the character of theology in itself; *theologia*—the science of the things of God. That there is such a science in the Christian view is contingent upon the act of God. It is that contingency which this book is concerned to explicate. And the author would contend that the explication itself testifies to the rational character of theological investigation.

If we are concerned more with the relations of God and man than with God in himself, that itself is not to be wondered at when our background is that of a theology of revelation. For God is revealed first and foremost in his mighty acts of power. Frequent reference is made in the following pages to the "demonic" element in human life. It is an element with which we are all too familiar today, but we are sometimes tragically unaware of the demons to whom we are ourselves subject. The demonic is the natural denaturalized. Often this denaturalization takes the shape of bestowing an almost supernatural significance on what is a natural good. That is certainly the characteristic attitude of the frustrated, and it is to such phenomena that attention is being called by those who in sociological commentary speak of the demonic element in human affairs. When we talk of God's mighty acts of power, we are talking precisely of his achievement in overcoming that which is demonic in the human situation.

It is to the acclamation of *Christus Victor* that the Christian society must today call men out of a world that is incapable of resolving its own frustrations. The character of that victory is a paradox. Its trophy is a scaffold. Yet, that there is the power of God unto salvation, the empty tomb attests.

The church itself today is under judgment. For though it is the very body of Christ, its members have no small responsibility for the predicament in which our world is bound. The dialectic of life and death, of grace and nature, goes on within it. If its members are to respond, in this hour of unutterable spiritual, moral, and physical catastrophe, to the exigencies of the situation, it must be with a clear vision of their end and of their origin. It is with that vision that this book is concerned, and if its uniqueness and transcendence seem stressed to a degree that involves the author in paradox and inhumanity, he would remind his reader that in his thinking too that universal dialectic must exhibit itself.

For, to him as to others, in respect of that natural order, whose disintegration is the dominant fact of our time, it is easier to say: *Gratia contra naturam*, than: Grace perfects nature. Yet, though the restoration of the natural is itself the work of supernature, the natural is not denied, only "crucified with him that it may also be glorified together with him."

Chapter 1: The Paradox of Revelation

There can be no way from man to God unless there has been first set in the wilderness a way from God to man.

That sentence formulates perhaps more aptly than any other the first emphasis of the Christian dogma of the redemption. It is a confession of failure, the very possibility of which presupposes that that failure has first been remedied by the gracious act of the transcendent God.

For the Christian, the revelation of God is at the same time the exposition of the predicament of man. We see in the Gospels the Son of God publicly executed. We read his superscription, and we see it in our own language. For some of us are Jews, some are Greeks, some are Romans. We make boast of our piety. Our devotion then becomes the tongue in which we can best express our own individual contempt of God. Or we are learned men, maybe. Then our philosophizing will furnish us with the terms in which we can best suggest our estimation of our Creator. Or perhaps we set store by some historic cultural or political achievement. Such achievements are at least in part, if not entirely, marred by the perfection of their understanding of man's actual state. We do well to remember that in Latin, as well as in Hebrew and in Greek, the title was written.

And that crucifixion in the Biblical narrative is set before us preeminently as the supreme act of God in history and as the final revelation of his glory to man.

Any exposition of the Christian doctrine of God must point first to the cross. For Christians, theology is, and must be, a *theologia crucis*, a theology of the cross. Our concern in this book is with the point of view characteristic of Christian theology. For if a theology may be said to possess such a point of view, it will be most surely manifest in its doctrine of God.

It was the purpose of the first volume of this series to set out a diagnosis of the contemporary intellectual and cultural predicament of human society. It will be the aim of this second volume to exhibit the very significance of that predicament. I have said that Christian theology is a *theologia crucis*. For it reveals God as the hero of the story of his own rejection. And clearly such a God is not easily accepted by man. For to accept him, man must first learn to see his cultural achievement as it is, to set no store by the multiplicity of his spiritual exercises, and to acknowledge both the finitude and positive unreliability of his intelligence. And he must go farther if he is to plumb the full irony of that superscription, which was God's so tragically shrewd comment on human achievement. He must see that his very futility ministers to the glory of God, and is, as it were, an instrument whereby his purposes are accomplished.

Christianity is not simply a religion. True, within the framework of the life that the Christian lives, an important place is occupied by worship, and by acts that betray unquestionable similarities to the practices of historical religions. But the Christian gospel is first and foremost an affirmation that thus and thus is God, and that thus and thus has he done. We may reject this gospel. It is open to us to do so, and any believer may, at some future date, be convinced that its affirmations are false. To some extent, however, he would understand what was involved in that act of rejection. When first Christ came forth and proclaimed the imminence of the kingdom of God, he urged on those to whom he spoke the duty of repentance. The word he used, to judge from the Greek, signified far more than a mere contrition, with avowal of amendment of life. *Metanoia* (for this is the Greek, which our English Authorized Version translates "repentance") connotes an alteration of one's entire outlook on the world. It is frankly catastrophic in its suggestion.

We know, of course, that though Christ came to his own, his own would not receive him. They would not undertake that *metanoia* which he demanded. Rather, in their conceit, they hung him upon a tree.

When, therefore, men reject Christ, we are not wise to see in their rejection merely a decision to absent themselves from divine worship, or even to revise in certain aspects their adherence to a code of conduct that stands in some relation or other of dependence upon the Christian sanction. Rather we must see a conscious or unconscious refusal to undertake that *metanoia*, without which no man can enter the kingdom of God. For, though the powers of that kingdom, as it were, invaded the historical series in the person of Christ at one time and in one place, they are nonetheless always operative in judgment and mercy. Their verdict on our apostasy must ever be negative, but the "'No" of rejection is transformed into the "'Yes" of acceptance through the cross of Christ. We are face to face with God the Living and the True. That is our situation, and often our lives are intelligible only in terms of an unconscious desire to escape from the recognition of its implications. There is Christ, there you and I, and we are face to face with him. We are the prisoners of the strong one, but there without the prison yard is one, who in his weakness is stronger than he. Had he not come, we had not had sin. But now that he is at the gate, we are called by him, and our whole situation is transformed by that invitation.

We can say "No." Around us, furnishing the center of our natural life, is an elaborate social structure that is the fruit of human apostasy. We are its prisoners more intimately than we know. We are stung to the quick of our pride when the proclamation of the good news of God the Living and the True first pierces our deafness. Only, perhaps, when we have said "Yes" to him and "No" to ourselves, can we discern the character of the situation in which we are imprisoned and the strength of the forces that urge us to say rather "Yes" to ourselves and "No" to him.

In what follows, I shall attempt to scrutinize these forces, to estimate their power and to characterize their achievement. My interpretation of their significance is definitely an essay in theology—that is to say, I am seeking to present them as they are exhibited in the light of a divine revelation. I shall start with religion, for, as the Fourth Evangelist so surely saw,[6] the greatest and most insidious danger that confronts the Christian claim is the transformation of the faith of Christ into a religion.

1. Is this a paradox? There is indeed a sense in which religion is a specifically human exercise. It is an *Ascensus ad Deum*. Man seeks to cross the wilderness himself without waiting for the Moses that is sent to guide him. God is, as it were, an object of his particular desires. It is as the satisfaction of some specifically human longing that the religious quest is undertaken. The God of the New Testament is the subject of the tale that is there told. When we say that God is the subject of the tale, we are simply repeating in other language what is the very heart of the New Testament message. God is the seeker; we are those who are sought by him. We do well in our circumstances to emphasize to how great an extent our knowledge of him depends upon his quest for us. Nor must we forget that when he finds us, we may not ourselves find then precisely what we were seeking before. The Jews sought for Messiah, but yet failed to discern him in the just one whom they surrendered to Pilate.

In that liberal culture, which we all inherit to a greater or less degree, religion is an adventure of the privileged few. Certainly no estimate of the natural achievement of man would be complete that did not devote some space to the consideration of his religious aspirations—indeed, of his spiritual achievement. That man is in a measure a religious animal is a fact of scientific observation that cannot be gainsaid. Again, that there have been spiritual geniuses, in whom that natural religiousness has been developed to an unprecedented degree, is also true. We cannot deny that their lives furnish us with an enormously interesting subject of study, nor that the attempt to establish some factor, common to all their individual attitudes, is a profitable exercise in the scientific study of man.

But, when all is said and done, in our culture religion is, as often as not, a subject of academic interest alone. It is remote from the life of

6. See the Eucharistic teaching of John 6.

the marketplace. For one thing, its cultivation takes time and demands a certain freedom from the economic struggle. It is, in a very true sense, the "flight of the alone to the alone." The incommunicability of its object, which is as often as not its distinctive characteristic, renders the exercise of little practical relevance save to the individual devotee.

Or else perhaps we find an envy of the state of mind of the religious person. He is regarded as someone who has found an answer to a practical question that is urgent in many minds at this present. He has learned a technique whereby he may adjust himself to the agonies and excitements of life in a time of world crisis, such as we are living through. "One must have a religion." "I wish I had religion." (The omission of the indefinite article is perhaps significant.) We are all of us familiar with these expressions of vague longing for a state of mind whose character is not fully understood, but which, it is thought, remains somehow unaffected by the pressure of external circumstance.

Yet we cannot disguise from ourselves the fact that such vague longings are, in essence, relative to our situation. They suggest our readiness, as it were, to make our need, as we discern it, the measure of the divine initiative. God is not for us the Living and the True. Rather he is the object of an introspectable, psychical state, which we court for its psychological efficacy as a barrier against individual distresses. We are not seeking God as he is in himself. We are coveting our own good, seeking an experience—of which we suppose that he is the object—of something that is likely to contribute to our mental well-being. Our piety, if we can call it such, is self-regarding. We seek him not for himself, but for what fruit the experiencing of him may bring to us in the ordering of our natural lives.

To both attitudes alike, to that admiration of the subject of religious experience, which characterized liberal culture at its best, and to the desire for that experience as a means to a Stoic tranquillity, the answer of the gospel is to point to the intrinsic contradictions of the quest. Between the realization of our own good, *as we conceive it*, and the purposes of God the Living and the True, there is a great gulf. The word of that God is ever sharper than a two-edged sword.

But that interpretation of religion that is implacably hostile to the gospel has in this our day not merely penetrated the popular mind, but is itself a root cause of that subjection of theology to the exigencies of apologetic, which is among the most lamentable aspects of the contemporary failure of the intellectual to answer to the demands of his vocation.[7] Even the sketchiest acquaintance with the history of Christian thought since Kant will incline the reader to endorse the judgment, shared by disciples of Aquinas and Barth alike, that apologetic has become the mistress, and not the handmaid, of theology. Now it will be argued in this book that the definition of apologetic is itself a theological question; for that definition cannot be achieved unless first the character of the human situation, as revelation discloses it, is appreciated.

We cannot deny that in the whole Modernist experiment, now perhaps in its concluding phase, we have witnessed a perfectly sincere attempt to preserve Christian influence in a decaying secular society. Of the specifically intellectual side of the Modernists' work, I shall say more later in this chapter. At present, all I am concerned to do is to suggest their significance, in so far as they have created within the Christian Church itself, as well as outside it, an estimate of religion that is fundamentally contrary to the character of the gospel of the mercy of God.

The Modernist experiment is perhaps best characterized as the attempted subordination of dogma to spirituality. *Lex orandi, lex credendi.* The subject and predicate alike of this expression furnished a title to that most tragic of Roman Catholic Modernists, George Tyrrell. But that subordination of belief to the exigencies of the spiritual life, which the sentence implies, leads inevitably to disaster. For, whatever content one may give to the phrase "spiritual life," one is not talking simply of an abstraction. The complex of devotional and mortifying

7. What M. Julien Benda named so expressively *la trahison des clercs* [the treason of the intellectuals]. See Julien Benda. *La Trahison des Clercs* (Paris: Éditions Grasset, 1927).

exercises, which is said to constitute that "spiritual life" with which so many post-Tridentine directors seem to be preoccupied, is only intelligible when set in the context of a particular dogma of man's origin, nature, and end. To suggest that the dogma be retained as a necessary condition of the continued pursuit of the life necessarily implies that the life is itself regarded as an intrinsic good. If we are to behave "as if" the Christian faith is true, we must presumably be convinced, on quite other grounds than that of its congruity with the Christian end, that the life of Christian men is good. We must, in fact, be sure that that form of life, which is the embodiment of the religious idea, is of all forms the highest. Our allegiance to Christian dogma (if behaving "as if" that dogma is true can be accounted allegiance) is contingent upon our continued appreciation of the form of life that can only be lived in such a dogmatic context.

We cannot insist too strongly, however, that thus to approach the Christian fact is, in effect, to pass it by upon the other side. The protest made by the Fourth Gospel[8] against the idea of the cultus-Christ, which Roman Catholic Modernism was concerned to revive, is decisive on this point. To conceive the Christian faith as supplying what one might term an occasion of spiritual achievement is to mutilate its cardinal article of faith. The coming of Messiah is the condemnation of religion. In that solemn rite, which on the eve of his passion he instituted, he uttered a divine "No" to all spiritual exercise and endeavor that had not been grounded in an unflinching appreciation of the fact that, apart from the bruising of his body and the shedding of his blood, the way was and is fast barred from earth to heaven. The daily celebration of the Holy Eucharist is the church's "No" to all man-centered religious activity.

No Christian apologist should be concerned to commend a pattern of religious exercise, or to suggest that in religious experience (whatever that phrase may signify) the nature of "Ultimate Reality" is disclosed to the subject of the experience. Rather, it should be his concern to bring into the consciousness of men and women, throughout that succession

8. Again see John 6.

of individual occasions that constitute human history, the mercy of God revealed in Christ. For God the Living and the True is no object of human quest, no satisfaction of human striving. Rather he it is, who, in the Word made flesh, has nowhere to lay his head, and whose life and death remain a condemnation of religiosity in the name of God.

2. Of the intellectual situation at the present moment, more must be said. I remember that, some years ago, in the examination of the final Honour School of Theology in the University of Oxford, the following question was asked: "Is the conception of divine revelation philosophically tenable?" Suppose that the asking of that question might be termed a last tribute to monistic idealism.[9] For, as far as I can understand it, its asking is only legitimate if one presupposes that conception of philosophy which is traditionally associated in this country with the names of "Oxford idealists."

Mercifully, we are now sufficiently alive to our great debt to Hume (here, as so often, on the side of the angels) to realize that, as it stands, that question is a nonsense question. Hume's simple recognition that no individual proposition about a contingent matter of fact could be established *a priori* holds good here as elsewhere. It is not for philosophy, whatever philosophy may be, to tell us whether or not God has intervened in the way in which he must have intervened for that intervention to merit the name of revelation. That he has or has not is a matter of fact. We can only look and see. We can only scrutinize evidence; we can only bring ourselves, or allow ourselves to be brought, face to face with him, to whom both scriptures and prophets testify.

But first we must clear our minds of irrelevant prejudgments. An appreciation of the lively skepticism of Hume and his empiricist successors[10] is perhaps a necessary first step in the case of those who,

9. By monistic idealism is denoted that class of philosophical doctrines which suggest that the actual world is in some sense both a manifestation of, and a moment in the self-constitution of, an absolute mind or spirit, which is regarded as the sole Reality. They are, of course, highly technical doctrines, but in a slightly bowdlerised and considerably simplified form they have exercised a very considerable (and, in the opinion of the present writer, an almost entirely detrimental) influence on modern theology.

10. In other words, those philosophers who have expounded and developed his fundamental insight that no proposition asserting a particular matter of fact can be established *a priori*.

in spite of its manifest contradiction and futility, speak of the universe as itself the expression and fulfillment of rational intelligence. Those who see in revelation a breach in the continuity of a cosmos that is, as many idealist philosophers have expressed it, "in its history the self-disclosure of an intelligible absolute," must first no doubt learn to think sanely in the school of the empiricists. Nonetheless, it may be questioned whether the reasoning, whereby the rigour of empiricist logic empties of their plausibility the grandiose pretensions of idealism, even begins to pave the way for the admission of the possibility of revelation.

Indeed, whether or not there has been, or could be, a divine revelation is not a matter that philosophy can decide one way or the other. An admission that that is so could soon be gained from an opponent in debate. But even so, the nerve of the question would not have been touched.

Time need not be wasted upon such questions as whether a divine revelation is a philosophically tenable conception. Rather an attempt must be made to characterize the intellectual prejudices that constitute so firm a barrier against the consideration of its possibility.

It was suggested above that Modernism was essentially the subordination of dogma to cult, and that this subordination was of set purpose apologetic. Now apologetic does not operate in a vacuum. To some extent its form is conditioned by the intellectual climate in which the apologist discharges his task. To speak crudely, his concern is primarily to "get his stuff across."

The error of Modernism, as we have seen, resided not so much in its apologetic fervour as in its appreciation of that for which it was concerned to apologize. The task of the apologist is a valid, and an urgent, task, but he is failing utterly to fulfill it when he misconceives that for which he is apologizing. What made the Modernists' misconception so plausible was the general climate of their period, pervaded as it was with a sense of the dignity and worth of human achievement. To commend the Christian dogma as a mechanism of religious achievement was a plausible, and to them a commendable, undertaking. It brought the Christian history (in its broadest sense) within the context of the history of human aspiration and endeavor. It suggested that life, in order to achieve its highest quality, must be transformed by being made the material for the embodiment of the distinctively religious idea. It offered men the machinery, whereby this transformation could be effected, in the whole apparatus of Catholic faith and practice.

And the character of the situation has, in many respects, not materially altered since the termination of the Modernist episode. We are still clinging to the vestiges of our own achievements that remain to us. "These be thy gods, O Israel." Our gaze is directed upon ourselves. We will find the significance of our life, not in terms of that which is over against it, but in terms of itself. A sense that human life is, as it were, a country that God in the person of his Son has invaded, is hostile to our natural immanentism.

Can it be said that we honestly appreciate this immanentist prejudgment for what it is?[11] It is a conviction hard to exorcise, for we see other things in terms of it. It is a permanent part of our intellectual equipment, a conviction that our problems are problems that we ourselves can solve. We have lost all sense that our life is in any respect finite, and it is for that reason, perhaps, that we set increasingly little store by our own individual personality.

It is a prejudice with which we are concerned. It is in no sense a philosophical theory. For that reason, I characterize it, by the use of metaphor, as a "denial of the horizon." There are no bounds that we cannot pass.

This is the cultural fruit of that relativism of which Kant is the father.[12] To some extent, we do regard the world as of human making.

11. By "immanentist prejudgment" is meant that characteristic of so many post-Renaissance world-views, which we may call the refusal to admit the possibility that the world in which we find ourselves does not carry its significance in itself. An indication of this emphasis may be seen in the fact that in post-Renaissance philosophy, metaphysic has given place to epistemology. In the latter study, we seek not to understand what is, but rather to validate and justify, by appeal to the transcendent, our previous comprehension of it. The notion of God is introduced as a ground of the validity of our own intellectual processes. It is never suggested that we cannot understand what we encounter, except by reference to him. On the substitution of epistemology for metaphysics in modern philosophy, see Casserley, *Fate of Modern Culture*, chap. 2 (33–48).

It is that which has been formed in and through our awareness of it. Its order is a function of our intelligence. We can only understand an object as existing if it is in some relation to ourselves. Our intelligence, our fancy, our will, is to some extent the measure of the world.

It cannot be doubted that a great many thinkers are still prevented by this attitude, which T. E. Hulme stigmatized as romanticism, from considering the very possibility of the entrance of the divine invader *ab extra* into the context of human life.[13] The hardness of the apologetic task is no excuse for refusing to undertake it. Our pride in our own achievement is crumbling amid the impact of events, that manifestly hurl us hither and thither. To the menace of Hitlerism, the naturalist can offer no solution save by a war, which must only create other problems in its turn without resolving those it was undertaken to resolve. The revelation of the demonic element in human affairs may shatter the immanentism that makes difficult our comprehension of these problems. Certainly we can hope that the intrusion of the demons may remind us of him to whom they are subject. But we cannot be sure that it will. There remains the barrier of which I have spoken.

It is the whole prevailing cultural temper that forbids an acknowledgment of the possibility that we are finite. We are so sure of ourselves that we cannot conceive even that we are creatures, called out of nothingness, by a Love ever diffusive of itself. It is not, as some disciples of Karl Barth aver, a predicament that is reducible to terms of the victory of the Hellenic over the Hebraic spirit. It is rather the fruit of a preoccupation with the temporal, historical series, which refuses to take account even of the possibility of meta-history over against it. We have made an absolute of a historical achievement. It supplies our perspective; we cannot, we will not admit God over against it. I have spoken of a "denial of the horizon." I might have generalized the

12. Kant's *Critique of Pure Reason*, certainly one of the most widely influential philosophical works ever published, still remains historically the inspiration for all those various types of philosophic doctrine that suggest that the order and necessity which are exhibited by the processes of the phenomenal world are in some sense *read into that world* by the perceiving subject.

13. An English thinker of the first two decades of this century, whose papers on various topics, collected posthumously under the title, *Speculations* (London: Kegan Paul, 1923), are remarkably illuminating.

metaphor by speaking rather of a "denial of the end." I do not mean that we refuse to recognize death as a biological fact. We do recognize it, but to the spiritual significance of death, we are blind. We read so many detective stories in which the fact of human finitude is exploited for our entertainment that we are no longer conscious that in the circumstances of death arise questions that will not go unanswered.

It is for that reason that we find the gospel of God the Living and the True so dark and terrible a thing. In our fear, we empty it of its catastrophic suggestion. We refuse it, because it is a condemnation of our achievement. Or more subtly, we strive to bring it into line with our facile belief in inevitable progress. We make the character of Messiah a fulfillment of our own relative aspirations. Hymns are sung, which acclaim the Son of Man, our judge, and by the mercy of God, our redeemer, as "our hero, strong and tender."[14] To the familiar strains of the "Londonderry Air," Christ is addressed in terms, not of reverence or awe, but of sickly sentimentality. The very publication of *Songs of Praise* is an indication of a spiritual sterility. He, who is our judge, has been made our hero, and the price of the transformation cannot be evaded.

We cannot, or will not, acquire the perspective of the gospel. For the gospel asserts in language too harsh to be misunderstood that, apart from the coming of Christ, we can never know ourselves.[15] Sometimes Barth speaks as if his coming were necessary to create the gulf that separates us from God. We may not go as far as that. But at least we must agree that his coming has revealed to us the depth of our impasse.

What then? We persist in striving to comprehend our world by the employment of modes of thought, which are incapable of expressing to us its fundamental predicament. The pathos of our present flight from reality is too obvious to require comment. Its sign is an infantile Utopianism, a weary futurism. We look outward, forward, never

14. *Songs of Praise* (Oxford: Oxford University Press, 1925), 611. This hymnbook is today primarily of interest as a historical document illustrating the attempt made by theological Liberalism to revise the Christian gospel by eliminating its message of redemption.
15. See John 15:22–24.

inward. We cannot look inward until first we are face to face with God in Christ.

For though his coming is judgment, it is also creative of the very conditions of our restoration. Through that act, unique and unrepeatable, which was his Death, he has exhibited himself to us. *Stat crux, dum volvitur orbis.*

The tragedy of our situation is that God can speak no other language to us, and that is the language we find it hardest to understand. For that sets over against human achievement divine failure. It is not a transvaluation, but an inversion of human value. If we strive, as Liberal theologians have undoubtedly done, to bring the episode of Christ within the history of human achievement, its character goes. We empty it of its significance; indeed, we have done this so effectively that we are paralyzed when we are told that there history and meta-history intersect, that there is God, ever active in history, face to face with man. We say: "No." It is a moment, only a moment, in a process that is an absolute, man's gradual ascent, his ever-widening achievement.

In the New Testament, the cross is indeed a moment, but it is the moment whereby the hours, the days, the years are judged. We can date the event. The Roman historian Tacitus mentions it in his Annals. It was a public spectacle. It was in time—yet the Lamb was "slain before the foundation of the world."[16]

In the approach of the modern intellectual to Christianity, the stumbling block is here. Finitude and sin—to both these characteristics of human life, the cross bears witness. (And what is the latter if it is not the refusal to recognize the former?) We must stand there. No other place will do as well. The word is only audible in that place. And we must accept. We must acknowledge the justice of the edict if we are to know the beatitude of the sons of God.

3. Concerning the barriers created by the political preoccupations of our generation, I do not intend to say much here. For these

16. Rev. 13:8.

preoccupations are closely connected with the immanentism of which I have already written at length.

One cannot deny that few aspects of the verdict of the cross seem harsher than its apparent condemnation of political action and institutions. The circumstances of the confrontation of the kingdom of God—which came with power in the person of Jesus, with the kingdom of this world, in the person of the Roman procurator—suggest an intolerant and harsh verdict upon the latter. Of the impact of the kingdom of God upon the kingdom of man, I will not speak, save to say that in the dialectic of their mutual relation resides the significance of the history of the church. But in that critical moment, the supreme crisis of all history, when Christ is face to face with Pilate, the fact is exhibited that not from within the kingdom of man is salvation to be found; rather is it to be found only in him, who in his rejection, and therein alone, declares the absolute sovereignty of God.

Not through human institutions can man achieve that insight into his actual situation, which must inevitably preface any intimate amelioration. For the institutions in which he trusts are, in a measure, the reflection of his estimation of himself; if that estimation be perverted, the whole social frame is itself of necessity distorted.

There is no indictment of the virtue of justice in itself, only an explicit rejection of the assumption that existing human institutions, built on a false estimate of human dignity, can be a genuine mechanism of social and individual fulfillment. They too are under judgment, the judgment of the cross.

Thus it is that from the cross our aspirations seem condemned. For the crucifixion is in itself an act wherein, by the costliest obedience human flesh and blood has ever borne, the sovereignty of God is acknowledged. In Christ crucified his kingdom came, and in and through baptism we are brought within that kingdom, set over against the kingdoms of men.

The whole Christian life is a dying unto the world and a living unto God, a contempt of the world's values, and through their denial, a recreation of their worth. The Christian Church is the place wherein the opposition of the kingdom of God to the kingdoms of man is continuously manifest. For the church is of his decision his body, and his bride.

Chapter 2: The Scandal of Particularity

In this phrase, which is borrowed from the German theologian Gerhard Kittel, is expressed most exactly the perplexities we sought to analyze in the first chapter. It is undoubtedly to many minds a stumbling block and a snare to find themselves compelled, if they are to come to terms with the characteristically Christian claim, to admit that at one particular time and in one particular place is accomplished the act on which depends not merely their temporal, but their eternal destiny.

I have said that in the cross of Christ history and meta-history intersect; that it is the moment whereby the hours, the days, the years are judged. Persons nurtured in the inheritance of our liberal culture find it an almost intolerable burden to admit themselves as dependent, not merely for some easily renounceable good, but for their very character as human individuals, upon the accomplishment of a bloody execution. We have so long thought of the natural order as itself in a measure an absolute. What significance, if any, it possesses must be sought in the ebb and flow of its processes. The recognition that, so to speak, significance is only bestowed upon it when it is transected at one point by that which is over against it and from which in the beginning it had its origin, is shocking and even frightening.

If we are to understand, we must look not at the universe but at one particular; we must not seek first, within the historical series, universal laws of its development in terms of which we can, so to speak, interpret the fact of Christ; we must not seek to bring him within the terms of our own thinking, but rather to recast the whole of our intellectual frame of reference by constant recollection of his particularity.

If we admit revelation, then, into our thought, into our whole appreciation of human existence, we have introduced an almost intractable dualism. The very word "dualism" is harsh to modern ears, but it is the cardinal article of the Christian faith, that God so loved the world that he gave. Again and again the simple past tense is used of that giving. It is not a progressive disclosure of some immanent intelligible purpose that constitutes this divine giving; rather, it is here now, at one place, at one time. Today the events that constituted that giving are past; they are items in history books. But still we must bring ourselves face to face with them in all their crudity, their well-nigh intolerable harshness. We are not to escape by first constructing our worldview and then, within its frame, setting the figure of Christ. We must refuse to allow the achievement of our intelligence to suggest to us that our intellects are capable of prescribing the character of the divine initiative. We must admit that there is something in ourselves, a tangle, as it were, which looks for its resolution, not to the temporal succession of our cultural achievement, but to an act that is the fruit of an initiative that has its origin *ab extra.*

The function of the church is in every age to bring the individual and the society in which his life is cast face to face with the judgment of God, once revealed in the execution of Christ. There is a sense in which the need of man varies from age to age. The successive exposition of the moments of the historical dialectic brings to the surface different aspects of his tortured and divided being. The consequent conflict and the willful ignoring of finitude, which is sin, compel him to seek now in one, now in another element of his divided nature the ground of his significance. The Christian understanding of history reveals in the life of man a continual tragedy of frustrated achievement. There is in the Christian scheme an analogue of the classical Greek virtue of *sophrosune.* It is the continued recognition, within the development of the historical series, that each emergent cultural moment carries within itself the seed of its own decline. Only when that sense of individual cultural form is retained can there be any sure basis for Christian social action. To some extent, the Christian baptised into the death of Christ must always, if he is loyal to his Master, be a disruptive force in society. For in and through his baptism he accepts the verdict of rejection pronounced from the cross upon man's cultural achievement and is thereby irrevocably committed to the task of pointing the whole social frame to its origin beyond itself. The church in its members is both involved in, and independent of, the historical cultural moment. It is involved in it, for it is compact of individual historical men and women who are here today and gone tomorrow, but it is independent of it, for it is at the same time the body of him who is the dissolver of all cultural forms that destroy and impede the attainment by the creature of his true status. The instrument, whereby the subhuman processes that ever threaten to absorb the individual persons are themselves revealed as demonic, is the revelation of the cross of Christ.

The tragedy of our predicament is, as I have suggested, the recognition that we cannot realize it, apart from being brought first to an admission of the historic intersection of history by meta-history in the life of Christ. Only through the grace of God can we come to see that we are sinners; and that perception is contingent upon our being brought face to face with his revelation. The act of God in history is at once the condemnation and the restoration of the whole historical series. But we must, if we are to undergo that condemnation which is a condition of our release, assist at that assize; we must make the journey to the courtroom of Golgotha if we are to behold him. We cannot see him elsewhere. To the exigencies of that journey all our philosophizing must, for the time being, be subordinated. We must admit as at least possible that our spirits are incapable of measuring the whole scale of the relations of the eternal with the temporal. We must allow it as at least not inconceivable that we cannot read ourselves unless we look at what is come to our level from above and without.

In contemporary Protestant theology, there is most unhappy opposition between faith and reason. The suspicion is widely prevalent that to admit theology is in any sense systematic, or to allow that philosophy is a true handmaid of theological science, is to ignore the final condemnation of monistic idealism that admission of the Christian fact demands. Thus the God of the philosophers (a metaphysician's entity) is opposed to "God the Living and the True." The suggestion that God enters as an object into the processes of human ratiocination is denounced as equivalent to a denial that he is known to man uniquely in man's encounter with him in the face of Jesus Christ. To the philosopher, argue these theologians, God is the name of the solution of a problem. For the Christian, the coming of his Son in the likeness of mortal flesh is rather the relegation of all such questioning to the status of pseudo problems. In the face of Jesus Christ, we see God, and his Voice that we hear is an emphatic "No" to all efforts to reduce him to the status of a term in our own speculations. To suggest the very possibility of such a reduction is to deny that transcendence or otherness, which is his fundamental characteristic when set over against us.

Moreover, it is suggested that, however restrained its claim, the admission as possible of a natural theology, in some sense affording the language in which the theological explication of the data of revelation can be set out, is to deny the very sense of the term "revelation." It is argued that if revelation is admitted, then natural theology, metaphysics, and the like are relegated to the status of inevitably sterile speculations. If it is admitted that only through the penetration of the historic series by God, Judge and Redeemer, can man and God be brought face to face, then surely it must be seen that the point of contact between them is set there and there only. Surely, if it is justifiable to assert that man's predicament can only be revealed to him when he is brought face to face with God, who has entered history for his rescue, then it is impossible to imagine that, apart from that act, he can in any sense comprehend God's relation to himself.

The problem is one of the most acute in contemporary theology, but it may perhaps be suggested that the fact that it has been posed in precisely this form is, in a measure, due to the theological and philosophical background against which it has been raised. The opposition of outlook that it discloses is at least in part created by the character of the setting that has made it so acute. In the conflict of idealism and transcendentalist dualism, the issues are obscured by the character of the former position. It is, in effect, what we have called the "denial of the horizon" invested with a spiritual significance.

The process of history is regarded as an absolute, and God is, as it were, conceived as the condition of its possibility. Now there is a sense in which the adherent of the classical philosophical tradition of Christendom who accepts God as First Cause would employ just such language to describe his relation to the manifold events of the temporal series. But the sense that his words would bear would be quite different. For him, God is the condition of the being of everything that is. His interest in what "is" is conditioned the whole time by his preoccupation with its origin. The finite character of contingent existence is thus ever in the foreground of his consciousness. When he asserts that but for God we are not, he is not simply referring our existence to its transcendent ground in virtue of a prior approbation of the worth of that existence. God is not for him known by description simply as the guarantee of a human valuation. His judgments are ontological in that they concern the character of distinctively human existence. The premise of his ascent to God is an appreciation of human finitude. It is not in any sense a "value judgment." It does not claim that the process of human life is as it were intrinsically valuable and therefore must be conceived as in some sense related to a transcendent intelligence that will guarantee that the process shall continue to embody those ideals that are the primary object of its valuation. He does not say (to put it crudely), "There must be a God to keep man going or to give man stature or significance or what you will." Rather he says, "There is that in man which demands his reference to a ground that has its being eternally within itself."

Nor does the Christian philosopher ignore that constraint laid upon man by his fallen state to seek his significance within himself and not outside the temporal order. (Of this more will be said later.) He is in absolute agreement with the Barthian Protestant in admitting the primacy of the Biblical revelation. He would contend, indeed, that the whole distinctively Christian problem is created by the impact upon human social, intellectual, and moral activity of a claim that carries with it its own certification. As T. S. Eliot has pointed out,[17] there is

17. In his contribution to *Revelation*, ed. John Baillie and Hugh Martin (London: Faber and Faber, 1937).

no greater gulf fixed between one man and another than that the one should admit and the other deny the incarnation of the Son of God. For the incarnation entails the entrance into history of a new and supernatural fact. Here is a breach with continuity. Of this the virgin birth is the sign. Here in a natural process a supernatural power is at work. Not of any fortuitous human decision is the birth of Messiah the fruit. To Mary, Gabriel is sent from God, and her response is to a divine initiative.

We cannot deny, moreover, that there is a direct congruity between this entrance into history of the God-Man and the whole distinctive outlook of the prophetic theology with its underlying assumption of divine revelation. The call of Abraham is the first episode in that whole series of events, which are the unique intersection of history by meta-history and of which the climax is the cross. We may discern analogies to God's dealings with Israel in his dealings with other societies and other individuals, but we must remember that we would only there discern those analogies if first we had seen the pattern of Israel's history certified as uniquely revealed by the coming of the God-Man.

So, in a sense, we are back where we started. There is the supreme either-or. Do we or do we not admit in the incarnation and in the passion and resurrection the act of redeeming God? If we do, our whole pattern of thought is distorted. We are bound, in a measure, to revise our frame of reference. We cannot look at the world, after the admission that God has entered it, as we did before. We must recast our entire scheme of things; we cannot rest content with the shadows of an imperfect intellectual achievement that is shot through and through with the tragic effects of sin. The coming of God in history and our invitation to share his own eternal beatitude through our participation in his death has compelled us to revise our scheme. In the next chapter we shall consider some effects of that revision, and we must remember that that revision is a fruit of, or, if you like, is itself an exhibition of, the divine activity in history. It is an event in time that is the fruit of the intersection of time by eternity. It is the mission of the church, the mystical body of Christ, to be his instrument for the extension of that irruptive and disruptive activity that was his coming. In a memorable phrase, Kierkegaard described the incarnation as God's attack upon man. There is a sense in which the Christian cannot but pray that the church at this present hour will be so sure an instrument of his purposes that she will embody his attack upon Europe in 1940.

Chapter 3: Man Before God

Our scheme has been to lay bare the whole character of the impact of the saving work of Christ upon our particular cultural situation. The church exists for no other purpose than that through its ministry and life it may continually refer human conflicts to the point in history at which they find their resolution. Apologetics properly conceived is the allotting to successive human aspirations and human tragedies of their place within the whole context of the Christ-drama. The apologist is continually concerned to discern that point in which man seems most ready to respond to the all-embracing compassion of the cross. It has been a demerit of Christian apologetics that it has so largely concerned itself with suggesting moments in man's life when he seems himself to be already set on a path of self-improvement and not with pointing to those opposing moments that must inevitably frustrate his every achievement. The apologist must appeal to man's sense of frustration rather than to his sense of achievement. Such a verdict inevitably sounds shocking in our ears. For so long we have thought in terms, not of the radical evil that infects our aspirations, but of the accomplishments that are already there apparently, but awaiting their perfection. Yet the verdict of the cross upon them is one of unhesitating condemnation. It is not there that we are to find our point of contact with the living God, but rather in that recognition of helplessness and contradiction, which is the mode whereby to the sinner the natural fact of his creaturely dependence upon God must reveal itself.

The apologetic task is primarily one of confrontation. Man is to be brought face to face with God in Christ; only thus can he know himself, for Christ alone, in the words of the Fourth Evangelist,[18] knows what is in man. Yet one is compelled to ask oneself more precisely concerning the character of that which is thus brought face to face with God in Christ. In the English translation of some of the later works of Dr. Emil Brunner,[19] the term "verbicompetence" has been used to characterize that capacity of response with which man is regarded as being endowed. In his great book *Man in Revolt*, Brunner offers an analysis of the frustrations and contradictions characteristic of man's natural life apart from the impact upon it of the supernatural, which in many respects recalls the analysis offered by such Catholic thinkers as Jacques Maritain and V. A. Demant.[20] Brunner describes the essential inhumanity of the human situation apart from that impact in a manner that yet allows him to conceive man's response to a divine initiative as a possibility.

There is much in Brunner's language which recalls St. Thomas. His sense of human impoverishment does not compel him to dismiss as nothing but "sound and fury" the suggestion characteristic of St. Thomas that man is at least *capax rerum divinarum*. Where he differs from Aquinas is in the suggestion that it is in a capacity for decision rather than in a capacity for understanding that man's "verbicompetence" resides. It is not so much in the comprehension of his situation (as St. Thomas allowed that by the *quinque viae* he might in a measure comprehend it) as in the power to respond to the new factor, which in the coming of Christ has entered the context of his life, that man's character is revealed. We may see here, as Brunner himself admits, a fruit of Kant's mistrust of metaphysics and exaltation of the practical reason. In the sphere of decision, rather than in that of intelligence, is to be found that potentiality of true humanity that Christ in his coming actualizes. Thus Brunner, here clearly under the influence of such thinkers as Kierkegaard and Martin Buber, opposes

18. John 2:25.
19. The eminent contemporary leader of Protestant theological thought, who, with Dr. Karl Barth (from whom on several points he has diverged), sounded the clarion call that brought the theology of the Protestant churches out of the waste land of Liberalism. Many of his books have been translated into English, and all are deserving of close study and attention.
20. cf. Jacques Maritain. *Humanisme Intégral: Problèmes temporels et spirituels d'une nouvelle chrétienté* (Paris: Fernand Aubier [Éditions Aubier-Montaigne], 1936) and Vigo Auguste Demant. *The Religious Prospect* (London: Frederick Muller, 1939).

to the intellectualism of St. Thomas a doctrine of decision as affording the differentia of the human individual.

We would do well to see in this substitution an appreciation of the historical character of the Christian faith that may perhaps be obscured in some of the writings of scholastic theologians. It has been already said that the appreciation of the character of apologetic is properly a theological task, and perhaps the significance of that assertion will now be becoming clearer. Apologetic is, as I have said, the mechanism whereby the Christian Church seeks, as it were, to effect the confrontation of the individual or the social group with the judgment of the cross. It is, therefore, an act or operation that possesses not merely a theoretical purport; it is the direct interjection of a new factor into the configuration of an individual or social situation. It is the presentation to the persons or groups within that situation of their judge and their redeemer. It is, therefore, no presumption that sees in the task of the Christian apologist a directly intrusive function analogous to that of the incarnation itself. The confronting of history with the moment at which history and meta-history intersected is itself, one might almost say, a prolongation of that moment into the here and now.

Thus in so far as the task of the theologian is a task that he performs as a member of the society of the church, it can be regarded as furnishing the occasion on which he himself and others with him may be confronted with the decision to accept or to reject Christ. The phrase "acceptance of Christ" is one that sounds harshly in the ears of the twentieth-century intellectual, not least, perhaps, because of its associations with a false individualism and a crudely fundamentalist appreciation of Holy Scripture. Nonetheless, it does call attention to the character of decision that attaches to the attitude of an individual to the Christian claim, which an excessive intellectualism might tempt us to ignore. The late Dr. B. H. Streeter once said that there is a sense in which *we* are the primitive church. In that phrase, he called attention to a point that we are sometimes inclined to ignore—namely, that we, in virtue of our membership in the church, are in a sense the bearers into history of that meta-historical factor that in the Person of the Messiah entered its series. If we remember that capacity of decision which Brunner rightly emphasizes, we will not be slow to understand the importance of that vocation continually to renew before the eyes of men the historic act of God in Christ.

We cannot deny that in the acceptance of the Christian faith there is an element of decision, but we need not, I think, follow Dr. Brunner in his complete subordination of intelligence to will. We can and must so scrutinize the human intelligence as to understand how it is that man can even in a measure comprehend the possibility of an intersection of the historical by the meta-historical. It is impossible to maintain the primacy of the practical reason in face of the necessity that man should, at least in a measure, comprehend the character of that which has shattered his conceits. We may well agree that of themselves, comprehension, explication, and the like are insufficient components of the complex act of acceptance of the Christian claim. We may indeed say that that acceptance involves (as perhaps does every act of judgment) an element of decision that primarily concerns the will. But the character of that act of decision is itself open to a distinctively intellectual scrutiny. Its character as decision is discerned by an act of definitely intellectual recognition.

We have emphatically repudiated the suggestion that the intelligence could in any sense prescribe whether or not a divine revelation should happen, but we have not supposed in so doing that, in the occasion of such a revelation, there is anything that is necessarily contrary to the expectation of a properly functioning intelligence. When we say that revelation and its mode are hardly predictable, we are not suggesting that the capacity for intelligence is necessarily so bounded as to refuse to consider that abstract possibility. Indeed, in the criticism of monistic idealism to which part of our first chapter was devoted, the premise was the incompatibility of such a metaphysical system with the admission of the possibility of divine intervention. We suggested that the insight of theology compelled us to condemn such a view simply insofar as we saw in it the proper prerogatives of theology usurped. Need we suppose that in any other doctrine where these prerogatives are not thus disregarded we may not discern at least a nearer appreciation of the possibility of such an irruption into the natural order as, according to the Christian contention, has actually occurred?

Such acts of discrimination are intellectual. Their presupposition is, in a measure, the possibility of constructing some formal abstract schema of the relations of God and man. We dare not. Unless we were to condemn ourselves to a mere irrationalism that regards the Christian decision as taking effect in a complete vacuum, allow ourselves to deny that the construction of such a picture of our situation is possible.

Where, I think, we may find a valuable corrective to scholasticism in the insight of Dr. Brunner is in his emphasis on the historical context in which our decisions are taken. We cannot regard our theological activity as in any sense remote from the practical situation of our lives. It is within—rather, it is over against—a configuration of events that our decision is taken. It is an act that must in some respect be regarded as affecting the situation in terms of which it takes place. It is, as I have urged, a moment in which the Christ-impact is renewed. It is to this that I think the late Sir Edwyn Hoskyns was calling attention when he suggested that the proper theological preoccupation—indeed, the primary task—of the church was the study of the New Testament. We cannot suppose that if the task of the church be thus defined it can be regarded as one that is purely theoretic. Rather, its concern is the realization, in successive historical situations, of the act of the living God. If we have said that, we have suggested the root of the inevitable and the invariably present tension between intelligence and will. We cannot say that intelligence is the servant of will; rather, we must suggest that will and intelligence function coordinately, yet not so as to avoid acting one upon the other. Within the whole complex act, which is response to the Christian claim, there is a decision to consider, an act of consideration, a decision based upon that consideration, a further decision to reconsider what had hitherto been assumed, a decision upon that reconsideration, and so on.

There is within the situation created by the coming of Christ a continued swing from scrutiny to practical action, and back again to scrutiny. We have got to realize that the whole complex admission of the scandal of his death as the source of life is a process maintained over a period of time. It is the dominant interest of Christian theology. Again and again the theologian is driven to suggest further readjustments of our natural scheme demanded by the admission of Christ's claim. Christian theology is a *theologia crucis* simply in so far as it is the operation whereby the human intelligence adjusts its own appreciation of the human situation in the light of the impact upon it of the divine word. It may seem strange that the subject of theology should so preoccupy us in an essay that bears the title "God the Living and the True," but theology ceases to be theology if it is other than itself the maintenance throughout the historical series of that primal act of God in history, which is its origin, its object, and its end.

When, therefore, our concern is with God the Living and the True, our concern is at once with the past, with the present, and with the future, for we are concerned with a strand of history that intersects history, that is more than history. Into this strand we are ourselves, as it were, woven in through baptism. A theology of God the Living and the True carries with it, of necessity, an ecclesiology or doctrine of the church. For the church is nothing if it is not itself the extension of the unique act on which we are dependent for our redemption and for the restoration of our inheritance.

The paradox of Christian theology resides in its steadfast determination to take time seriously. Such language as "God the Living and the True" calls attention to just that fact. For the whole association of such a phrase is with the Biblical history of the vocation and destiny of Israel. One is not then speaking of an object of philosophic enquiry, one is rather speaking of an agent who calls Abraham, leads his chosen by the hand of Moses across the desert, takes David from among the sheepfolds, and so on. He is the subject of a historical drama, not a term in an intellectual quest. Yet if the fulfillment of his purposes is to be possible, that much must be granted to those whom he calls to tasks of his own foreseeing, that they should be capable in some measure at least of representing to themselves the relations to himself into which he has brought them.

T. S. Eliot, in his play *The Rock*, includes the following chorus:

> Then came, at a predetermined moment, a moment in time and of time,
>
> A moment not out of time, but in time, in what we call history: transecting, bisecting the world of time, a moment in time but not like a moment of time,
>
> A moment in time but time was made through that moment: for without the meaning there is no time, and that moment of time gave the meaning.

That is the paradox of the Christian doctrine of God. The opposition between the Hellenic and the Hebraic conception resides here if anywhere. The Greek God's primary goal, of an intellectual endeavor, is to render intelligible the world of becoming. Always for him the movement is one of ascent. The metaphor is as old as Plato. In the Hebrew and the Christian traditions, the movement is reversed. God, in the likeness of mortal flesh, enters the sphere of human decision. He becomes the object not of intellectual scrutiny, but of contempt and rejection. There in historic events he is disclosed. Now the Ancient of Days is an hour or two old. Now the Word by whom the heavens were made is stripped naked and hung upon a cross.

But when we have said this, we have not suggested that the Greek achievement has been in vain. Rather, we are assessing more shrewdly its significance. The analytic of the human intelligence, which was the achievement of the Platonic and the Aristotelian tradition, remains as a norm of all investigations of its subject, that same subject which is brought face to face with God in Christ. Through revelation and the impact that revelation makes, we are more properly able to assess the precise character and limitations of that achievement. We have seen how tenuously man retains hold upon that sense of the transcendent character of the ground of his existence. We have seen again and again in human history how that intuition of finitude, which is the most profound natural human intuition, is debased and how the infinite, by reference, to whom alone man discerns his individual finitude, is located within and not without the historical process. The possibility of that intuition nonetheless remains itself a guarantee of the at least partial validity of human ratiocination and of the possibility of man's being not unable to represent to himself the content of that which in Christ is revealed to him.

Thus so many differing lines of thought seem to illumine the character, the distinctive and peculiar character, of the Christian doctrine of God. It is a doctrine that suggests that not in the ascent of man through intellectual and spiritual exercise is the end for which he was created attained, but only through the invasion of his frustration and solitude by that very word through whom he was made and whose purposes he has so often frustrated and gainsaid.

Chapter 4: Renewal of the Understanding

It is, perhaps, a commonplace that Christian theology is rooted in history. In what has gone before, I have thought to expound in a measure what is entailed by this rooting. I have argued that in the Christian affirmation that in the life, passion, and resurrection of Jesus Christ history and meta-history intersect, is involved an adherence to the particular, which is a scandal to those who seek in the particular only a universal significance.

In the lexicographical method in New Testament studies pursued by such students as Hoskyns, Dodd, and the majority of the contributors to the great New Testament *Wörterbuch*, edited by Gerhard Kittel, we see a conscious orientation of theological study by the admission of the authority of that particular. It was Hoskyns who said that New Testament Greek was the language of the Holy Ghost, and in that epigram is enshrined perhaps the surest appreciation of the necessity of proper control of New Testament study by the end which it seeks to further—namely, the explication of the historic act of God in history. The church is distinguished by its possession of a book; it is not only the guardian of a tradition, it is the keeper of a written record; and in the Biblical record, its function as the extension of the incarnation is made unequivocally clear. It is, therefore, by the church's appreciation of its own character, as that book reveals it, that its conformity with the divine purposes is effected. It exists for no other purpose than to perpetuate throughout the stream of history the impact of God upon its course in the incarnation.

The Christian doctrine of God is, and must be, first presented in historical terms. As Father Thornton has said,[21] the fact of the incarnation is regulative of the peculiar form of the distinctively Christian theism. In that event, we do not merely see the infinite reduced to terms of the finite. The gospel narrative does not simply describe a series of events, beautiful, tragic, tender, cruel, in which the meaning of the infinite is, as it were, shown forth. The Word that is made flesh is no mere immanent intelligence in whom all things consist. Rather it is the active, creative principle, of which the prophets spoke in their mention of that Word of God that would accomplish the purposes for which it was sent forth. We are not to think of revelation simply as disclosure; we are to think of it rather as a saving act.

Man's destiny, eternal as well as temporal, is affected by what took place on Calvary, apart altogether from his appreciation of its significance. That particular event of the crucifixion is for the Christian determinative, not simply of his finer appreciation of ultimate reality, but of his being. Not primarily our knowledge of God, but our relation to him is affected by that tremendous occurrence.

"God the Living and the True"—our theme in this book has impelled us to emphasize history. For God the Living and the True, is the God who has disclosed himself in the concrete actuality of historical events. In those events, we have not merely beheld him, we have known the impact of his redeeming power. We spoke in the last chapter of the relevance of the theologian's work to the individual historical situation. The theologian is himself located within the stream of

21. cf. Lionel Spencer Thornton. *The Incarnate Lord: An Essay Concerning the Doctrine of The Incarnation in its Relation to Organic Conceptions* (London: Longmans, Green, and Co., 1928), throughout.

history, and insofar as his task is apologetic, he is concerned to intensify his contemporaries' appreciation of the tremendous fact that upon history, in Christ, meta-history has catastrophically impinged.

We can believe that at least part of the distinctively Christian theological insight is the power to comprehend historical events *sub specie aeternitatis.* The Christian—himself assuming, as it were, the grace of God to be an instrument of his eternal purpose—can comprehend the relevance to that purpose of the ebb and flow of human history. We can expect—nay, we must expect—that in the appreciation of such phenomena as war, the Christian insight will go deeper than that of the man who is compelled to interpret such events by means of a defective scheme of categories. But are we to suggest that the task of the Christian theologian is, as it were, exhausted by the exposition of the relation of the historical series to the kingdom not from hence? Must we deny that the impact of God in history affords to those who have seen him not merely a power of comprehending *sub specie aeternitatis* the events of which history is compact, but also in a measure a power of comprehending God as he is in himself?

In the history of Christian thought, the problem of the reconciliation of faith in revelation with human intellectual achievement has always been the most acute. We cannot, if what has been said above of the distinctive character of Christian theology is at all intelligible, be surprised that this is so. It is the inevitable fruit of the emergence within a situation of a factor that is novel and unpredictable. The gravity of the situation is intensified when the moment of the intrusion *ab extra* is accompanied by a paradox as grave as that of the cross.

Let us look this thing in the face. In that intellectual tradition of which we are all, more or less, the heirs, the vision of God has always been the goal of the most intense mental and spiritual discipline and struggle. In the Eleusinian mysteries, the *epopteia* (vision of the divine) was the coveted privilege of the initiate. In the whole of Greek philosophical tradition—which, in its origins in Platonism, knew in a measure the influence of the mysteries—the vision of the ultimate reality has ever been accounted a good, even *the* good, which is in its enjoyment most natural to man. In the comprehension or in the vision of the eternal, the highest potentialities of the human individual are actualized. The gravity and pain of the individual are actualized. The gravity and pain of the ascent to that beatitude are more than compensated for by the grandeur of the final achievement.

Yet in the New Testament what do we find? It is the narrative of the descent of the Son of God. In describing the cardinal moment of its narrative, the Nicene Creed lapses into language that is crudely historical: "Who for us men and for our salvation came down from heaven." But it is in the character of the reception wherewith the Son of God is greeted that the contradiction of Greek and Christian theology is clearest. It is a curious fact, perhaps not only of academic interest, that the Fourth Gospel, of all books in the New Testament the most consciously anti-Hellenic in spirit, should have been regarded by many as the first essay in Christian Platonism. The opposition between the Evangelist's theology and that of Plato is seemingly absolute. The prologue itself is no easy baptism of a Philonian Logos-doctrine into Christ. Rather, it makes it clear that the coming of God to earth only reveals the radical character of the gulf that separates him from man. The doctrine of a historical fall is a premise of the Evangelist's argument. The whole burden of his tale deepens our sense of humiliation as we read it. It is indeed the description of a divine attack upon man in mercy and a corresponding counterattack of man upon God in hate.

It would seem that the gibbet of Calvary testifies to the end of time to the very idolatry of human search for God; that the choice between faith (as expressed in acceptance of God's revelation in the Crucified) and reason was absolute. Either the one or the other must be chosen, and if we decide for reason, we fear at first sight that our choice may partake of the character of the rabble's cry for Barabbas.

This is the nerve of the problem of the relation of reason and revelation as it confronts the theologian. For the theologian is of necessity one who has admitted the occurrence of the unique event of the incarnation. There is no escaping this problem, and none who cherish the classical tradition of Catholic theology can regret the harshness with which that great teacher, Dr. Karl Barth, has posed the opposition.

But must we admit this choice is inescapable? Let us look again for a moment at the character of the human impasse from which God in Christ would deliver us, and let us look at it as it appears when it is posed in terms of speculative thought. I have said above that man's highest intuition is his awareness of his own finitude. It is the recognition that his being is contingent upon the necessary Being that is over against him and that constitutes the deepest intellectual appreciation of which he is capable. And the corollary of this discernment is the recognition that we do not know what God is; we know only what he is not and what relation everything else has to him. We cannot deny that this particular metaphysical assertion is vested with the ethical character of genuine humility. In the individual, the appreciation of his own contingency is a psychological event that is fraught with a consciousness of his own insignificance. It is surely plain that such a recognition is distinguishable both in content and quality from the suggestion that man's significance is discernible in his own spiritual and material achievement.

When regarded as a propensity of intelligence, idolatry is most surely interpreted as that kind of naturalism that would find man's ground in the exposition of his own achievement. What is condemned from the cross is the inversion of the metaphysical intelligence upon itself and the consequent denial of those limitations that must circumscribe its progress at every step. We are not, in metaphysical thinking, discerning or seeking to discern the conformity of what is with the pattern of our own hopes and aspirations. Our activity is rather to discern the relation in which everything whose existence is not contained within itself must stand to that which of necessity exists. Metaphysics, properly regarded, is a continued denial, not merely of the pretensions of the human intellect, but of the claim of the finite individual to exist. It is to be regarded as an intellectual discipline, the continually renewed construction of a schema whereby the contingency of that existence and the limits of its intelligence may be represented. We do not, as metaphysicians, profess to scan the nature of that which we call the "ultimate reality." The very use of the term "ultimate" should be a safeguard against such a pretension. It is, after all, a relative term; and in this fact perhaps is contained a warning to the metaphysician that the "first cause" that he seeks he knows primarily as cause, and therefore primarily in terms of his relation to that world of finite and contingent things of which he is himself a member.

The metaphysician invites the condemnation that awaits the idolator when he denies the absolute distinction of the necessary and the contingent and lips into that immanentism that suggests that the opposition of these two is not absolute but can be resolved in some higher synthesis. Nonetheless, though the resolution of the tension between necessary and contingent being is a temptation that besets the metaphysician constantly, it is not one to which of necessity he must yield. We must admit that it is at least logically possible for a philosopher to represent the relationship of finite to infinite so as never to forget the unlikeness in which their very likeness itself is surrounded. The doctrine of the analogy of being[22] is a formal schematization in metaphysical terms of the creature-creator relation. Nor does the formal character of the schema preclude our admitting the dynamical or, if it is preferred, the dialectical character of their relation. Metaphysical comprehension of human finitude and of man's ontological contingency is abstract and formal. When we say that man exists, we are merely recording a fact that is capable of empirical verification. When we say that the ground of man's existence is not in himself, we are merely suggesting that there is in man at least a formal "verbicompetence." His gaze is not directed continually upon himself. His attention is not, as it were, absorbed by the flux of becoming in which he is located. He poses a being over against himself that is self-

22. It is impossible here to do more than suggest the enormous importance alike for metaphysics and for theology of this cardinal doctrine of St. Thomas Aquinas. Its admission in some form or other would seem to be inevitable if we are to allow that human thinking concerning God and the things of God can be intelligibly conducted.

existent and therefore is not himself. That being is the ground of his existence. Of it, he can say that were it not, he would not be, but were he not, it would be unchanged. Of its relation to him, he can say nothing, only admitting that, apart from its own initiative, he cannot hope to comprehend it as it is.

A facile opposition of the ontological to the dialectical fails altogether to comprehend the significance of the former. We need claim no more for natural reason than that it equips man with a formal capacity of response. But we can claim for grace that where that formal capacity is absent, it is as it were supplied by the catastrophic irruption of Messiah's coming.

The relation of God and man is not adequately represented by such a formal schema of likeness in unlikeness. The relationship, however, as mediated through Christ, is of a character that man could not of himself anticipate. It is dependent on a divine initiative. Man is brought face to face with God, not through his effort, but through his failure. That is the paradox that lies at the very heart of the New Testament—indeed, of the whole Biblical theology.

When the end of man's supernatural life is characterized as the vision of God, it should be noted that it is the end of his supernatural and not of his natural life that is referred to. Man's end will be this, not in consequence of his natural achievement, but in and through the mercy of that God who has brought him into a new relation with himself, whereby he may indeed enjoy the vision of his beatitude.

As creation is prior to man's awareness of his finitude, so the accomplishment of redemption is prior to man's achievement of the end of that redeeming work. We are not to think of history as possessing any other hero save that God through whom time in the beginning came to be.

For the Christian, then, the doctrine of God is at once a metaphysical and a historical study. It is a metaphysical study in so far as it is concerned with the Ultimate; it is a historical study, for it is the foundation of Christian theology that there is a strand of history that is the power of God unto salvation.

Chapter 5: Ascent and Descent

It may seem strange that a study of the Christian doctrine of God should have progressed as far as this without any reference to the mystery of the Holy and Undivided Trinity. Yet, perhaps, a little reflection will suggest that it is by no means so surprising as at first appears. The vision of God is the supernatural end of man, and man will enjoy it as an adopted son of God. The character of adoptive sonship, which the merciful act of redeeming God has won for man, is a precondition of his comprehending in any measure the mystery of the Trinity.

We so often ignore, in our own thinking, the primacy of being over thought. We are before we are conscious that we are. Through baptism, which is an instrument of God's merciful purposes, we are incorporated into the mystical body of his Son. We become the adopted sons of God, and as the adopted sons of God, the objects and the subjects of that love, which the Father ever bears his Son and the Son the Father. We are already proleptically enjoying the beatitude that is the fruit of our participation in the very life of God. It is as thus caught up into the life of the Trinity itself that we are aware of the mystery of relation obtaining within the Godhead. For we are in Christ and in Christ are objects of that love which unites Father and Son—namely, the Holy Ghost.

God has descended, man has ascended. The ascension is the complement of the incarnation; it is the manhood that is assumed into the heavens. The tale of God's dealings with man must be told before ever we approach the mystery of the Trinity. For had those events that the Gospels record never happened, then that assumption of redeemed humanity into the life of God, which is the fruit of his redeeming work, would never have been achieved. The act of God in history is the condition of our knowledge of him in eternity. For though the existence of God, Trinity in Unity, is itself the primal ground of the existence of all that is, yet that interior life of God would remain forever remote from his creatures, who in some measure reflect its perfections, were there not first a mediator between God and man—namely, Christ.

It is the history of his redeeming work that reveals the condition of man's possession of his supernatural dignity. It is the possession of that dignity that qualifies him to comprehend God in a measure as he is in himself. Thus we say that the descent of God is the condition of the ascent of man. In our first chapter, we said that Christian theology is, and must be, a *theologia crucis*. Such it must be, for it is the cross that is the condition of that ascent whose fulfillment is the vision of God. We tell the tale, for the tale is the story of how it has come about that we are even attempting to set forth that doctrine of the primal reality, which makes boast of being the specifically Christian doctrine of God. Before our thought of him, we know his acts of power. For it is through these acts of power, and through them alone, that we can make our first stuttering effort at expounding his glory. Before, therefore, we begin our exposition of the doctrine of the Trinity, we do well to look back.

There is a strange simplicity in our scheme. Constantly we have found ourselves compelled to retrace our steps to one fundamental place upon our road—indeed, one might say, to the starting-point. What again and again we have found ourselves compelled to assert and to emphasize is that Christian theology must repeatedly recall its students to the contemplation of an act, an act without which neither its highest goal could be attained nor its humblest beginning enunciated. For that act is, in the fullest and deepest sense, the very condition of its possibility.

Chapter 6: As He Is

The emphasis of Christian theology has often lain more upon what God has done than upon what he is in himself. If one looks at such a classical formulation of the Christian faith as the Nicene Creed, one sees that its climax resides, not in its metaphysical analysis of the relation of Son to Father within the Trinity, but rather in the affirmation that that Son came down from heaven. It is for that reason that we learn to speak of the Christian story before ever we come to comprehend the Christian faith. The life of Jesus is indeed a tale that is told. We find here surely an indication of that truth that is perhaps the supreme insight of the distinctively Christian doctrine of God—namely, the primacy of the divine initiative.

If the knowledge of God that revelation brings transforms our intellectual comprehension of reality, we possess that knowledge simply and solely because he has brought us into that state wherein we can know him and what he is. Our confession of God as Trinity in Unity is contingent upon his act. Where so many expositions of the doctrine of the Trinity err is in their failure to admit the dependence of our confession upon the divine initiative. It is through the cross that we are enabled to pass from death unto life. We cannot, therefore, hope, apart from the cross, to have understanding of God in his eternal Being.

We are not to suppose, however, that when we speak of the primacy of the divine initiative, we are talking of anything except our own knowledge of God. Of God's eternal possession of himself in his own self-sufficiency, we can only say that that is neither before nor after but timelessly the same. When we speak of the primacy of the divine initiative, we are making clear that in redemption as in creation we are known by him before ever he is known by us. And in our knowledge of him, it is that comprehension on our part that he has known us, whether in creation or in redemption, that is the necessary prelude to our achievement of a comprehension of his Being.

What he is eternally in himself we know through what he has done. In the incarnation there is, I have suggested, that moment in history wherein all history is illumined and its achievement judged. Our knowledge of God incarnate is the starting point whence dimly we may start to comprehend him as he is. Again, we are confronted by the "scandal of particularity." We can never start upon our journey until, with the centurion, we have said of that figure upon the gibbet, scarred, hideous, and filthy, "Truly *this* is the Son of God." That is the first step, and, until it be taken, we are impotent. It is of this thing on the cross that we must say that it is God's Pact, where human rejection is the occasion of a divine acceptance. "So God loved the world that he gave," and this is the giving, this sight at which we shudder, the Son, that he gave. It is in the character of the giving that we can best see the nature of God as he is in himself. Had we not first said that God so *loved* the world, had he not, in effect, in the passion of his Son so loved it, we could not have said that he in himself is Love. The confession that God is Love is our first articulation of the fact that he is Trinity in Unity, and Unity in Trinity.

We know that God is Three Persons in one Godhead, solely through what he has done. Were it not that the Son had revealed the Father to those whom the Father had given into his own hands and had imparted to them the gift of the Holy Ghost, who is eternally the bond whereby Father and Son are united in love, we had not known either Father or Son or Holy Ghost. It is through the mediation, through the redeeming work of the Son, that we are in his relations to us but in a measure as he is in himself.

For our knowledge of God, we are dependent on his act of power, and therefore for our knowledge of ourselves as well we depend on that act. For that we exist we know is not due to ourselves, but to him. Likewise, what we have become and what we yet may be is contingent upon what he has done. And as through first knowing this act of power, we have come to know him as he is, seeing with ever increasing insight that that act is an expression of his Being, which is love. Through first seeing ourselves, confronted by God in the darkness of Calvary, we have come to see in a measure what we too are, who thus are loved by him. It is through redemption—which is wholly God's act, whose very occasion is not merely man's extremity, but his pride, lust, and cruelty—that we are enabled to see the world in its relation to him as the expression of his love.

Thus we see that the primacy of the divine initiative whereby in the redemption we were repossessed of God is, as it were, analogous to his self-sufficiency. Eternally he is, Three in One, and One in Three. What we are, and the very fact that we are at all, we owe to him. Creation is the expression of that love which is ever diffusive of itself.

But in creation, that love is not impaired. God, the archetypal society of Persons, Three in One and One in Three, maintains his life unimpaired and unaffected. Thus we can say that, even though by divine *fiat* we were to cease to be, he in himself would remain as eternally he is.

For the Christian, in creation and redemption alike, God is the subject of the tale. The world is only intelligible when it is exhibited in its relation to him. This was the great insight of St. Thomas Aquinas's natural theology. It supplied, as it were, a formal schema of his relation to the world. In no sense did it foreclose that fuller comprehension of his nature and therefore of the nature of that which depended upon him for its being, which his mighty act of power would make possible. In no sense, moreover, did it suggest that human sin, original and actual alike, had not impaired and obscured the character of that primal intuition. It may be that at moments in the history of the world it is not merely a greater fullness of understanding that we can hope for from the mercy of God, revealed in history, but rather a restoration of our sense that the world is, in principle, intelligible at all.

It is surely at such a moment as this that we stand today. The liberal experiment has collapsed, and in an apostate Europe we witness a senseless battle of the demons. Man assuredly today sees himself fast bound by the chains that his own sin has fashioned. Even among the members of the church there has appeared an impotence moral and spiritual of so grave a kind that men have asked whether that society is not itself another self-seeking human corporation. Among the sons of men, there are none found who may point the way of escape.

But may we not see the significance of man's present agony as the learning of a lesson, that most desperately he needed to understand? If we look again at the tragedy of the cross we can, perhaps, dimly discern the purpose of these awful judgments. If the cross bears witness to the love of God, it also attests the utter bankruptcy of man. Its paradox is inescapable and we must accept its "No" to our achievements before our natural life can ever, through the grace of God, be restored.

"There are times," to quote the Dominican writer already referred to,[23] "when, if men are to regain faith, their reason must be abased; when to

> have hope they must be driven to despair. It is the bitter lesson which it would seem divine love has determined that our age should learn. . . . For the agony of our time is less the unprecedented physical suffering than the agony of the triumph of unreason, the being 'trampled to death by geese,' the loosing of the irrational forces of destruction. *Le monde entire retentit de cette colere des imbeciles.* It is the *impasse* of the practical reason before the insoluble dilemmas of events: the impotence of might in the service of right. It is the paralysis of the 'rational-ethical' before moral issues which confront it; 'the ultimate problem and the deepest anguish of mind . . . when the Christian finds himself faced with a situation in which he is convinced that war is a duty, but the methods of war a crime': the ineluctable dilemma of the unjust war and the unjust peace; the irrationality of events which demand destruction calling upon destruction; to destroy destruction—the casting out of devils by Beelzebub."

The shallowness of so much of the "theology of the incarnation" current in the early days of this century is powerless in the face of such depths of human tragedy. Too long we have used language that denied the frightful gulf separating not merely God and man but the state of the creation in the beginning and the state of the creation after the fall. Too long have we ignored the awful truth that the restoration of the *natural* order demanded of God an intervention that was in every sense supernatural. We have even suggested that Christ came to reveal to us the perfectibility of man, and that it was by his life rather than by the shedding of his blood that we are saved. In this present hour of judgment, God is surely recalling us to a comprehension of the utterness of our dependence upon him. He is revealing to us the bankruptcy of our every achievement apart from the impact of his grace, which, in its gift of forgiveness, raises us to the enjoyment of a life that transcends our natural good. We are to learn today the primacy of the divine initiative, the primacy of the supernatural.

Not through our achievement are we brought from death to life. The occasion of that transition is an episode that reveals to us, beyond all measure of doubt, the depth of our wickedness. It is through man's cruelty that the glory of God is revealed. The lesson that these years

23. White, *Blackfriars* (1939).

would teach us is assuredly the lesson that if we would see him as he is, we must first look at the cross.

So God loved the world, and the "so" designates the cross. If we would see him as he is, we must first see what in his power he has done for us. We can only come to ourselves through the death of ourselves, and the place of our burial we share with him whom we crucified. To know our worth, we must admit that we are worthless. Rather, to say that we are, we must first say that we are not.

The work of the cross remains, and if we have eyes to see, we can comprehend its power amongst us at this hour. It is the weakness of the Crucified that lays low the kingdoms of men and brings the bewildered, through the admission that it alone is the place of God's revealing, to trust again their own intelligence.

As he is. We need to see him as he is. When we so see him, we are at first shocked that his face is marred above the sons of men. But as he confronts us, we are enabled to see of what stuff we ourselves are. Then no longer does it surprise us that there is no beauty that *we* should *desire him*.

The Church of God

Donald M. MacKinnon

Preface

In the preparation of this book, my main debt has undoubtedly been to the late Sir Edwyn Hoskyns's writings. More perhaps than any other English theologian, he has helped many of my generation to understand the character of Christianity as a revealed religion. In the later parts of the book, I owe a great deal to the more recent writings of Mr. Christopher Dawson, especially, perhaps, to the chapter "Christianity and Polities," in his book *Beyond Politics* (Sheed and Ward, 1939).

My colleague here, the Rev. J. D. M. Stuart, has helped me considerably with the preparation of the manuscript, and various pupils have read and commented on the book in typescript. To all of them I extend my thanks.

D. M. M.
Keble College, Oxford
June 1940

Introduction

We are concerned in this book[1] with the positive exposition of the mystery of the church of God. It is not an introductory textbook of church history, but rather the presentation of the relation of the church to the gospel of God—indeed, of the church as an integral part of that gospel. Disputes concerning the character, function, and dignity of that society are at bottom disputes concerning the very nature of the gospel. When we seem to be exercised concerning the claims or organization of a human corporation, it is rather with the ultimate simplicities of God's dealings with his creatures that we are concerned.

In an earlier volume in this series,[2] the fundamental character of that gospel was expounded. We were concerned there with the nature of divine revelation, of the mystery of life through death, of the uniqueness of Jesus. All this must be remembered if what follows is to be in the least intelligible. We cannot understand the church if we have misunderstood Christ. Conversely, we may make bold to say that an understanding of Christ necessarily entails an understanding of the church. For the church is the body of Christ.

On the occasion of the death of the late Pope Pius XI, and of the election of his successor, it was remarked by more than one commentator in this country that never for centuries had such interest been displayed by its citizens in the election of the head of the Roman Church. It should be remembered, moreover, that the election to the Papal chair and the coronation of Cardinal Eugenio Pacelli took place before Hitler's occupation of Prague and the collapse of all popular hopes of the avoidance of war. How, then, can the widespread interest—one might almost say concern—aroused by the election be understood? It is possible to dismiss it as a profound indication of "failure of nerve," or as yet a further sign of the flight from reason. Liberal observers will presumably thus interpret the phenomenon, and

1. Originally published as D. M. MacKinnon, *The Church of God*, Signposts, ed. J. V. L. Casserley and E. L. Mascall, no. 2 (Westminster: Dacre Press, 1940).
2. See D. M. MacKinnon, "God the Living and the True," in *Kenotic Ecclesiology* (Minneapolis: Fortress, 2016); Hereafter, cited in text as GLT.

wring their hands over man's willingness even to trifle with "outworn dogma." The familiar clichés somehow fail, however, to carry any conviction in a world whose interior frustrations are hourly more manifest, and whose visible predicament grows ever more terrible.

Rather perhaps we should see in this sudden, unaccountable enthusiasm of a predominantly Protestant England for the Vatican an expression of an awakening sense that we have no power to help ourselves. In the earlier volume mentioned, we contrasted certain emphases of the Christian faith in *God the Living and the True* with the departure and method of speculative philosophical theology. The harshness of certain oppositions was consciously emphasized, and critics of the book accused its author of "irrationalism." Yet it might be argued that the same disposition was expressed in this sudden concern of ordinary men and women with the Roman Pontiff. One can call it failure of nerve if one likes, but none can deny that it is a failure profoundly akin to that of those disciples of the Christ who said, "Lord, to whom shall we go? Thou hast the words of eternal life."[3] We can accuse them, if we will, of superstition. For in the narrative of St. John, the Master addressed had affirmed, to the grievous scandal of many of his listeners, that unless they chewed (for this is the force of the Greek word) his flesh and drank his blood, they were spiritually dead.[4] The reference may or may not be exclusively to the Eucharist, but at least the claim is uncompromising. What is demanded is the acknowledgment of the flesh of Christ as the place of the absolute and final revelation of God. The individual, transitory occasions of his earthly life—above all, the mortality by which it is conditioned, and in which it issues—there and there alone are the "words of eternal life."

So, today, after generations in which the distinction of the church and the world has been a natural scandal to the educated, men and women are suddenly aware again of that distinction as the sole ground of hope in a world increasingly at the mercy of impersonal forces they cannot control. The fact is that to men and women, groaning in the

3. John 6:68.
4. Cf. John 6:53–54.

agony of an unintelligible passion, the church of God suddenly again stands for something. And that something we may describe as the final and absolute revelation of Almighty God, given in the Word made flesh.

We see the popular expression of the collapse of that philosophy that distinguished the Liberal optimism of the past hundred years in this tentative acknowledgment of the church as a transcendent society. It may well be that it is through the *fact* of the church that the men and women of this age will come to understand the gospel. That statement must sound almost infinitely shocking to the mind of the Liberal humanist. For, as Christopher Dawson has repeatedly pointed out, in the mind of such a one the identification of the Augustinian "two cities" is reversed.[5] It is the world that is his city of God. Certainly no honest Christian will deny the terrible blots upon the history of the church. For its members are every one of them sinners in need of the mercy of God. Within the mystical body of Christ itself grace continually struggles with nature. But—that church is, and is alone, the city of God. For its character, as such, rests not upon the will of its members, but upon the act of the Son of God himself. To him, and to his flesh, it points. Its authority is his, and its mystery and scandal are the mystery and scandal of the Word made flesh.

To the church, then, men and women are looking, to the church that is part of the gospel of God, to the church that manifests that gospel to their necessity. This book is written in an endeavor to make that church intelligible, and also perhaps to assist those who read it in the further comprehension of the gospel, the good news of the Word made flesh.

Chapter 1: Flesh and Blood

The language of the New Testament is at once familiar and unfamiliar. There are few words employed in the writings that compose it that are

5. The contrast between the city of Man and the city of God was the theme of St. Augustine's *De Civitate Dei*, a work written at a time when the foundations of ancient civilization were crumbling; in it the author opposed the transitory character of human institutions to the permanence of the church of God.

technical, in the sense that such terms as "category" and "electron" are rightly regarded as physics. Even in such a work as St. John's Gospel, this principle holds true. If we find that writing hard to understand, its difficulty is not that of a philosophical treatise. We find such a work as Kant's *Critique of Pure Reason* difficult to understand principally because of the formidable apparatus of technical terms the author employs. We ask ourselves again and again what he is trying to say.

Now with the evangelist, the position is quite different. Certainly his language often involves nuances that escape us in consequence of our natural unfamiliarity with the Septuagint,[6] with Jewish apocalyptic[7] of the last century BCE, and with the whole interior complexity of Hebrew theology. But it is surely significant how often his thought is presented to us not in abstract but in concrete terms, how often indeed in concrete terms referring to physical particulars that are the objects of sensuous perception. He is no metaphysician, though often his work is as difficult to understand as any metaphysical treatise. Its difficulty is precisely due to the fact that in it we are brought face to face, within the normal context of everyday human life, with that which is final and absolute. There is no shrinking from any aspect of that context. Not least is its physical groundwork recognized by the evangelist. The particularities of time and place receive an almost forced emphasis. Again and again we are reminded that the scene of his tale is not just anywhere. It is Galilee—Judea—Jerusalem; the particular geographical region is emphasized, and the cultural and religious traditions of a single people exhibited as the background of the universal crisis of humanity. Again and again, too, we are bidden to remember the limitations of time. To say that the gospel is "a myth, a parable of eternal truth" is grossly to misrepresent the evangelist. How can such an interpretation be reconciled with the repeated insistence on the hour that "is not yet come,"[8] and that on the night of betrayal

6. The Greek version of the Jewish Bible.

7. The name given to writings purporting to set out in their exact order those events foreordained by God to usher in the end of the world and the final accomplishment of his purposes; e.g. the book of Enoch. For a full discussion of the importance of the apocalyptic outlook, see J. V. L. Casserley, *Providence and History*, Signposts 11 (Westminster: Dacre Press, 1940).

8. John 2:4, 7:6, 7:8, 7:30, 8:20.

at length "has come"?[9] How are the references to the year of the priesthood of Caiaphas as "*that* year"[10] to be rendered consistent with such a view?

The gospel is, in part at least, a message of universal salvation. But it has its roots in history. Salvation was wrought out for man in the flesh of Jesus. In a particular human life, in an individual "flesh and blood," a work was wrought that was the very work of God. "What was insupportable for the Greek, as it is to the modern man," writes Pastor Hermann Sasse, "was that a man, who had lived at a definite time, and in a definite place, and whose death was an established historical fact, should be the revelation."[11]

The language of St. John is legitimate if we grant him the premise of his prologue. "The Word became flesh."[12] His whole narrative is an exposition of that theme. It is a rendering explicit of its implications. By the term "flesh," he refers to the conditions of distinctively human existence. It is a curious paradox that his prologue has served so many would-be "Christian metaphysicians" with their starting point. It is true that it is concerned with the fundamentals of the relations of God and man, but its climax is a sentence that focuses attention, not on universal principles, but on a concrete, particular occasion. We forget the particularity, the limitations involved in "fleshliness." As Professor Karl Adam has written,[13] "The eternal appears subject to succession, living a day-to-day life; the infinite finite, limited; the perfect fragile and fragmentary; the holy in 'a body of sin'."[14]

The difficulty that the Fourth Gospel presents to understanding is a reflection at the level of self-conscious intellectual activity of the whole "scandal of particularity," of God the unfamiliar manifested in the particular and familiar. And what is true of the scandal of the gospel is true of the scandal of the church. After all, the church is

9. John 13:1, 17:1.
10. John 11:49, 11:51, 18:13.
11. Hermann Sasse, *Mysterium Christi*, ed. G. K. A. Bell and Adolf Deissmann (London: Longmans, 1930), 101.
12. John 1:14.
13. Karl Adams, *L'Eglise est une*, ed. Pierre Chaillet (Paris: Bloud et Gay, 1939) as quoted in *Theology* (Sept. 1939): 164.
14. Cf. Rom. 8:3, in the likeness of sinful flesh.

just one historical phenomenon among many. Historians whose metaphysical premises are frankly naturalistic must take account of it. It is a "thing of flesh and blood," a concrete, visible institution, its members individual, mortal human beings. An atheist can write an account of the church, at some period of its history, of its impact upon the social and economic institutions of that time. We need not question the validity of his methods. Church history can be regarded as a proper subject of empirical historical study. But there, affirms the Christian, is the power of God unto salvation.

Our language reflects our condition. When Kant wrote of space and time as forms of our experience, his insight was sound in that he called attention to the most pervasive features of that experience, and to the factors that most characteristically limit and impede scope. The events of the physical world succeed one another in time and are separate from one another in space. It is to the physical world that the church belongs, and our exposition of its character is infected by the fact. The church is historical in a sense analogous to that in which we say that Christ was historical. When we read that the church is an extension of the incarnation, our attention is being called at least in part to this analogy existing between a particular individual and an institution. We are also reminded of what may be called the priority of the incarnation. That is the primary fact, which it is the function of the church, as it were, to extend to earth's remotest end and time's ultimate conclusion. The incarnation—"a dagger thrust in the heart of the world"—to adopt a striking phrase of the late Sir Edwyn Hoskyns—is the starting-point. But between the mystery of the incarnation and the mystery of the church, there is an analogy. Reflection on the mystery of the one may well serve to illuminate the mystery of the other. Yet the incarnation remains primary, the incarnation, that is to say, understood in the light of the cross. We fail utterly to understand the mystery of the flesh and blood of Christ if we ignore the mortality that it entailed. The statement, "the Word became flesh," is not to be regarded primarily as a basis for philosophical construction. It is the affirmation of man's redemption. In the reading of the first chapter of St. John's Gospel at the end of Mass, priest and people kneel at the words "And the Word was made flesh" as an acknowledgement, not of the dignity of the creature, but of the humiliation of the Creator.

"Everything," wrote that great Anglican divine, Bishop Butler, "is what it is and not another thing." Those words might well be inscribed on the walls of any theologian's study. The temptation to over-systematize what is in itself "creative and unmanageable" is surely the besetting sin of the theologian. If sacred theology consists of the application of the human understanding under the guiding light of faith to the fuller comprehension of the mysteries of divine revelation, the theologian, though he may not realize it, is neglecting the aim that he has himself avowed as soon as he permits, in thought, the reduction of his material to the status of anything other than itself. What he is concerned to comprehend is unique:

> Once, only once, and once for all, His precious life he gave.[15]

The passion and resurrection of Jesus are unique events. We may indeed detect all kinds of analogies to their efficacy. The very description of them as effective, as in some sense causal processes, presupposes that there is some kind of likeness-in-unlikeness between them and (let us say) an event in the physical world. But the theologian's task is difficult because he is dealing with something that is of the very nature of the case quite simply beyond him. The initiative is divine. What he is trying to understand cannot be reduced to terms of anything except itself.

The same difficulties that beset us in the sphere of the doctrine of Christ, and of the work of Christ, beset us again when we come to deal with the church. The church is a society, possessing a visible structure. It has, as we have said, played a very important part in history. School examination papers still ask for short notes on prominent ecclesiastics. But the church can only be properly understood as an evangelical fact, as an aspect of the gospel.

15. William Bright, "Once, Only Once, and Once For All," in *Hymns Ancient and Modern*, Standard Edition, 1875–1924, ed. H.W. Baker (London: William Clowes and Sons, 1922), no. 315.

The church is there to be understood, as Christ was once there to be understood. The givenness of the church recalls the givenness of its Lord. "God so loved the world that he gave."[16] In that sentence the glory and the scandal of the gospel is given concrete form. The world is the object of God's love. That is the ultimate ground of Christian hope. But "God so loved the world that he gave." The structure of the sentence exhibits the mode of the giving as a consequence of the manner of the loving. We are to see the love of God manifest in the gift. We may refuse the gift, which is the flesh and blood of Jesus, and there is much in its character that invites and encourages our refusal. But the fact that it is God's gift remains, and in our refusal of it, we are rejecting the very love of God towards us, which it manifests and would make operative in our lives.

So with the church. When a man confesses that the church is the body of Christ, he must acknowledge that it is not flesh and blood that has revealed this fact unto him, but the Father, which is in heaven.[17] The church is a mystery of faith. It is only when through faith we have acknowledged its authority that its paradox can become at all intelligible to us. In accepting the church, a man accepts a society, which, though visible and distinguishable among many others, is not as those others are. When Bill Jones joins the Ancient Order of Buffaloes, his life is not radically affected. He has contracted certain new obligations. He may even wear a distinctive badge. But he remains Bill Jones. When, however, he is baptised, and made a member of Christ's church, the whole context of his life is altered. As we shall see, it is his inmost nature that is affected.[18] Membership in the church involves a participation in the death of Christ. It carries with it so intimate and so terrible a change in a man's relationship to the world that St. Paul does not hesitate to talk of his entry within the church as involving his death and resurrection.[19]

The church is, as we have said, the extension of the incarnation. And

16. John 3:16.
17. Cf. Matt. 16:17.
18. See below, chap. 10 (152–55).
19. Rom. 6:3ff.

when a man is made a member of the church, he himself becomes, as it were, part of that extension. He could not, of course, be saved at all were it not for the original sacrifice of the obedience of Jesus offered to God in isolation, anguish, and dereliction. We are utterly and absolutely dependent, in respect of our very humanity, upon the accomplishment of that act. But nonetheless it is the function of the church to manifest the very mystery of the flesh of Jesus until he shall come again. The Christian is indeed healed by his stripes, for there is salvation in none other. But it is in and through a visible society that God has ordained that that Christ should be manifested unto the world.

That is the paradox of the church's situation, a paradox that is only resolved when we have grasped more intimately the primacy of the divine initiative. Enough, however, has perhaps been said to make clear what it is that this book is concerned to do. We are not concerned with details of ecclesiastical organization. We are, in the most literal sense, concerned with the gospel. Our interest is solely evangelical in that it is concentrated upon the redemption wrought out by God in human flesh and blood.

Our first task is to expound the relation of Christ to his church, and that perhaps, because it is our first task, is our hardest. There we are at the center, not as it were on the circumference, of the problem of the very relation of God to his creatures. Then that problem there can be none more ultimate, nor any whose solution carries with it more far-reaching implications. For God is our origin, and our final end is intelligible only in terms of his most excellent glory. We cannot therefore expect to find our task an easy one. Our concern is with the ultimate, with that beyond which there is nothing, with him who was, and is, and ever shall be himself.

Chapter 2: My God, My God, Why Hast Thou Forsaken Me?

The very strangeness in our ears of the title of this chapter is an index of our curiously imperfect grasp of the evangelical significance of the church. We are familiar enough with this first verse of the twenty-second Psalm, which was, according to the record of St. Mark and St.

Matthew, spoken by Jesus upon the cross. But at first sight, it seems that such a cry can have little or nothing to do with the subject of this book.

"The word 'Church,'"[20] said Sir Edwyn Hoskyns, "means 'Belonging to the Lord' (*kuriakon*); hence the Slavonic *Cerkov*, the German *Kirche*, the Scottish *Kirk*, and the English *Church*. The word is therefore not a translation of the Biblical word *Ecclesia*, but an admirable paraphrase of it. *He Ekklesia* in the Greek translation of the Old Testament means the Hebrew people considered as the chosen people of God, his peculiar possession, concrete flesh and blood, men and women, selected from all other peoples for the worship and for the glory of God in the world. The holiness and the complete purity of worship involved in this selection remained in the Old Testament unrealised; but the prophets looked forward confidently to the future realisation of the righteousness of God, and declared the certainty of the advent of his true worship. Upon this unfulfilled Old Testament background and in the midst of the Jewish people our Lord wrought out his mission as the Christ, the fulfilment of Old Testament prophecy."

This quotation has been made to emphasize the fact that the church shares, with its master, an Old Testament background. No more is the church intelligible apart from the "fulfilment of Old Testament prophecy" than is the life of Jesus. The roots of the church are in that life, and it is as the fulfillment of the expectation of Israel that the direction of that life is to be understood.

We are living at a moment of unparalleled opportunity for the preaching of the gospel. The sudden recovery of a vision of the church as in some sense a transcendent society, to which we drew attention in our introduction, is not entirely attributable to anxiety concerning the future, even though it is provoked in part by material fear. In part we may discern, in that recovery, a hankering after that which only the good news of the flesh of Jesus can supply, to wit, a ground of

20. In a short, but brilliant, paper read to the Anglo-Catholic Congress in 1930 on the apostolicity of the church; cf. *Report of the Anglo-Catholic Congress* (Westminster: Catholic Literature Association, 1930), 85ff. In what follows, as throughout this book, I am immeasurably indebted to the writings of this theologian.

hope.[21] Very few men and women retain that reverence for their own collective achievement, which marked the period of their blindness to its implications. Again and again one hears it said (admittedly in less technical language) that there is no way out on the natural plane. In a situation, which patently defies rational comprehension, men and women are willing to allow the possibility that only the terrible paradoxes of the gospel, to which the church bears witness, can reveal its true import.

It is perhaps too early to assess the manifold crosscurrents of English theological thought in the latter half of the nineteenth century and the first three decades of the twentieth, or to say that, despite their conflict, they nonetheless manifested a common direction. But they may be not unfairly described as in the main influenced by a refusal to admit that Christianity is fundamentally an "evangelical, biblical way of salvation." We have mentioned elsewhere the Modernist experiment,[22] and it is, of course, an extreme instance of the tendency suggested. But a subtler form of the same error can be detected in what underlay a fashionable jargon of the later 1920s and early 1930s. When Liberal theologians spoke of Christianity as "Incarnationalist," or suggested that, whereas the central emphasis of Protestantism rested on the Atonement, that of Catholicism rested on the incarnation, they failed to realize how utterly they were misrepresenting the primitive Catholic gospel.

The gospel is a thing of terror, and we are not merely paying lip service to Kierkegaard when we say so. In the primitive narrative of St. Mark, we are not asked to attend to a profound metaphysical teaching. We are asked to watch a series of events that move inexorably to a catastrophic and terrible issue. Even in the earliest chapters, there are hints of what is to come, and when the climax of Caesarea Philippi and the confession of Peter is past, the narrative is dominated by the approach of an event whose sheer horror must inspire dread in the bravest.

21. Cf. on this, the chapter dealing with the church in Peter Drucker's *The End of Economic Man* (London: William Heinemann, 1939).
22. See MacKinnon, GLT, chap. 1 (48–62).

The New Testament is the fulfillment of the Old. We are quite familiar with that truth. But we pay little attention to its implication. It was Amos who spoke of "the day of the Lord" as a day of "darkness, and not light"[23] many centuries before "there was darkness over all the land."[24] It is Jesus who fulfills the Old Testament. "The Son of Man goeth as it is written of him."[25] It is by him that the sovereignty of God is acknowledged; in the moment of his final obedience, God's kingdom indeed comes with power. There upon the cross was the fulfillment of Israel's hope, a fulfillment made possible by her very apostasy. "We have no king but Caesar."[26] Thus upon the day of the Lord do God's chosen people, his peculiar possession, make their contribution to the realization of their ultimate hopes. Not through the loyalty of the historic, visible Israel to her vocation is the purpose of that vocation fulfilled, but rather in and through an apostasy that thrust the whole burden of the acknowledgment of divine sovereignty, which was her purpose and her hope, upon the isolated figure of Jesus.

"When the Messiah, in and through whom alone the vocation of Israel as the people of God could be realised, stands alone before the high priest, deserted even by the chosen disciples, his rejection is a turning-point, decisive both for the Messiah himself and for Israel who rejected him. He is the sole representative at that moment of God's holy people; he bears in his own Person the whole burden of Israel's appointed destiny."[27]

Christ before Pilate affirms that for this cause came he forth (not from Galilee, but from the Father) to bear witness unto the truth. That is the vocation fulfilled by the Son of God made man. It is a vocation fulfilled by him on an occasion constituted by the apostasy of the very people of whose hopes he was the fulfillment. As Fr. Gregory Dix has written: "Even in the darkness and dereliction of Calvary, God still is, he is still God, he is still proclaimed 'My God.' I suppose that is what is

23. Amos 5:18.
24. Matt. 27:45.
25. Matt. 26:24.
26. John 19:15.
27. William Temple, ed. *Doctrine in the Church of England: The Report of the Commission on Christian Doctrine Appointed by the Archbishops of Canterbury and York in 1922* (London: SPCK, 1938), 102.

meant by the coming among men of the *basileia tou theou*, the *kingship* of God, in the power and the glory of it; when a man in the might of the Spirit surrenders himself to the ruling of God, against all human hope and without possibility of retreat, without one last little reservation for 'the arm of the flesh' by which to reassure himself."[28]

Dix's brilliant comment explains the title of this chapter. In those words, we are to see a cry of triumph in dereliction, the attestation of the sovereignty of God, the coming of his kingdom. The truth of divine sovereignty, to the attestation of which among the nations Israel was called, is here acknowledged in act in the perfect obedience of Jesus. And the truth he attests concerning the being of his Father is at the same time the truth concerning himself. *It is as a claimant to Messiahship that his own people reject him.* It is *himself* that his crucified flesh attests. His act is no mere human act, but an act of God wrought out in human flesh and blood.

So the church emerges on the plane of history as the new Israel of God, a society that exists to attest the achievement of Israel's hope. To quote Hoskyns again:[29] "His rejection by the Jews was the rejection of the Christ of God and the end of the old Ecclesia of God. In their place was brought into being the new Ecclesia, the new people of God, and this new people was formed from those who obeyed the Messianic call to repentance and gathered round Jesus, the Messiah. To those Messianic disciples the teaching of Jesus was primarily directed. The crowds in the Gospel narratives were men and women from whom the Lord confidently expected the new people of God to emerge; and the new people of God were extracted from the crowds one by one."

The new Israel and the old are divided by the crisis of the coming of Jesus. For the coming of Jesus is the coming of the kingdom of God. The destiny of Israel depended, as indeed that of all mankind depends, on acceptance or rejection of the Son of God. It was Israel's rejection of him that constituted the occasion of the fulfillment of the purpose for which he was manifest. If we are to understand the church at all,

28. Fr. G. Dix, OSB. "The Prophet and the Church: Dogma and the Mystical Body—I," *Sobornost* 19 (Sept. 1939): 19.
29. E. C. Hoskyns, *The Anglo-Catholic Congress* (London: Anglo-Catholic Congress Committee, 1930), 85ff.

we must see in it the new Israel, which claims the fulfillment of God's purpose in the flesh of Jesus, as attested by his resurrection from the dead.

So it is that the origin of the Christian Church is found in the act of God wrought out upon Calvary. Its members are those who in baptism have made that act their own, have become, in the language of the Prayer Book Catechism, "members of Christ, children of God, and inheritors of the Kingdom of Heaven." Of the mystery of membership of Christ, we shall have much to say later.[30] At present, we would suggest the significance of the last of the triad. The church is constituted of those who acknowledge the divine sovereignty, or rather of those in whom has been realized the infinitely costly acknowledgment of that sovereignty wrought by Jesus. Members of the church are under the very sovereignty of God, and in consequence they enjoy already a foretaste of that beatitude that is the portion of those who acclaim his absolute dominion.

The church is surely then rightly regarded by those who understand even dimly those things that are now coming on the earth as the ground of man's ultimate hope. The very nature of the church as the new Israel is itself testimony to the strength of God. It was the very apostasy of his chosen, of those whom he had knit to himself by the closest of ties, that supplied the occasion of his self-vindication. It was in the mangled flesh and shed blood of Jesus that his sovereignty was acknowledged; it was through the very frustration of his purposes that his glory was revealed. All this, the church attests, and, as the body of Christ, proclaims the everlasting sovereignty of God, Alpha and Omega, the first and the last.

And it is in its Liturgy, in its "showing of the Lord's death till he come," that the church stands most assuredly as witness to a tortured world that, where its self-contradiction was most hideously manifest, in the apostasy of the very chosen people of God, there was Christ attested as victor in his resurrection from the dead.

30. See below, chap. 8, 9, 10 (134–55).

Chapter 3: Apostles of God

We have seen how the whole mission of Israel is fulfilled in the accomplishment of the passion of Christ. The whole burden of the destiny of the people of God was borne by him. His manifestation in desolation is, of course, a paradox to us as to his contemporaries as long as we persist in ignoring the contradictions of our human predicament. The coming of the Messiah does not reveal the fact that human things can easily be made perfect, but the fact that they labor under a massive contradiction. As Hoskyns has rightly said, the place where the Christ is crucified is the place where the tension of human life is greatest. It is a paradox that the historical context of Calvary is the apostasy of the very people of God. Israel was God's peculiar possession. It is by those whose whole outlook on the world is dominated by the sense of a divine call that Christ is brought to death. It is within a setting that God himself has provided by the whole history of his relation with Israel that these terrible events take place. It is the very spiritual opportunity of Israel that creates the condition of the rejection of the Messiah.

All this is infinitely shocking to the humanist, to the believer in progress, to the comfortable "Incarnationalist" theologian. That the people of God, brought face to face with his Son, should thus refuse to accept him is bad enough, but that the whole ground of their action should have emerged out of the glory of their past, should clothe itself with the character of an act of allegiance to God the Living and the True is a paradox to humble the strongest. Yet how else can we understand the words of the high priest: "What need have we of witnesses? Ye have heard the blasphemy?"[31]

Though in the narrative of the gospel there is set before us the account of the calling of the new Messianic people, nonetheless the work of the Messiah is wrought out in isolation. In the primitive record of St. Mark, the Lord is an utterly isolated figure. His disciples, even as the crowds from which he has called them, persistently misunderstand him; finally, they forsake him and flee. St. Luke, always the humanist of

31. Mark 14:63.

the evangelists, tends to mitigate the severity of his isolation, but here, as so often, in St. John, the theological kinsman of St. Mark, it is harshly reaffirmed.

What has been said here justifies the choice by a recent Anglican writer[32] of the title "The Church and the Passion" for the first chapter of his book. It is to the gospel of God that the church bears witness, and the gospel of God is simply Jesus crucified, but attested Son of God by his rising again from the dead. Where the contradiction and frustration of human life was revealed at its most intense, there was the very act of God wrought out; there did he himself, in the depth of mortal weakness, vindicate his character and his claim. "For this cause came I into the world that I should bear witness unto the truth."[33]

No one can attempt to write of the church of God unless he has first allowed himself to be in a measure broken by the shattering paradox of the New Testament revelation, which the church attests. The meaning of the church is the death and resurrection of Jesus, and it may even be said that the meaning of the death and resurrection of Jesus is the new Israel that is constituted thereby. We are to concern ourselves in the following chapters with various aspects of the church's life. In all our discussions, we will find that again and again the paradoxes we encounter become intelligible when we refer them to the paradox of the passion of Christ.

We have said that the hardest moment of our problem is the determination of the relation between Christ and his church. We might have said that it was the determination of the precise sense borne by the conjunction "as" in the formal commission given by Jesus Christ to his apostles after his resurrection: "As the Father hath sent me, even so send I you."[34] Anyone attempting to look at the New Testament as a whole must agree with St. Mark that, historically speaking, the "beginning of the Gospel of Jesus Christ, the Son of God,"[35] was the coming of John the Baptist. In the actual observable sequence of

32. A. M. Ramsey, *The Gospel and the Catholic Church* (London: Longmans, 1936).
33. John 18:37.
34. John 20:21.
35. Mark 1:1.

events, the earthly ministry of Jesus was preceded by that of the Baptist. To the human observer, that is the starting place of the whole short series of events. Of course, behind Jesus was his individual background, his home at Nazareth, his mother, his kinsfolk. As man, he had a particular individual background from which he emerged to transform the religious situation, which had been created by the preaching of the Baptist. But behind that background was—what? That is the underlying question. Throughout the whole Gospel narrative, the debate of Jesus's critics with his disciples and himself, and among themselves, centered on that question. In what sense can the work of Jesus be regarded as a mission?

"As the Father hath sent me, even so send I you." The language is so simple and so familiar that we easily fail to grasp its significance. The verb "send" is common and everyday. Why is it that if we ask "Is Jesus sent?" the question is of such tremendous import? The import of the question becomes intelligible when we realize that we are so using the word "sent" that we cannot answer the question in the affirmative unless we can say, "Sent by God." We are perplexed and disturbed because, when we ask that question, we are wanting to know whether we dare look for the origin of a whole series of historical events to that which is utterly beyond history. When we ask if Jesus is sent, we want to know if he is the Apostle of God.[36]

We are familiar enough with the application of the title "apostle" to the members of the Twelve, but we do not perhaps realize that the character of their apostolate is determined by the character of the apostolate of him who sent them. We can understand any leader or teacher instructing and commissioning followers to carry on his work when he is dead. If such a leader has himself evoked in those who knew him an affection bordering on reverence, we can understand how, in the eyes of later generations of adherents to his teaching, those who were his most intimate followers should be held in like regard. But the dignity of the followers of such a human leader can, after all,

36. Cf. F. N. Davey, "Biblical Theology," *Theology* (Mar. 1939): 166–76. The word "apostle" is derived from the Greek noun *apostolos*, meaning "one sent"; the corresponding verb, *apostellein*, is used by St. John of the sending of the Son.

be no more than a relative dignity. They are the intimates of a man among men, albeit a great benefactor of mankind. We do not ask such a benefactor the same question as we ask of his champions, "Who put you up to this?" We do not thrust the question further back, as we must do in the case of Jesus.

But with him it is different. The records of his teaching and life reveal to us not a teacher of ethical principles commissioning followers to propagate a peculiar doctrine. Rather, we are face to face with one who is presented to us as embodying in his presence the occasion of a final decision. He is spoken of as calling men unto him, of making demands upon them that are intelligible only if we grant the underlying assumption of the whole tale: that here is the End, the place of final revelation, the occasion of ultimate decision.

If we like, we can dismiss the whole thing as a farrago of nonsense. We can refuse to ask ourselves the questions that the gospel thrusts upon us, we can refuse to ask if Jesus is indeed the Apostle of God. And, if we do, the apostolate of the Twelve ceases likewise to be a problem for us. They are no longer the patriarchs of the new Israel; they are simply twelve rather pathetic, misguided individuals.

What we think of the apostolate on which the historic church rests will depend on what we think of the mission of Jesus. If we can explain the latter without reference to the supernatural, as some of his would-be biographers have tried to do, then the former, too, we will understand in the same way. The question of the character and claim of the church is not settled when we have shown that it was founded by Jesus. No one who is prepared to allow any historical weight to the Gospel narratives would deny that Jesus did in point of fact call together a peculiar intimacy, and that it would seem that this group did form the nucleus out of which emerged the Christian Church. Scholars whose presuppositions are frankly agnostic would admit a sense in which they must allow that Jesus did indeed found a church. But what matters is not simply the natural continuity between the first disciples and the present; it is rather the setting in which the call of those early disciples is cast. Is that setting supplied by the natural observable processes of human history? Jesus may be said in some sense to have sent the disciples. But can we say that he sent them even as his Father had sent him? That is the crux, the final and ultimate question to which any attempt to grapple with the fundamentals of the Christian faith must drive us back again and again. In discussing the doctrine of the church, if our theological insight is sharp enough, we shall find ourselves thrust back on the question of the person of Jesus, of the revelation that he brought, or rather of the revelation that he himself was in his life and above all in his passion, as that is made intelligible by the resurrection that followed it.

These are ultimate questions, and even as we say that they are so, we are realizing that we are not using the word "ultimate" quite as we had been accustomed to do before we were led to ask these questions. When we ask questions about the gospel, we are taken by roads that seem familiar enough to places where what was hitherto familiar is infected by novelty and paradox. For the gospel of Christ is something utterly and absolutely unique, and the path whereby we are led to assimilate it (for this is our end, as *we* see it) is in every sense a Way of Sorrows.

Did the Father send the Son? That is the question, and on our answer to that question, our whole attitude to the church depends. If the church is to be understood as sent by the Son, even as he was sent by the Father, we are indeed faced in the church with the power of God unto salvation. For though the victory over the evil powers was won by the Messiah "without the aid of his disciples and in spite of their unbelief,"[37] none the less, "they are the fruit of his victory and to them its general redemptive proclamation was entrusted."

The church, the new Israel, is the fruit of the Messianic victory. We can even say, elaborating the metaphor, that the cross is the tree of which the children of the church are the fruit. They are themselves as close to Christ crucified as that; their dependence upon him is as complete.

37. E. C. Hoskyns, "Jesus, the Messiah." In *Mysterium Christi: Christological Studies by British and German Theologians*, edited by G. K. A. Bell and D. A. Deissmann (London: Longmans, Green and Co., 1930) 86.

The church is the society in whose members the victory of Christ over the powers that hold men in thrall and render frustrate their every effort and achievement is manifest. They are his members, and by baptism in him, they have passed from death to life.

Yet in the world, the life of God was fully manifest in the death of Jesus. The coming of the kingdom of God in him revealed itself in terms of the very frustration of natural human hope. The centurion confessed him the Son of God, when he hung lifeless and pitiful upon the cross.[38] There is the kingdom of God—not where, in pomp of outward circumstance, lip service is paid to the church by the great ones of this world, but where, amid mockery, contempt, and loneliness, the body of Christ dying unto the world reveals by its very incognito that it is alive unto God and victorious in the power of that victory that was and is his alone. For even as Christ himself was the slave[39] of the Father's dominion, so his body, in the concrete occasions of its historical life, must strive to exhibit his sovereignty as alone absolute and unconditional. It is in the Liturgy, where formal oblation is made of his passion, that the imperfections of its witness are blotted out by the all-sufficiency of his act.

To this truth, in a Eucharistic hymn familiar to generations of Anglicans, the late Dr. William Bright gave powerful expression:

> Look, Father, look on his anointed face,
> And only look on us as found in him:
> Look not on our misusings of thy grace,
> Our prayer so languid, and our faith so dim;
> For lo! Between our sins and their reward
> We set the Passion of thy Son our Lord.[40]

"Our misusings of thy grace." It is in the purpose of the church that we see the purpose of God's grace, which is one with the purpose of creation—his glory. We are incorporated into the church, into the very body of Christ, to acknowledge the sovereignty of God, to be the

38. Matt. 27:54; Mark 15:39.
39. Cf. Acts 4:27: thy holy child (slave) Jesus.
40. William Bright. "And Now, O Father, Mindful of the Love." In *Hymns Ancient and Modern*, Standard Edition, 1875-1924, edited by H. W. Baker, (London: William Clowes and Sons, 1922), No. 322.

witnesses of his kingship, even as Christ attested it in the dereliction of Calvary. But though in him we are dead to the world, yet still in ourselves we are intensely alive to its attraction. It is not a paradox that the church, which in itself is to bear witness unto the Truth of God among the nations, is ever thrust back upon the admission of the passion as alone the attestation of his sovereignty. Rather, as we shall see, the whole character of the life of its members is infected by the tension of being at once within Christ and without, at once of him and dependent upon him. For the church is sent by Christ to witness to Christ, and, in the achievement of his work, he, who is in his church, is there outside it in his fullness, to be attested by it as other than itself.

"As the Father hath sent me, even so send I you."

Chapter 4: The Revelation of the Mystery

The method of Christian theology in all its departments is prescribed by the peculiar character of its material. It is not primarily a speculative study. For it is the elucidation of a gospel, of good news brought to men and women at that point where their predicament was revealed most acutely—namely, at that place where the Christ was crucified. It is for that reason that any account of the church of God must begin with the exposition of that to which the church bears witness, and that which, in a measure, it makes accessible to men—to wit, the mercy of God revealed in the face of Jesus Christ.

The theme of the New Testament is God's relations with man, whom he has created; a theme treated not as technically expert metaphysicians might treat it, but treated by men who have learned to see the whole pattern of these relations in the light of a particular individual history. And the Christian theologian, if he is to be loyal to his character as Christian, must likewise in all his investigation view his immediate subject-matter not in abstraction, but in relation to the flesh of Jesus. Thus in discussing the doctrine of the church, and of the sacraments, one must avoid all forms of reasoning that suggest that their mysteries can be understood apart from the revelation of God in Christ.

In discussing what are called the "Sacraments of the Gospel,"[41] all appeal to the "logic of the sacramental idea" must be rigorously excluded until the character of these rites as indeed sacraments of the gospel has been made absolutely precise. Similarly, as long as we seek to approach the mystery of the church by way of reflection on man's social nature, on the fact that he is certainly capable of sympathy and affection, we are only going to find ourselves confused and bewildered. Certainly the order of grace illuminates the dimly comprehended facts of the natural order. Of that we shall have much to say later. But at present, we are concerned only to utter an urgent warning against supposing that the giant themes of Christian theology can be approached without reference to the revelation of God.

An apologetic who seeks to commend the sacramental life by the argument that it fits in with man's actual, present situation is literally sub-Christian. If we have begun to grasp the import of the sixth chapter of St. John's Gospel, we shall see that much talk of the "sacramental principle" (a theme beloved by conventional apologetics) is frankly out of place when our concern is with the commendation of baptism and the Eucharist. We may contrast the precise theology of the Prayer-Book Catechism, where emphasis is laid on the dominical institution of the sacraments. "Ordained by Christ himself." We should not suppose that "himself" to be altogether without point. It is their institution by Christ himself that in part constitutes the sacraments of baptism and the Eucharist as sacraments of the gospel. Their performance is not primarily concerned with the stimulation of our devotion, but with the rendering accessible to us of the very saving act of God, wrought out in the flesh of Jesus.

Similarly, the church is set before us as a visible fellowship attesting that act. Its outward order is, as we shall see, intelligible only when it is understood as relating it to that very history that it attests. The life and death of Jesus, to which the church bears witness, is not a mere dramatic exposition of certain general principles that might, by a sufficiently farseeing intelligence, be grasped apart from it. Were that

41. Cf. Article XXV of the XXXIX *Articles of the Church of England.*

so, there might be something to be said for the suggestion of certain Liberal theologians that the function of the church was to make itself unnecessary, to guide men to a utopia, where they would have no further need of its witness; for at length they would have made their own the principles embodied in the life of Jesus, and would be able to dismiss their tutor. But we see now that we must rigorously reject such an attitude as utterly foreign to the gospel. The life, passion, death, and resurrection of Jesus are not thus to be dismissed as a mythological presentation of universal principles. Indeed, when we approach them, we must first jettison, at least for a while, our conventional distinction of universal and particular. There, in the concrete particularities of an individual occasion, *is* the act of God.

Thus our concern is with the nature of the gospel— even, one might say, with the question: Is there a gospel? Our perplexities concerning the character and office of the church cut as deep as that. In this present day, we do indeed see that men and women are turning to the church as the witness to the gospel. For how else can we understand that phenomenon to which we called attention in our introduction? It is not that men and women are blind to the manifold imperfections of the individual members of the church, especially of those called to high office therein. The Spanish tragedy threw them into sharp relief. It is to the church as bearing witness to the gospel of God that men are turning, and it is to it therefore as fulfilling its office of compelling men into that place where "the tension of human life is sharpest—even the place where the Christ was crucified." It is the example of the martyrs that is compelling men to reconsider the mystery of revelation, and that is inevitable. For in martyrdom unto death, the whole witness of the church is made concrete.

The martyr is, in a sense, an isolated figure. But his witness is unintelligible apart from the dogma of the group of which he is a member. It is that which he attests, in the moment of its conflict with the dogma of a rival group, by his willingness to die. So with the Christian martyr. It is to the Christian dogma that he bears witness, and the Christian dogma has its roots in the primitive apostolic proclamation of the word of God in Christ, with which it is directly continuous.[42] The Christian martyr bears witness to Christ and to the work of Christ. He attests the vindication of divine sovereignty wrought out upon the cross. His martyrdom is a formal attestation of the gospel. But it is a burden laid upon him not merely by a special vocation, but by his membership of a society compelled by its very origin to witness to the Truth.

The church is a martyr church. One of the great keywords in the New Testament account of the church is "witness."[43] Its use is not governed by a completely uniform rule, but its emphasis is constant. The church is not commissioned with the proclamation of universal truths of morality and the like. It is concerned to attest a concrete life and death as the very act of God. This might once have seemed a rather narrow task as contrasted with (let us say) the encouragement of "just solid service and nothing more."[44] But in this crucial moment of history, which has aroused man's slumbering sense of his need of redemption, men and women are discerning in that gospel, and in the fact of its attestation, the only ground of their hope. Of the full theological significance of this, more will be said later.

But we have said enough, perhaps, to show the significance of the title of this chapter. The Christianity of the individual is no nice, ordered pattern of spiritual exercise. It is the rigid conformity of the individual to the inexorable demand of a final and an absolute revelation. The antithesis (beloved of journalistic theologians) between spiritual and institutional religion is utterly without basis in the New Testament. In the Gospel of St. John, which was called by Clement of Alexandria the "spiritual" gospel, the function of the Holy Ghost, whom the Father sends in the name of the Son, is rigorously prescribed. "He shall take of mine, and shall shew it unto you."[45] Of

42. Cf. C. H. Dodd, *Apostolic Preaching and its Developments* (London: Hodder and Stoughton, 1934). See also Fr. G. Dix, OSB, "The Prophet and the Church: Dogma and the Mystical Body—II," *Sobornost* 20 (Dec. 1939): 5.
43. From the Greek word, *martus*, meaning "witness," the English word "martyr," with its narrower sense, is derived.
44. In these words, Dr. Cyril Norwood has expressed his conception of the aim and scope of Christian education; see *The English Tradition in Education* (London: John Murray, 1932).
45. John 16:15.

mine—of the things that belong to the flesh and blood of Jesus. The flight from institutional religion is a flight from history, a flight from a gospel that is rooted in history.

The church is a scandal to those to whom religion is a technique of spiritual achievement. For it attests that Christianity is concerned primarily, not "with man's love for God, but with God's love for man."[46] Within the church, the Holy Ghost, who descended upon the apostles at the first Pentecost after "the Passover of God," takes of the things of Christ and shows them unto the members of his body. Its visible institutional framework attests its source, and the ground of its unity. It is not a collection of individuals brought together by a community of interest and enthusiasm. It is a new creation, a new people of God, having its roots in a concrete historical act, whose interior purport and significance are its own.

Its direction is Godward before it is manward. It is the sphere in which the kingship of God is acknowledged. There is a direct continuity between its mission and that of the national Israel, in this regard. It is the fact of divine sovereignty, which is its first concern, and of divine sovereignty as attested and vindicated by him into whom the members of the church are incorporate, and who constitutes its unity—even Christ, crucified and risen.

We pass now to consider the several aspects of the church, its external organization, its pastoral and prophetical ministry, its liturgical life, its authority and teaching office, its relations to the world in which it is set, and the relations of its members with one another. All alike are intelligible when, and only when, we have grasped the church in its primary relation to the gospel, and in its essential character as the new Israel formed of those who are incorporate into the Messiah. The paradox and problem of its life are the paradox and problem of the life of a society that at once manifests, and is dependent upon, an act, which is the act of God.

We seem now to move outward from the heart of the gospel. But we shall find that in moments of perplexity we are thrust within it again.

46. Michael Ramsey, *The Gospel and the Catholic Church* (London: Longmans, Green and Co., 1936), 67.

To the Christian, the gospel is absolute. Its finality is complete. Though it is manifest amid the relativities of human existence, it is of God, not of man. For when we have said that Christ is of Nazareth of Galilee, we have not said enough. Only when we have acclaimed him as the Word, by whom the heavens were made, as the very utterance of God, can we rest, and even then our peace is his, not our own, nor as the world gives.[47] For then we are face to face with an ultimate demand.

Chapter 5: Unto All People

The second century, for the church historian, is a century of the Gnostic controversy,[48] is therefore a century in which we hope to find many lessons valuable for our own time. It is not that the danger of any large-scale revival of second-century theosophy is imminent, though such a revival is by no means impossible. Although astrologers, Palmists, and other such persons are claiming an ever-increasing number of clients, little heat is given to precisely the type of speculation, which the followers of Valentinus and Marcion indulged. Nonetheless, only an excessively simple reading of the situation would fail to recognize that we have our Gnostics.

In one of the introductory essays to his recently published work on the Fourth Gospel,[49] the late Sir Edwyn Hoskyns discusses the influence of that Gospel in the second century. The essay is of great value as revealing the true import of the work of Irenaeus,[50] and at the same time, it profoundly illuminates the whole problem of the authority of the church and of ecclesiastical order. It suggests that in the controversy with Gnosticism, what was involved was the whole character of Christianity as an evangelical, biblical way of salvation. It would seem that in the history of the church, at moments of peculiarly acute crisis, it is often just this that is involved, and of recent years, it is with the issue of the gospel that we have been concerned. Our

47. Cf. John 14:27.
48. On Gnosticism, see E. L. Mascall, *The God-Man*, Signposts 5 (Westminster: Dacre Press, 1940), 29–31.
49. E. C. Hoskyns, *The Fourth Gospel*, ed. F. N. Davey, 2 vols (London: Faber and Faber, 1940).
50. Bishop of Lyons in the second century, and author of a compendious word, *Against the Heresies*, in which he dealt effectively and thoroughly with Gnostic theology.

contemporary Gnostics have flirted with very different conceptions from those which attracted their spiritual ancestors of the days of Irenaeus. There is a real kinship between them. Both alike have sought to translate the stark simplicity of the gospel into the language of an intellectual minority, and both alike have failed to recognize that in the act of translation, they were transforming altogether what they were translating. Modernists and so-called "liberal churchmen" were in the main recruited from the ranks of those who had time and opportunity to imbibe the fullness of a culture, which was in its underlying assumptions fundamentally anti-biblical and anti-Christian. It was the ideals, the underlying assumptions or dogma of that culture that they erected into an absolute. They hardly ever entertained the possibility that the assumptions of the culture in which they had been educated required scrutiny. Rather, they regarded the Christian faith itself as the presentation, in a form suited to the uneducated, of their own unquestioned dogmas. Few can acquit English Liberal Christianity of the indictment of an intellectual arrogance from whose fruit we are still suffering. The tendency that "English modernism" crystallised was the tendency to make the scholar the arbiter of Christian truth. It is hard to imagine an impertinence more thoroughly disastrous or more calculated to undermine the fundamental character of the Christian gospel.

It is no coincidence that such a revolt against the gospel was accompanied by a mistrust of the hard, tangible signs of the church's external structure. Such marks of her "fleshliness" as the episcopate, the sacraments, the fixed creeds, were regarded as barriers set by the ignorance of foolish men in the path of the achievement of pure, spiritual religion. It is in no partisan spirit that attention is called to this theological mood, discernible alike in *The Modern Churchman*[51] and in the popular Sunday newspaper. We are concerned with it as a topical illustration of that flight from the flesh of Jesus, from the revelation once given, which is again and again in history a temptation

51. *The Modern Churchman*, the review of the Modern Churchman's Union, published monthly by Blackwell, Oxford.

to Christian thinkers. The phenomenon we have mentioned is so near us that its contrast with the whole emphasis of the New Testament should be easily manifest.

There is a sense in which the gospel is profoundly popular; it is, as Christ in the synagogue of Nazareth proclaimed it to be, "good tidings unto the poor."[52] It is, indeed, tidings brought to every creature by One who is sent by God. It is God-given for the simple reason that the Son of Man, who is its burden, is the Apostle of God. It is to human beings as human beings that the word of God is uttered. It is always a temptation to the intellectual to substitute for a gospel of mercy spoken unto every creature a philosophy, a set of specifically human ideas, and to bring a message of salvation to terms with the dogma or assumptions of a passing phase of culture.

One who, like the present writer, is a professional philosopher is hardly likely to be tempted to underestimate the importance of the task of the Christian scholar. But it is, and must remain, a subordinate task, subordinate, that is, to the proclamation of the everlasting gospel of the mercy of God. It is always the temptation of the intellectual to resent the restriction laid upon him by the fact of the gospel. To him that fact is scandalous, that is, it is a stumbling block, in a quite peculiar sense. Its "fleshliness" oppresses him with an intensity that manifested in the ingenuity wherewith he seeks to escape its burden. It is he who is aware of dogma (in the strict theological sense) as a restriction. Its presence inhibits him from erecting into an absolute a prevailing mood of thought. It is not those who, in the eyes of the world, are accounted poor and simple who crave release from the cramping frame of Christian institutions. To them, the giant affirmations of the Nicene Creed are tiresome restraints imposed by an arbitrary authority. They are a lasting signpost to the fact that they were so loved of God that he gave for them his only begotten Son.

"The return to dogma" on the part of certain younger adherents of the Christian tradition, which some of their elders seem to find so shocking,[53] is not inspired by any desire to be reactionary. It derives

52. Luke 4:18.

from an act of humility, from the recognition that the outward institutional framework of Christianity (dogma, episcopate, sacrament) is essential to the recognition of Christianity as the gospel of the mercy of God. Here, as so often, to borrow a paradox from T. S. Eliot, "it is the spirit that killeth and the letter that maketh alive."

It was his recognition of the fact that the institutional frame of Christianity was necessary for the maintenance of its character as the gospel of God that gave peculiar value to Canon Ramsey's study, *The Gospel and the Catholic Church*. The first part of this book, dealing with the New Testament period, is a masterly demonstration of the thesis that it is as the gospel that Christianity demands an institutional frame. If one treats the problem of the apostolic succession as primarily one of the ecclesiastical organization, one fails altogether to grasp its import; it becomes academic and dull. But when one has set it within the whole context of the church as the manifestation of the gospel of God in flesh and blood, its character changes. It is no longer a historical, but a distinctively theological, problem. We are thrust from the external visible facts of history into a realm where the finite, the perceptible, and the mortal is caught up into God and made an instrument of his purposes.

In our discussion of the apostolate, we have seen how the notion of 'apostle' became intelligible only when it came to rest on Jesus, the Apostle of God. The flesh of Jesus is the realization of the new Israel, an Israel that possesses its own patriarchs.[54] The New Testament evidence for the work of the apostolate in the primitive church is clearly set out and discussed by Ramsey in the sixth chapter of his book. They were the links whereby the individual Christian communities were bound to one another and to the historical act of the constitution of the new Israel by the rejection and passion of Jesus.

To quote Ramsey's own words, "Can we now draw any general conclusion? About the title *apostolos* we cannot always dogmatise. Its use no doubt has varied, and may possibly have been at first vague

53. Compare e.g. Canon F. R. Barry, *The Listener* (Mar. 15, 1940).

54. The character of the Apostles as Patriarchs of the new Israel is suggested by a saying of Christ's that occurs in different contexts and in different forms in Matt. 9:28 and Luke 22:30.

and wide, and later restricted, St. Luke showing this tendency to restriction. Yet apart from names and terms, we can be certain of this; there was a ministry, restricted in numbers and of definite authority, not attached to local churches but controlling local churches on behalf of the general Church. This ministry included at least the Twelve with St. James, St. Paul, and St. Barnabas in addition, and its functions were (i) to link the Christians with the historical events of Jesus from whom this Apostolate has received a solemn and special commission; (ii) to represent the one society, for only in the context of the one society can a local church grow into the fullness of Christ. Amid all the uncertainties of the Apostolic age, it is clear that there is no Church mentioned in the New Testament which does not own the authority of an Apostle or apostolic man who represents the wider general Church."[55]

It is the contention of the Catholic that the "developed structure of episcopacy in the Church fulfils the same place and expresses the same truths as did the Apostles' office in Samaria and in Corinth and throughout the Apostolic Church."[56] It would seem, from the evidence of the letters of St. Ignatius,[57] that in his view at least, the episcopate fulfilled the same function as that of the apostolate. The reader may be referred to Ramsey for a convenient summary of the evidence. The principle is clear enough. The historic episcopate is an organ of unity and it is from this function, as linking the individual local churches of Christ into one and joining them all to the historic act of their origin, that the peculiar doctrinal authority of the episcopate is derived. We are not to think of the episcopate as a collection of isolated individuals of exceptional gifts, to whom in virtue of those gifts special tasks have been allotted. They are organs of a society with a special pastoral responsibility to the "little ones" among its members. Their responsibility and the limits within which they may exercise authority are

55. Ramsey, *Gospel and Catholic Church*, 73.
56. Ibid., 77.
57. Bishop of Antioch, martyred at Rome early in the second century. His letters, written on his way to martyrdom and addressed to the churches of Asia Minor and Rome, provide invaluable evidence of the emphases of Christian theology in the subapostolic period.

prescribed by their function in relation to the whole body. One might say that they represent the poor man's safeguard against the intellectual arrogance of the theologian who subordinates the gospel to philosophy.

The point was admirably made by Hoskyns in his address to the Anglo-Catholic Congress in 1930:[58] "In our modern controversies we Catholics are not concerned primarily with a question of organization. We are concerned with the nature of the Gospel, at a time when there is much vague talk about the independent motions of the Holy Spirit. Taught by the New Testament, we are bound to think of the Episcopate as preserving the witness of the Apostles, and to demand this of the Bishops. The Bishops are not mystical persons to whom we owe some strange kind of undefined mysterious obedience. The Bishops are responsible to bear witness to Jesus Christ, the Son of God, and to hold the Church to that witness. Nor does the Episcopate offer an opportunity to gifted individuals to occupy an exalted position and to tyrannise over those who are endowed to a lesser degree with intellectual or other gifts. The authority of the Bishops depends solely on their link with the Apostles, though we may hope that this link may be productive of virtue and courage and of intellectual and spiritual insight. . . . Nor (and I would like to emphasise this in an assembly of Catholics) do the Bishops represent the whole history of the Church and bring the whole weight of this history crashing down upon our shoulders. There is much in the history of the Church, which we should do well to forget or be entirely ignorant of. The Bishops represent the history of the Church only in so far as that history has been controlled by the will of God perfected in Jesus Christ. In this sense they link the past with the creative work of God in the present and in the future."

The whole exterior framework of the Christian Church is the poor man's protection against the tyranny of the wise who would rob him of the heritage of the gospel. In a sense, one might say, too, that its visible structure, its articulate doctrinal standards, its ordered sacramental practice, represent the very lashing of the church itself to its historical

58. Hoskyns, *Anglo-Catholic Congress.*

moorings. The whole church is an organ of the gospel. Of the burden that that character imposes upon its individual members, we shall speak later. Those aspects of its life that most perplex hankerers after a "spiritual religion" are due to the fact that it proclaims, not a possibility of spiritual achievement, but a work of redemption wrought by the Son of God in human flesh and blood.

Again and again we have seen the pressure of external circumstance upon individual members of the church, who have held high office within it and have usually been endowed with great personal gifts, a pressure that issues in individual demands that the gospel of God be transformed into a human philosophy. And it has been the external organization of the church, in itself attesting the character of the gospel, that has preserved its saving truth for Christ's little ones. It is through the institutions of the church that the gospel is preserved from the idiosyncrasies of its members.

We shall see how great an issue is the issue of the relation of a church that is thus the bearer of an everlasting gospel to successive cultures and civilizations. Indeed, for the Christian, it is this conflict of the city of God and the city of man that underlies the whole to-and-fro movement of human history. We are living at a moment of the profoundest spiritual crisis. Liberal capitalism has given place to totalitarianism, individualism to ruthless collectivism. The human person, whose natural dignity it was not the least historic achievement of the Christian Church to vindicate, is menaced as never before. What tasks may confront the Christian Church, as this post-Christian age unfolds itself, we cannot tell. It may well be that we are nearing a situation when martyrdom unto death is the only language that can be spoken. But at least we can be thankful that the Christian Church's external organization, pointing it back to the moment when the word of God was uttered upon the cross, has preserved it from being absorbed in the morass of a secular Liberalism whose issue was inevitably that totalitarianism that at present oppresses men's spirits everywhere.[59]

It is the "little man" who is at this moment looking to the visible church as the safeguard, as indeed the only hope, of his humanity. It is the witness of the church to the truth of the gospel that is at this moment thrusting men back upon the word of mercy that is there spoken to them in the depths of their need. It is through that word of mercy and that alone that they are given, in the admission of their poverty, a new vision of their dignity. For through the gospel, they know that they are the objects of the love of God in Christ and that no weight of outward oppression can rob them of the sure knowledge that they are in Christ sons of God and inheritors of the kingdom of heaven.

The wisdom of men has issued in frustration so appalling that the whole world finds itself threatened with catastrophe. In the midst of that world, the church is set, a visible separate society, pointing to the flesh of Jesus, Apostle of God, as the hope of its restoration. In this historic moment, it is the separateness of the church, of which its external organization is a necessary instrument, that transforms the situation into an occasion when the revelation of God may be made known to his children. For the church attests the ultimate demand, of which the coming of Christ in the flesh was the occasion, and by its presence, brings that demand into relation with the whole anguish of the world today.

Chapter 6: He That Heareth You Heareth Me

It was Sir Edwyn Hoskyns who suggested in language paradoxical enough to be almost shocking, that the primary duty of the church was the study of the New Testament. The paradox, of course, was in part due the narrowness wherewith the term "study" was interpreted. Clearly, if it is taken to refer only to the activities of the professional biblical scholar, it is pure nonsense. To affirm that the primary task of the church consists in the study of the New Testament is, however, not to say this. It is rather to suggest that that task consists in bringing into the open a deposit of faith, which is, to a quite remarkable degree, concentrated in the New Testament writings.

59. On the relation of liberalism to totalitarianism, see V. A. Demant, *The Religious Prospect* (London: Muller, 1939).

It is in the New Testament that the primitive apostolic preaching is, as it were, given a permanent form. It is there that we find our earliest record of that gospel, of that good news, which it is the task of the accredited teachers of the church to safeguard and to proclaim. When the church authoritatively defines a dogma, it is simply unfolding some item of that primitive deposit of faith that is enshrined in the New Testament.

In Professor C. H. Dodd's valuable little book *The Apostolic Preaching and its Development*, an effort is made to state the precise nature of the primitive apostolic theology, and the student of the history of Christian doctrine must be impressed by the remarkable way in which the emphases of that theology agree with those of the authoritative creeds of Christendom. There is in both the same absence of abstract metaphysical interest, the same concentration on concrete historical fact as the occasion of the accomplishment of the work of God, and the conclusion, to which this comparison points, is fortified by a historical study of the history of Christian doctrine to 451 CE, the date of the Council of Chalcedon.[60]

The superstition that the establishment of fixed standards in the shape of creeds, and the elaboration of formal definitions by councils, represented the arbitrary imposition on an ignorant and compliant laity of the abstract speculations of theologians is an unconscionably long time in dying. But there are signs that its hours are numbered. So flamboyant a misunderstanding of the whole character of the teaching authority of the church is due to a number of causes, among which we may perhaps give pride of place to the "myth of the simple Gospel," to which, it should be remembered, it was first and foremost technical theologians who sought to recall the unlettered children of Christ.[61] The idea that Jesus gave nothing but a body of ethical teaching, which he illustrated by the "lovely story of his life and death," rests, of course, on a treatment of the New Testament documents arbitrary enough to make the responsible historian shudder. It is hard to believe that

60. See Mascall, *The God-Man*, 36–38.
61. Such as Adolf von Harnack in Germany and C. W. Emmet in this country.

such interpretations have not been given the coup de grâce once and for all by Hoskyns' great book, *The Riddle of the New Testament.*[62] But nonetheless it was an interpretation that appealed to the optimistic mood of Liberal Europe. The New Testament scholars were thought to have rescued Jesus from the hands of cruel theological oppressors who had successfully kept generations of innocents from their inheritance.

In the whole debate, of course, it was the very nature of the gospel that was at stake, and, however much we may regret the suffering, bewilderment, and grief occasioned by the Roman Church's authoritative condemnation of the cognate error of "Modernism," it would be hard now to deny its perspicacity in recognizing the true character of what was involved.[63] We are now, however, increasingly aware that what the authoritative doctrinal formulae of the church accomplish is the safeguarding of the gospel from the distortions to which it is liable at the hand of successive generations of irresponsible speculative theologians.

To call such an attitude "Barthian irrationalism" may help to relieve the critic's feelings. But the danger of the speculative theologian remains, especially when he assumes the guise of discoverer. Hoskyns was acutely alive to such dangers, and in a passage at the conclusion of his essay on "Jesus the Messiah" in *Mysterium Christi*, summed up the situation thus,

> The New Testament scholar, who is also a Christian, cannot patiently permit the dogmatist or the philosopher to expound the doctrine of the Incarnation *on the basis of an analysis of human nature illustrated by the humanity of Jesus.* He was unique; and this particularity rivets the Christian doctrine of the Incarnation to the Christology, and to the history involved in the Christology, and presents an awkward material to the philosopher, who is operating with a rigid doctrine of evolution. There are metaphysical implications in the Christology; and the New Testament scholar, who is compelled to adopt a *rather crude conception of revelation*, precisely because he is a historian and has to interpret a movement of God to man, and not of man to God, has nevertheless the right to demand that the Christian dogmatist should start *from this particular revelation*, and

62. Written in collaboration with F. N. Davey (London: Faber and Faber, 1931).
63. Cf. Fr. Victor White, OP, "Von Hügel—a Modern Heresiarch?" *Blackfriars* 18, no. 213 (Dec. 1937): 910–16.

> that the philosopher should at some point or other in his philosophy make sense of it by some other means than by ignoring the particularity of the Old Testament, and by refusing to recognise that in the end the particularity of the Old Testament is only intelligible in the light of its narrowed fulfilment in Jesus the Messiah *and of its expanded fulfilment in the Church.*[64]

By "evolution," of course, Hoskyns does not refer to the family of more or less similar hypotheses in empirical biology that we normally refer to by the shorthand phrase "theory of evolution." He is referring to those immanentist philosophies[65] that regarded the whole process of world history as in some sense the gradual self-constitution and self-discipline of an absolute spirit, philosophies to which the whole conception of a divine invasion *ab extra* is fundamentally abhorrent. The biblical conception of revelation we find crude simply through our approaching it with prepossessions created by a long, more or less unconscious, adherence to the philosophical dogmas in question. Between such views and the biblical theology, no truce is possible. That perhaps may be granted readily enough, but what of the apparent depreciation of the "doctrine of the Incarnation" suggested by its subordination to the "Christology"? That too is intelligible to one familiar at once with the history of English theological thought in the past thirty years, on the one hand, and with the movement from the first speech of Peter at Pentecost to the definition of the Council of Chalcedon, on the other.

The subtlest temptation that besets the Christian student is the substitution for the gospel of an abstract metaphysical scheme, the temptation to start from certain ideas about the nature of things in general and to force the Christian facts into conformity with them. In recent years, the most enticing forms of such speculation have come to be widely known as "Incarnationalism." The title is hideous, but the doctrines do certainly possess a certain spurious attraction. Commonly the starting point is the prologue to the first chapter of St. John's Gospel, arbitrarily torn out of its setting in the gospel as a whole. The

64. Hoskyns, *Mysterium Christi*, 89. The italics are my own.
65. Cf. MacKinnon, GLT, 57.

fourteen verses are then treated as if they were a short metaphysical treatise, with a definite Platonist bias. Created things in different degrees manifest the perfection of God. The universe as a whole is an intelligible scheme, for it is in its complexity the work of the divine Logos or creative intelligence. Such writers are careful not to go the whole way with Dr. J. F. Bethune-Baker in saying of the universe that "the whole is Incarnation."[66] But the difference between the manifestation of the divine creative intelligence in each item and in the whole of the created world, on the one hand, and its manifestation in the incarnation, on the other, is one of degree, not of kind. In Jesus, the Logos[67] is incarnate; what is present in part elsewhere is here disclosed in its fullness. In the Holy One of the gospels, the very creative principle of the world is shown forth to us. Thus the harsh paradoxes of Chalcedon are avoided, and the basis of a Christian rationalism firmly laid.

But what relation does this rationalism bear to the doctrine of Christ, the Christology of the New Testament? The sense in which we must understand the idea of incarnation, if we are to be loyal to the New Testament teaching, is quite other than that which is congenial to one who takes his stand on a Platonic metaphysic of degrees of goodness. It is a sense much more closely akin to the savage paradoxes of Chalcedon.

If we look at the history of Christian doctrine, we find that again and again the reason why the church's authorities have intervened with a definite formulation of dogma was that some thinker had forced the gospel into a scheme of ideas of his own and in so doing had radically distorted it. This is true perhaps most markedly of the work of the

66. J. F. Bethune-Baker, *The Way of Modernism and Other Essays* (Cambridge: Cambridge University Press, 1927), 85.

67. The notion of the Logos or Word first enters Christian thought in St. John's Gospel, where the background is perhaps almost entirely supplied by the Old Testament, and the Synoptic Gospels (see Hoskyns's commentary, ad loc.). In various of the Greek fathers, however, the use of the term with reference to Christ has a definitely technical-philosophical import, and it is perhaps better rendered as "rational principle" than as "Word." In Christ there is incarnate that rational creative principle in accordance with which the scheme of creation was set in order in the beginning, and which it continuously manifests. Such language was dangerous, as the distinction between God and man became easily blurred in consequence of its use, and the term "Logos" is not found in the official formulations of the doctrine of Christ's person.

Council of Nicaea, where the issues at stake did manifestly concern the very nature of that gospel. There certainly the abstract speculative interest suffered defeat, and the insistence of the great individual hero of the council, St. Athanasius, on the biblical theology of redemption was vindicated.

Of the issues of that council, Fr. Gregory Dix writes illuminatingly:

> It was not the relation of Jesus' manhood to divinity, but the relation of Jesus' divinity to ultimate Godhead which was disputed. The issue was once again whether God was truly one, whether this world can be the sphere of truly divine action, whether events in time can have ultimate significance. It was the old Judaic categories, monotheism, messiamsm, and eschatology, which Arianism challenged in the name of Greek philosophy.[68]

The background of the Arian controversy was the whole speculative movement, which we associate with the development of the Logos Christology.[69] And it is surely significant that Athanasius, whose position the council endorsed, should, in his famous treatise on the incarnation of the Word, have endeavored to employ that theology in order to express the fundamentally Hebraic gospel of redemption, and should have miserably failed. If one goes to the treatise seeking a systematic theological essay, one is disappointed. The author is too deeply conscious of the fundamental Christian emphasis on the redemption wrought by God in the flesh of Jesus to be at ease in the elaboration of a theological system.[70] For him, the Logos theology is only a set of terms, which he finds difficult to employ intelligibly. Yet fundamentally he was right. For he saw that such speculations were at best a pastime, at worst a means whereby the gospel of the mercy of God is withheld from Christ's little ones.

The authority of the church does indeed impose restrictions on the free play of speculative reasoning. But the church is the warden of a gospel that is of God. For it is the message of the advent of Jesus,

68. Gregory Dix, "Hellensim, Judaism and Christianity." In *History of Christian Thought*, ed. Selwyn, Christian Challenge Series (London: Unicorn Press, 1937), 43.
69. See above, note 67.
70. For the interests of Athanasius, cf. Aulen, *Christian Victor* (SPCK, 1931).

the Apostle of God. We have written elsewhere[71] of the constraints under which the Christian thinker labors. They are imposed by the fact of revelation. We are not to suppose that, even with the Thomistic clarification of the relations of sacred theology and metaphysical philosophy behind us,[72] the task of the Christian thinker is easy. The urge to reduce to human order that which obstinately remains the revelation of God, to which we must conform ourselves, presses ever hard upon him. The character of Christian theology as fundamentally a *theologia crucis*, a theology of the cross, reveals itself intimately to him in his speculations, and always he is compelled to remember that the real hero of the first five centuries of Christian thought, to borrow again from Fr. Dix, is the church as a whole, led by the bishops of the great apostolic churches, especially Rome. For it was their steadfast adherence to the Christian facts that preserved the gospel of the mercy of God for the little ones for whom his Son had died. And this is the fundamental end and aim of the teaching authority of the church.

Chapter 7: The Sacrament of the Eucharist

We pass now to a brief consideration of the Eucharist. In the Prayer Book Catechism, we read that the Sacrament of the Lord's Supper was ordained "for the continual remembrance of the sacrifice of the death of Christ, and of the benefits which we receive thereby." The rite of the Eucharist is thus thrust into its place in the very center of the gospel. It is a memorial (an *anamnesis*[73]) of the sacrifice of the death of Christ. When Christians come together for the celebration of the Eucharist, their attention is fixed not on themselves, but on Christ crucified.

Certainly of recent years there has been much misplaced emphasis in discussions of the theology of the Eucharist, some of it by learned theologians. All of it has shown the infection of that theological naturalism, which perhaps more than anything else impedes the

71. See MacKinnon, GLT.
72. It was the achievement of St. Thomas Aquinas (1225–1274) to make clear the mutual relations and rights of faith and natural reason.
73. The Greek word used by St. Paul in what is the earliest account of the institution of the Eucharist. 1 Cor. 11:24ff.

average man and woman from beginning to grasp the function of the sacraments in the Christian revelation. So many discussions of the sacraments start at the wrong end. Readers or listeners are bidden to reflect on the "idea" of a sacrament. Their attention is concentrated on a universal, sacramental principle of which individual, sacramental rites are the embodiments. We are told how appropriate it is that incarnate spirits, as men and women are, should, in their approach to God, use visible and tangible signs to express their relation to him. Some writers, who claim familiarity with recent developments of philosophical thought, insist that the present climate of philosophical opinion is unusually congenial for the vindication of Catholic sacramental philosophy. But when we ask these persons what exactly is this philosophy of which they are talking, and what precise relationship it bears to the sacramental theology of the Bible, we find in point of fact that they are really enunciating certain general propositions of a metaphysical character, whose relevance to that theology is far from immediately clear.

We must look this question of the character of the Eucharist in the face; for, unless we do, we shall not begin to get our minds clear concerning the doctrine of the church, wherein the Eucharist is set. The question at issue is simple as well as fundamental. We have got to ask ourselves to what principles we appeal in the understanding of the Eucharist. Do we talk of the natural propriety of sacramental religion to incarnate spirits, of the sacramental quality of artistic creation, of the sacramental universe? Is that the background against which the Eucharist is to be understood? For if it is, then, not only the Eucharist, but the gospel of the Word made flesh must be thrust against that background. We must use language with reference to that gospel that has no roots in the New Testament; we must learn to think of Jesus, not as St. John thought of him, but as writers think of him who like to speak of him as the Logos, in a sense completely alien to that of the Evangelist. It is precisely to such a flight from the gospel that our natural abhorrence of its particularity impels us.

The teaching of the Church of England, as of the rest of the Catholic

Church, on this point is absolutely definite. There is, in its precise sacramental theology, little sanction for the kind of abstract speculation mentioned above. Nor does the Liturgy itself give much excuse for such sentimentalism. We may draw wistful comparisons between the rite of the *Book of Common Prayer* and the rites of other parts of the Christian Church. But at least we must be thankful for the sternness wherewith it insists on the relation of the Eucharist to the gospel. The very brevity of the prayer of consecration at least should serve as a damper to the enthusiasm of those who would seek to absorb a sacrament of the Christian gospel in a natural process of human religious development.

The movement of the Christian life is towards the center, and this is reflected in the order of the Eucharist. "God so loved the world that he *gave*." We are drawn, as it were, into the very place of his giving, even into the very gift itself. If we like, we can so regard the fact of our baptism. As was suggested above, we are knit together into Christ to form the new Israel, a people of God. That is the background of the Eucharist, for it is as the baptised people of God that we assemble for its celebration.

If we are to understand what we are about in this action we must see that we are brought in it to the very center of the Christian revelation, to that place where the kingdom of God came with power. For the gift of the Eucharist is the gift of the flesh of Jesus. We are his body, who in baptism have been made his members. Our vocation is the vocation of Israel, the vocation of the people of God—namely, the call to realize his kingship. But our obedience, our witness, our faith is through and through tainted by the sin wherewith we are affected. Therefore, we are thrust back upon his obedience, upon his self-offering.

The Epistle to the Hebrews, in its tenth chapter, sees in the accomplishment of the passion of Jesus the fulfillment of the fortieth Psalm: "Burnt-offerings, and sacrifice for sin, hast thou not required: then said, Lo, I come."[74] It is the flesh of his obedience, of whom it was written that he should fulfill the will of God, that we offer in the

74. Ps. 40:9.

Eucharist. The rite is first and foremost a sacrifice, and we must agree with the universal and agelong tradition of the Christian Church in affirming simply that what is offered is the body and blood of Christ.[75] Such language is admittedly harsh and shocking to the refinement of twentieth-century spirituality, but its harshness is the harshness of the gospel, whose message again and again comes to rest upon the flesh of Jesus, and upon the shedding of his blood.

Each celebration of the Eucharist sets before us sacramentally the bloody act of Calvary. It is the realization of the coming of the kingdom in the obedience of Jesus.[76] It rehearses the achievement of his victory through the giving of his body unto death, and in it we anticipate "his coming again with power and great glory." The bread and wine of the Eucharist attest the first and the second coming of the Son of God; for it is by that first coming whose circumstances we rehearse and represent at the altar, that we can look forward with joy to that second coming, when his incognito shall be removed and his Messiahship made manifest.

Thus in the Eucharist we are indeed brought into the very heart of the Christian mystery. We make his act our own. In familiar language, by our sacramental oblation of his passion, we ratify his act by our own "Amen." What he has done, he alone could do. As was said above, the work of the Messiah was wrought out in isolation and dereliction. But that act remains as the only adequate homage ever paid on earth to the sovereignty of God, and it is to that act that the church, in the Eucharist, formally adheres.

"In remembrance of me." The words are familiar enough, but we often lose sight of their significance. It is then that we seek to understand the Eucharist apart from its setting in revelation and, in so doing, remove it from its context in the gospel. It is but another aspect of that flight from the flesh of Jesus, to which we have so often

75. For the doctrine of the Eucharistic Sacrifice in the primitive church, see Darwell Stone, *History of the Doctrine of the Holy Eucharist* (London: Longmans, Green, and Co., 1909), vol. 1, chap. 2–3 (22–132).
76. Cf. Dodd's piece in the symposium by eminent Free Churchmen, "The Lord's Supper in the New Testament," *Christian Worship* (Oxford: Oxford University Press, 1936).

referred, and against which we have suggested that it is the whole function of the visible, tangible structure of the church to preserve us. The authority of the church imposes on the life of its members a movement towards the center. This may express itself in various ways; for our present purpose, we may mention the obligation to be present at Mass. That may seem a narrowing thing, and indeed it would be, were the Eucharist to be regarded merely as an occasion of spiritual experience, or indeed, as it has sometimes been called, "the greatest of human experiences."

But the Eucharist is the sacramental oblation of the flesh of Jesus. It is the celebration of his great "Yea" to the divine claim, the realization of the kingdom of God.[77] At Mass, it is the privilege of the Christian to make intercession in the body of Christ for all mankind. If the movement to the altar is inwards towards the center, it is almost simultaneously outwards from the center, too. The piety of the altar is the piety of the gospel, and the piety of the gospel sees, in the acknowledgment of the flesh of Jesus as the place of revelation, the restoration of all things in him. "The whole creation groaneth and travaileth together." At the altar, we see in a glass darkly the transformation that yet shall be.

It is the mystery of the flesh of Jesus that compels us to repudiate the facile natural sacramentalism, which would wish to see in the natural creation, as it is, a sacrament of the divine handiwork. For the coming of Christ in the flesh exhibits, in the most acute form, the predicament in which the whole universe lies. It is, as St. John repeatedly insists, crisis, judgment. Such is the human situation that the kingdom of God could only be revealed, in the midst of it, upon the gibbet of a criminal. Only in humiliation and desolation could the self-attestation of God be wrought out.

But the resurrection of Christ revealed to the whole natural creation the law of its restoration: Christ the first-fruits, and his people in him. It is their adherence to him, their inherence in him, that is the

77. Cf. the writings of Dodd, especially his paper in *The Kingdom of God and History*, Church Community and State Series (London: Allen and Unwin, 1938), 13–36.

ground of the hope of inanimate creation. They are its priests, for in them its whole process attains to self-consciousness.[78] The frustration of its life is most intimately bound up with the frustration of their own. But when bread and wine are brought to the Christian altar, and become by consecration the body and blood of Christ, we see in their transformation the type of the renewal of the natural order.[79] In the Eucharist, we see the things of inanimate nature in a new context, used in fact as instruments of a divine movement towards man, and of a human movement towards God that is made possible by his own previous approach. There, what is profane and earthly is set apart (for that is the primary significance of consecration), taken from its setting in disordered nature, and given a new setting in the world of the gospel. Bread and wine in the Eucharist are directly related to the whole work of Christ, which is the manifestation of the kingdom of God, and its acknowledgment in the flesh of Jesus.

So, indeed, the Christian vision of the restoration of all things in Christ is kindled at the altar. For the consecration of the Eucharist is the archetype of the transformation of the whole natural order.[80]

If we are to understand what is meant by calling all life sacramental, we must look at the altar. We must not, in our efforts to comprehend the Sacrament of the Altar, look at what certain writers call "natural sacraments." That natural order is too intimately and too deeply perverted to supply us with an adequate pattern of comparison. We must rather look first at the gospel of the mercy of God, and at the sacraments of that gospel, if we are to form a properly Christian conception of the sacramental character of the world as a whole. Above all, we must look at the Eucharist, which is the sacrament par excellence, and as we grasp the relation of the elements of bread and wine to the body and blood of Christ, we shall begin perhaps to comprehend the condition of the restoration of all things in him, and the consequent endowment of all life with a sacramental character.

We have devoted this chapter largely to a consideration of the

78. Cf. Conrad Pepler, OP, "Cosmic Praise," *Blackfriars* 21, no. 238 (Jan. 1940): 33–41.
79. See below, chap. 9 (138–52).
80. Cf. Victor White, "Doctrine in the Church of England," *Blackfriars* 19, no. 216 (Mar. 1938): 163–76.

Sacrament of the Eucharist. In doing so, we have had in mind the Catholic tradition, which has seen in the Eucharist the archetypal sacrament. But what has been said of the Eucharist ought also to be said analogically of the other sacraments. All alike point to Christ, who is the Way, the Truth, and the Life, who in his historical actuality is the Word made flesh, the very utterance of the Father. In all alike, his activity is embodied.

Baptism and penance enshrine and effect that death and resurrection, which is the very foundation of Christian life. That life is the life of Christ in the members of his mystical body. But his work of redemption is the condition of its extension. "Except a corn of wheat fall into the ground and die, it abideth alone."[81] The Christian life has its source in baptism; therein we are indeed made partakers of Christ's death, that death, which, in the Apostle's words, he died unto sin once.[82] He is our way unto life as well as the life that we enjoy. Only in so far as we die his death, can we live his life. In the sacrament of penance, we deliberately renew that dying unto sin, which is typified by the font of baptism, and by the priestly absolution there bestowed, we are restored to the fullness of life in Christ. His is the death that we die, and his the life that we live.

The whole of our life is set within the context of this movement to life through death. For in that principle is set forth the truth of the gospel, the law of human renewal, which in the last resort is the Christ himself. He is the Way, the Truth, and the Life. We cannot better express the underlying principle of the Christian theology of the cross, to which the sacraments bear witness.

Chapter 8: The Priest of God

We have now spent some time in the consideration of the relation of the church to that gospel in which it finds its proper setting and true significance. We have done so because only if we have first set the church in its proper relation to the revelation and saving act of God

81. John 12:24.
82. Rom. 6:10.

will its authority, its worship, its paradoxical, and almost scandalous claims, become intelligible to us. It was in his contribution to the symposium *Essays Catholic and Critical* that Hoskyns, taking the bull by the horns, said: "For the Catholic Christian, '*Quid vobis videtur de Ecclesia*, What think ye of the Church?' is not merely as pertinent a question as '*Quid vobis videtur de Christo*, think ye of the Christ?': it is but the same question differently formulated."[83]

On that fundamental insight this book might be regarded as a comment. It is a fundamental insight, for it compels us to ask questions about the church in the only context in which their bearing can be perceived. Wireless preachers sometimes ask us if we have "understood Christianity," and sometimes go on to suggest that we have not, as in its stead the churches have inflicted on us a spurious substitute properly called "churchianity." To them we must reply, not by making an apologia for the behaviour of members of the church, who have for a while been overcome by the world, but rather by thrusting them back on the ultimate questions that the gospel compels us to ask. Has God revealed himself? Has he indeed "visited and redeemed" his people? Where? How?

The Christian answer to these questions involves the church, simply because the church is involved in the apostolate of Jesus. The authority of the church rests, not on the coherence of its dogma with the dogmas of the societies wherein it is set, but on the character of the Messiah as the revealing and redeeming act of God.

To the philosopher (and the present writer must own himself by profession a philosopher and not a theologian), the importance of the problem of revelation is plain. He cannot, if he would, evade the problem of the validity of the New Testament claim that Jesus is the End, the final and absolute revelation of God. Indeed, the only justification that a philosopher can have for writing a book of this character is the hope that his professional job, which is perhaps one of clarification rather than of construction, may in some measure equip him for bringing to the notice of his readers the ultimate character of

83. E. C. Hoskyns, *Essays Catholic and Critical*, ed. E. G. Selwyn, 3rd ed. (London: SPCK, 1929), 153.

those issues. The question of the church is an ultimate question; that indeed is part of what is meant by calling it an eschatological society, the full significance of this phrase, we shall be presently concerned.

Hitherto we have been concerned to view the church from outside. Now we are briefly to consider certain aspects of its interior life. First, the character of its ministry, then its relations with the world, and, lastly, the character of its members. But in all these considerations, we shall find ourselves again and again forced to remember its ultimate character, its finality. The life of its members derives its distinctive character from the tension between nature and grace set up within it by the fact of their baptism. They are within the *ecclesia*[84] of God, branches of the vine, members of Christ, adopted sons of God. These latter titles do not merely suggest "beautiful thoughts." They state cold facts concerning the being of the Christian. He is an adopted son of God, adopted in the Beloved, in whom was purposed the eternal purpose of God.[85] He had passed from death unto life.[86] With St. Paul he can say: "For I am persuaded that neither death, nor life, nor angels, nor principalities, nor things present, nor things to come, nor powers, nor height, nor depth, nor any other creature, nor powers be able to separate us from the love of God, which is in Christ Jesus our Lord."[87] His hope is grounded on what he *is*, a member of Christ, repossessed by God because he was baptised into Christ's death.[88] But if thus the Christian can rejoice in his character, it is a rejoicing set within a context of inescapable tension. Tension, strain, and uncertainty alike are embedded in the very heart of the Christian life. The tug of the world upon the individual member of Christ's body, the pressure of its assumptions and standards upon his judgment, the lure of some clearly cut, naturalistic substitute for the Christian theology of the cross, the absorption in a multiplicity of spiritual exercises—of all these we are fully aware. "Not as the world giveth give I unto you,"[89] said

84. See above, i.e., chap. 2 (98–103).
85. Eph. 3:11.
86. 1 John 3:14.
87. Rom 8:38–39.
88. Rom. 6:3.
89. John 14:27.

the Messiah on the night of his betrayal. The peace of God does not fill us with a Stoic tranquillity. It thrusts upon us ultimate questions, and shows us that our answers to them are fraught with final import not for ourselves only but for others.

This is the very priesthood of Christ in which the baptised share in virtue of their baptism, but which he calls various individuals to share in a peculiar degree of intimacy. It would ill become a layman to speak much of the priestly life, but a little must be said if this book is to be in any sense an adequate outline of the church.

To all members of Christ's body belongs in a measure the gift of priesthood. For they are crucified in him who made offering to the Father of himself. They are, as it were, incorporated into his perpetual oblation. It becomes their act, their confession of the sovereignty of God, their intercession for humankind. But to some is given an especial participation in this Godward act of offering. In them it is, as it were, made articulate. It is their privilege, formally, to celebrate the act in which it is visibly rehearsed.

The altar of God, Calvary, is the background of the Christian priesthood. It is the intimacy of their participation in Christ's self-offering that gives to the priests of the church their peculiar character, and imposes upon them a peculiar burden. For it is as priests that they are made the shepherds of Christ's flock.

The burden of the true priest, the *sacerdos magnus*,[90] is the heaviest burden man can bear. For it is the burden of the anguish of Christ for those who rejected him. The true priest knows that the advent of the Son of God is the very crisis of human life. He knows with what terrible consequences is fraught the confrontation of man with that love of God. It is his task in the ministry of the word to make that confrontation possible. But it is at the altar that he pleads the oblation of Christ's flesh that the meeting may be for salvation, and not for judgment.

He is the shepherd who gathers men into the flock of Christ, and it is his task to tend them with the intimate understanding that was his

90. Eccl. 44:16.

who alone "knew what was in men."[91] The life of the priest is a life of pain. He is oppressed at once with a sense of his unworthiness, of his own continual frustration of the work that Christ would accomplish through him, and of the hideous need of his people. His hope is the Christian hope, the hope that is set upon the cross, where, in the darkness, the centurion penetrated the divine incognito.

In the true priest, the tension of the Christian life is at its sharpest. For in the priest the shepherd calleth his sheep by name, and again and again the question, "Where is the flock that was given thee, the beautiful flock?" will drive him to the altar, where alone by the oblation of Christ's passion, the sins of Christ's members are made good.

Chapter 9: The Church and the World

We concluded our last chapter with some remarks on the priesthood, for it is in and through the priesthood that the Godward-directed life of the new Israel is made articulate. We saw that the background of the priestly life was the altar, whereas witness is borne to the fact that it is through the passion of Christ alone that we have access to, and fellowship with, the living God. The context of the Christian priesthood is created by the act of Christ's obedience. Yet it would be a mistake to imagine that the priestly life is the prerogative of the formally ordained. The life of every individual member of Christ's body is in its degree sacerdotal and apostolic. It is for that reason that the background of the life of the layman as well of the priest is furnished by the altar. The suggestion of certain spiritual directors, who have found their inspiration in the introverted piety of the Counter-Reformation, that in the daily life of the Christian layman, meditation is of greater importance than attendance at Mass, deserves an unsparing repudiation. For its emphasis is on the individual's appropriation of the divine bounty, not on the act of God, whereby his kingdom is established and man is reconstituted.

91. John 2:25.

If we are to understand the relations of the church and the world[92], we must recollect constantly that all Christian activity is related to the oblation of the Eucharist. It is in and through the offering of the body and blood of Christ that not only the individual, but also the social group of which he is a member, is made acceptable to the Father in the Beloved. It is the work of the church to "extend" that of its Lord. It is the place where men die in him and rise together with him. Its whole character is determined by its relation to the Lord. We shall see how it is indeed this relation that makes intelligible the paradox of the church's situation in the world. To this we now turn.

First of all, we must make certain that we have three points absolutely clear in our minds.

(1) The church is the new Israel, the body of Christ. Its "givenness" is the "givenness" of the gospel. We cannot choose to be Christians and not be members of the church. For the character of the church as the body of Christ is dependent on his will (we may be indeed thankful for this), and not upon the faithfulness of its individual members to the revelation entrusted to its keeping. The denial of Peter, the cowardice of his fellow apostles, the faithlessness of Thomas left unaffected the essential dignity of the apostolate. We are not made members in baptism of an "ideal" church. That indeed would be impossible, if membership of the church is, as we are told, membership "one of another." For all are alike, sinners who have come short of the glory of God.

(2) But if the character of the church is independent of the moral conformity of its members to gospel of which it is the guardian, we should not blind ourselves to the extent to which its members have allowed the spirit and standard of the world (in the theological sense) to affect and bias their judgment. In a valuable article, wherein he dealt courageously with this theme, Mascall said with truth: "Unscrupulousness is the cardinal sin of ecclesiastics: it has no place

92. The term *world* in the chapter title is here used in a technical theological sense, deriving from the usage of St. John's Gospel. Both there and here it is used to refer to the whole of human life in so far as it seeks to find its significance within itself apart from God, who is its origin and final end.

in God."[93] If we are realists, we will face these facts, and many others equally uncomfortable.

An estimate of the church's character, which recognizes its claim upon us to be fundamentally that of the gospel, and which will allow us to speak of it as indeed heaven on earth,[94] will not blind us to the measure in which the world holds its members, and not least those who hold high office within the church, in its sway.

(3) It is in the conflict of the church and the world that there resides for the Christian that principle that makes both history in the conventional sense, and the individual Christian life, intelligible. On the night of his betrayal, Christ made intercession for his disciples to the Father "that he should keep them from the evil one."[95] For though his passion was the victory wherein the prince of this world, in whom the world lies, was cast out,[96] yet, set in the midst of the world as they would be, he saw as inevitable the tribulation and affliction of those who followed him.[97]

It is for this reason that "in comparison with the optimism of liberalism the Christian view of life and the Christian interpretation of history are profoundly tragic. The true progress of history is a mystery which is fulfilled in failure and suffering, and which will only be revealed at the end of time. *The victory that overcomes the world is not success but faith* and it is only the eye of faith that understands the true value of history."[98]

Faith is the victory that overcomes the world.[99] In what was said above,[100] we saw the truth of this revealed supremely in Christ's attestation of his Father. And to quote Dawson again:[101] "Not only the individual, but the Church as an historic community follows the same

93. E. L. Mascall, "Judgment must Begin," *Christendom* 7, no. 28 (Dec. 1937): 274–79.
94. Cf. E. C. Hoskyns, *Cambridge Sermons* (London: SPCK, 1938), 28.
95. John 17:15.
96. John 12:31; cf. 1 John 5:19.
97. John 16:33.
98. Christopher Dawson, "Kingdom of God and History," in *The Kingdom of God and History*, edited by H. G. Woods et al., Vol. 3 of Official Oxford Conference Books (London: Allen & Unwin, 1938), 216. Italics my own.
99. John 5:4.
100. See chap. 2 (98–103).
101. Christopher Dawson, *Beyond Politics* (New York: Sheed and Ward, 1938), 129.

pattern, and finds its success and failure not where the politician finds them, but where Christ found them." The victory of the church over the world, which besets it within as around, is victory of faith. It is the function of the prophet to remind the whole body of the character of this faith, point to it as indeed the only victory that finally overcomes the world. That faith is the attestation of Christ as the very word of God made flesh, not merely by word, but by deed. For to the faithful Christian it is a commonplace that "revelation could go no further; he is Alpha and Omega."[102] Yet the victory of our faith is not ours, but rather is his who before Pontius Pilate witnessed a good confession[103] and thus brought to nothing the evil one in whose power the whole world lay.

We have gone far enough to see the terms of our problem, and in what follows, our concern will be to make explicit what is implied by the three points specified.

We are not going to begin to understand the problem of the relation of the church and the world unless we have first made efforts to understand the church. In earlier chapters of this book, we saw how intimate was the connection of the church with how our problems concerning the nature of the church began to disappear when we faced honestly the question of the character of that gospel. The ultimate character of the church is a manifestation of the ultimate character of the gospel.

Men may indeed find the idea of an ultimate revelation unbearable. They may oppose to it such Liberal slogans as "Absolute truth is not revealed." They may also flee from the harsh implications of such notions as the wrath of God and his mercy. The New Testament theology refuses to come to terms with their facile optimism, and accordingly they reject it. But what is becoming increasingly clear is that, when the idea of a final revelation is gone, the whole Christian structure is not merely impaired, but undermined. We are today faced with the alternatives of, on the one hand, adherence to the Christian

102. O.P. "Plain talks on fundamentals," *Blackfriars* 17, no. 200 (Nov. 1936): 841.
103. 1 Tim. 6:13.

dogma, or, on the other, a radical skepticism. There is no longer a convenient halfway house left to us in the bowdlerised faith of humanitarian Liberal Christianity. Such work as that of the late Sir Edwyn Hoskyns on the Gospels has undermined the very foundations of the Liberal building. The problem is no longer capable of being treated as one of historical uncertainty. (What is it that the Gospels say? etc.) It is seen now to be one of rival dogmas—the Christian dogma, and the immanentist dogma (in one or more of its various forms).[104]

Thus the problem of the church emerges once more. To the nineteenth-century Liberal (as to the English Modernist and to Dr. Rosenberg) the spiritual autonomy of the church is a grievous scandal. In the church is seen an institution that will not be domesticated, that will not come to terms with any worldview that finds the significance of man in himself, or rather in his own achievement. To that domestication, its loyalty to the gospel must ever bar the way. "Blessed be the Lord God of Israel; for he hath visited and redeemed his people." The opening words of the *Benedictus*[105] are so familiar that we forget what a stumbling block they essentially are. We bless God, because he "hath visited and redeemed" us, has come and loosed us from the prison in which we were fast bound. We confess our imprisonment, and we give thanks to God for coming to deliver us. This is simple evangelical language. But it is formally contradicted when the assertion is made that the end of man's being is to be looked for in his actual achievement and that sequence of historical events bears him almost irresistibly towards the kingdom of heaven, that, in Bethune-Baker's words, "the whole is Incarnation."[106] For if in point of fact this is so, the necessity of a deliverer, who enters from without, is done away. In the achievement of the future, the tragic conflicts of present will find their justification. The process is an absolute in relation to which alone the individual man must find his significance. In himself, he is only a moment in the constitution of that whole.

104. See MacKinnon, GLT, chap. 1–2 (48–68).
105. The canticle sung at morning prayer in the rite of the *Book of Common Prayer*; it is taken from St. Luke's Gospel (2:68) and forms the Canticle of Lauds in the Roman Breviary.
106. Bethune-Baker, *The Way of Modernism*, 85.

However unworthy some of the motives that prompted the ecclesiastical opposition to the Liberal dogma, nonetheless the insight, which discerned the formal opposition between it and the gospel, was exact. It was an insight that, in a marked degree, was enjoyed by the early Tractarians. Dawson, a Romaic Catholic writer, in a suggestive analysis of their teaching,[107] finds it oddly paradoxical that some of their successors should find the end of the Anglo-Catholic movement achieved in the emergence of a Liberal Catholicism. For, to the Tractarian, the gospel is the word, the very utterance of God, addressed to man in his extremity, and it is the function of the church to attest that gospel. To the Liberal, the gospel is impossible to accept, for it ruthlessly presents man as incapable of saving himself. It does not hesitate to reveal the depth of his need, or the inescapable tragedy of his divided being.

Yet men are today beginning dimly to recognize again that, in point of fact, this revelation of man's predicament, harsh and shocking though it is to the sensitive, is in itself a ground of hope. "God so loved the world." When we first read the tale of the crucifixion, we perhaps say to ourselves that, after all, had *we* been there, *we* would not have hounded Jesus to his death. The Liberal, as Dawson has pointed out, tends to invert the Augustinian scheme of the two cities, seeing in the city of man the city of light and in the institutional church the city of darkness. That assumption we more or less share. When we first read the tale of the crucifixion, our anticlericalism expresses itself in an inarticulate sense that somehow Jesus died as the victim of ecclesiastical tyranny. But when we come to understand more exactly the occasion of the passion, then we realize that in point of fact it is "men, busy, active, immersed, proud, independent, blind to the call of the God who made them, and who with infinite long-suffering continues to give them the rain and the sun, imagining that they are the centre of the universe, measuring, judging, weighing everything in balances"[108] who are themselves there weighed in the balances, and

107. Christopher Dawson, *The Spirit of the Oxford Movement* (New York: Sheed and Ward, 1933).
108. E. C. Hoskyns, *Cambridge Sermons* (London: SPCK, 1938), 61.

found wanting. Indeed, we come to see *ourselves* face to face with the Son of God, in those who crucified him. We cannot exempt ourselves in virtue of our achievement from that universal predicament of the human race, which the cross reveals at its highest tension. When modern Protestant theologians say that the coming of Christ creates the gulf that separates God and man, we may find their language strange and unintelligible. But they are pointing forcefully at an important truth—namely, that it is in a very real sense the manifestation of the Son of Man that creates, as well as reveals, the crisis in which humanity finds itself.

It is tempting for us to understand the word of God in terms of our own favorite myth. Yet, if we identify the gospel of God with the formal endorsements history that is of our own making, we empty that word of its character as a word spoken to us from outside our own world. It is this transcendence of the gospel that is the ultimate ground of our exercise of the theological virtue of hope. We can say, with the Liberals, that it was ecclesiastical intolerance and lust for power that brought Jesus to his death, but we shall say it for a very different reason. We must affirm it not as congruous with the Liberal view of human development, but as a part of the divine revelation, the tragic revelation that man's highest achievement is the occasion of his lowest fall. For in revelation, we learn to see the grim reality of the problem of power, of authority wielded without reference to its giver, and with no thought save of the self-aggrandizement of those in whom it is vested. In the New Testament, we read the terrible story of the decline and fall of Israel after the flesh, and these things are assuredly written for our learning.

But we have got to understand that in the gospel we are *all* brought face to face with the mercy of God, and found wanting. The coming of Jesus creates the crisis of human history. It thrusts man into a new situation, brings him to the judgment seat of God. To those who construe history solely in terms of the natural, its pronouncements are pessimistic. Yet that pessimism is the near neighbour of Christian hope. For the coming of Jesus reveals to man his eternal destiny. His end is achieved not within but outside the ebb and flow of temporal history. Judgment, mercy, redemption, these fundamental words of the Christian gospel are the very basis of human rights. "God so loved the world." It is the act of God in Christ that reveals to man his inalienable dignity. If, in the description of the human situation, we must allow place for the crisis of individual decision into which the coming of Christ thrusts the individual, we have asserted the right of the individual person against any collectivity that would seek to absorb him in its achievement. His character is not revealed by the ebb and flow of events, but first and foremost by those events wherein the arm of the Lord is laid bare, and by his finger the devils are cast out.[109]

The church attests the gospel. It is the new Israel, the Israel after the spirit, which supersedes Israel after the flesh. That character it possesses as the body of Christ, on whom the whole destiny of Israel rested, and in whose passion it was fulfilled. The church is a transcendent society simply in virtue of the transcendent character of that gospel of which it is the bearer. There is a sense in which we must admit that the church must stand outside the movement of human history, pointing men, as it does, to those events that alone give that history significance and redeem it from frustration.

Yet that transcendence is no mere *apatheia*, or incapacity of suffering. Within the body of Christ, the tensions of human life are at their highest. The writings of certain ascetic theologians may have suggested to those who are unfamiliar with their general frame of reference that the Christian life is one of almost Stoic tranquillity. As we shall see, that is not so. At present, it is sufficient to emphasize how clearly the history of the church shows that it is in its members that the whole conflict of nature and grace is revealed in its most intense form. The character of the society is unaltered by its members' failures. That is guaranteed by the ultimate character of the apostolate of Jesus. But we must not blind ourselves to the fact that, in a measure, the magnitude of those failures themselves attest the gospel. They

109. Cf. Vigo Auguste Demant, *The Religious Prospect* (London: F. Muller, 1939); Victor White, "The Christian Revolution," *Blackfriars* 15, no. 167 (Feb. 1934): 138–49.

reveal the church as the place of conflicts that in their character are truly eschatological,[110] concerned with those ultimate and final things, which the whole life of the church shows forth. In membership of the church, which is membership of Christ sinful, human individuals are brought into that place where the whole power of the kingdom of Satan assaults the city of God. We are in the place of an eschatological conflict, and apart from the recognition of this, our lives are unintelligible.

"Be of good cheer; I have overcome the world."[111] It is that victory that the church in every age is concerned to make its own. At the altar, it is indeed the church's own, for there the willful sin and imperfection of its members are made good by the obedience of its Head. There in the Mass is a catholic action, an action that is universal in its scope, and which, by its power, transforms to the honor and glory of God the sorriest of our negligences, and the most self-regarding of our failures. In the Mass, the act of God, wrought out in flesh and blood, is rehearsed with intention of the purifying and sanctifying of the faithful. Scripture, Liturgy, church: the witness of those three agrees, and by their witness, men are revealed as objects of a divine mercy, and as called to become no less than the sons of God—by adoption and grace.

If men and women are again to find their home in the body of Christ, it will be perhaps through the very depth of their need that they will make their way there. For it is to those conscious of a need, which it will be the concern of the last chapter of this book to describe, that in the first instance the word of God is spoken. We do ill service, however, to the cause of Christ, who is himself the Way, the Truth, and the Life, if we seek to mitigate the tragedy of the church. Its whole situation is paradoxical—to the Jew a stumbling block, and to the Greek foolishness.[112] But that paradox attests the further paradox, indeed embodies the ultimate paradox, of revelation. The church of Christ is

110. Eschatology is that branch of Christian theology that deals with the ultimate destiny of mankind and the universe.

111. John 16:33.

112. 1 Cor. 1:23.

in the last resort a scandal, a stumbling block, thrusting upon men as it does, both in its history and in its explicit teaching, the question whether indeed God has revealed himself, and boldly bidding them enter the place where the tension of their situation is made most acute, where is manifest the power of God unto salvation. The church is the hope of the world, for the church, the new Israel, the body of Christ, is itself the good news that it brings.

Despite its character as the new Israel, we must not look for perfection in the church militant here on earth. Its members are at war. In the world they have tribulation, and often the pull of the world upon them is too strong for them to resist.

There is great insight in the words of Professor Karl Adam: "Inasmuch as we live on earth as strangers and pilgrims, the true Christian theology must always be and must remain a theology of the Crosses. When an effort is made to whittle away the eschatological tension in the Christ himself, and its shadow in the Church, that must to some extent determine her outward form, the fundamental burden of the message of Jesus is misconstrued. . . . The Christian life is not the realisation of the fullness of God, but only the road that leads thereto. It is not the end of the journey, but only the last stage; it is an interlude that is full of tension and strife, of perplexity and danger, but also of certain faith and joyous hope."[113]

The facile Utopianism, which would deny these limitations, will never see its hopes realized. Within the body of Christ, we are members one of another. Yet it is no paradox that it is precisely in those places where these limitations are most clearly grasped that the spirit of prophecy is strongest. That is inevitable, for the prophet is not a "creative spiritual genius," but one who sternly insists that historical events be interpreted theologically—that is to say, in reference to the

113. From the paper entitled, "Le Mystère de l' Eglise: du Scandale à La Foi triomphante," in the work already quoted, *L'Eglise est une*: "Tant que nous vivons *in statu viae*, la théologie chrétienne véritable devra toujours être et demeurer une *theolgia crucis*. Quand on essaie d'atténuer la tension eschatologique dans le Christ, et son retentissement nécessaire pour la forme de l'Englise, on méconnaît le sens fondamental du message de Jésus. . . . Le christianisme n'est pas la plenitude achevée, mais seulement la voie qui y mène. Le christianisme n'est pas le terme, mais seulement la dernière étape; c'est un intérim plein de tension et de lutte, d'obscurité et de risque, mais aussi de foi certaine et de joyeuse espérance."

gospel of which the church is the bearer. It is also the work of the prophet to recall individual Christians to the rock whence they are hewn, at times when the prince of this world has blinded their eyes to the truth of Christ. Thus we find the spirit of prophecy realized in men as different as Jacques Maritain and Georges Bernanos, the one a technical philosopher, the other a novelist and man of affairs, but both united in their insistence that the issues of our time are issues of the gospel, and that it is in that light, and none other, that Christian men must see them before they act.[114]

We are living through the first stages of a veritable "hour of darkness." Indeed, Dawson has gone so far as to argue that the situation with which the church is faced is graver even than that which confronted it in the days of Augustine. We need today, perhaps more than anything else, to recover a true perspective in our view of the relations of the church to the world. Christian theology is inescapably a *theologia crucis*. It is the centrality of the cross in the gospel that should give us pause when we are tempted to go whoring after those delicately balanced systems of philosophical theology that academic teachers offer us from time to time. Not so easily domesticated are the savage paradoxes of the gospel. If we are going to understand to what tasks Christians are called at this present time, we have got to understand what it is that the gospel teaches us of human history. "Not as the world giveth, give I unto you."

"To Christians," writes Dawson, "the shock and the disillusionment should be less severe than to those who have put their faith in the nineteenth-century gospel of secular progress. For the Christian faith never minimized the reality of the forces of evil in history and society, as well as in the life of the individual, and *it has prepared men's minds to face the extreme consequences of the external triumph of evil, and the apparent defeat of good*. Yet nonetheless it is no defeatist philosophy;

114. The occasion of the "prophetic" activity to which we here refer was the Spanish Civil War. Maritain and Bernanos alike lodged truly prophetic protests against the identification of the cause of the church with that of the insurgents, both pointing out, the one in his open letter, *Sur la question de la guerre sainte*, the other in his *Les Grands Cimetières sous la Lune*, that such an identification involved those who made it in a denial of the church's independence of action.

it is a triumphant affirmation of life—of eternal life victorious over death, of the Kingdom of God prevailing over the rulers of this world of darkness."[115]

We are told today by some of the finest Christian minds that we are witnesses of the birth pangs of a new Christendom. The tragic and terrible conflict in which the nations of Europe are involved is fraught with hope for the future, according to these writers, and the gravity of the present hour is no occasion for despair. The Western Powers are not the champions of Christian civilization, or of an actual Christendom. But they are endeavoring to preserve, by their efforts, a situation in which such a realization is still possible. Moreover, the failure of the League experiment has convinced many of the impossibility of attempting to achieve a just order in national and international life on the basis of a naturalistic or agnostic estimate of man's origin and destiny. We ought to thank God that he has called us to live in such an hour of opportunity.

But there are others who take a different view. Such an estimate seems to them to rest on a dangerously inadequate appraisal of the situation with which we are faced. It is an hour of darkness, and not of light. It may be that the future does hold the promise of better things, even of a new Christendom. But the present is heavy with insoluble perplexities. "The dilemma of the unjust war and the unjust peace"[116] is inescapable. It is a situation fraught with possibilities of evil rather than of good. England and France did indeed take up arms in part at least from determination to preserve the human person from a dreadful threat. But their statesmen have sometimes shown an almost terrifying ignorance of the character of that menace, and of the circumstances that have produced it. It is indeed not without significance that the exact significance of political totalitarianism has been most surely gauged by such Christian writers as Demant and Dawson, or by such friends of Christianity as Peter Drucker.

115. Dawson, "The Hour of Darkness," *Tablet* (Dec. 2, 1939): pp. 625–26, an article that shows an unusually realistic view of the issues with which the Christian world is faced.
116. White, "Kierkegaard's Journals," *Blackfriars* (Nov. 1939): 810.

What gives the present situation its immense gravity has been ably expressed by Dawson:[117]

> The new mass dictatorships associate the highest and lowest qualities of human nature—self-sacrifice and boundless devotion, as well as unlimited violence and vindictiveness—in the assertion of their will to power. . . . As soon as men decide that all means are permitted to fight an evil, then their good becomes indistinguishable from the evil that they set out to destroy. The subordination of morals to politics, the reign of terror and the technique of propaganda and psychological aggression can be used by any power or party that is bold enough to abandon moral scruples, and plunge into the abyss. That is the greatest difficulty that faces us at the present time. For it is an evil that thrives by war, and the necessity of opposing by force of arms the spirit of unlimited aggression creates the atmosphere, which is most favourable to its growth.

There is a profound sense in which we can and must say that only the church can save the world. For the world is not the ordered cosmos of the first creation. In itself it is frustrated, introverted, demonic. Human life is radically disordered, and the disorder is manifest, not merely in the life the individual, but also in that of the society. The ceaseless oscillation between an anarchic individualism and a subhuman collectivism is an evidence of the depth of the perversion of the natural order. It is from the prince of the world that the Messianic victory has delivered mankind, and that victory, we must remember, was wrought out, not in might, but in weakness. For it was a victory of faith, of that faith that alone overcomes the world.

The world is overcome, not by the visible defeat of the "engineers of the mechanism of world power,"[118] but by the steadfast testimony unto the truth of God, borne by the Christ before Pilate. It may be that, if Christendom is to be reborn, the price of the rebirth will be a renewed realization by Christian men and women everywhere that the victory that overcomes the world is faith, and that their task is not to overcome its spiritual masters by their own weapons, but, by their

117. Dawson, "The Hour of Darkness," 626.
118. Ibid.

faithfulness unto the cross; to redeem from bondage those children whom such masters have enslaved.

When we look at the history of the church during the past centuries, we find much to shock us, much ready compliance with successive secular moods, much tolerance of social injustice that cried to heaven for vengeance. As Fr. Stratmann, the German Dominican, has written:

> Anyone who is acquainted with the spirit of both Catholic and non-Catholic cultivated and ignorant thought knows how depressing it is when everything to do with the Church is apologized for and justified. We know what a relief it is when shadows are acknowledged to be shadows, stains to be stains, puzzles to be puzzles. How much better it is to acknowledge and bewail that the Catholics in practical daily life, flay people, priests, bishops, popes, have to a great extent forgotten that the Church is the bearer of the Spirit and the Office of Christ, the Mother of all mankind, the Mystical Body of Christ, and that in the course of the world's history her members have fallen short and still fall short of her high calling. If this is acknowledged, the Catholic ideal stands much higher and is much purer.[119]

We have not exhausted the theme of the church and the world, and we will return to it in the next chapter. But for the present we have said enough to make it clear that in those relations, we see a perpetuation of the whole gospel situation. The life of the church is shot through and through with tension land crisis. The pull of the world upon its members sets up within it a strain that affects them all. We are members one of another. But in itself, the church attests a kingdom not from hence, it bears witness to the gospel of the mercy of God. If at the present hour what is at stake is no less than the status of the human person, inevitably the defence devolves upon the church. For it is in the gospel that the dignity of that person is formally and finally ratified.

If in the perspective of God there is no discontinuity between nature and grace, on the plane of human history the actual relation of the kingdom of God and the kingdom of man may often reveal itself to human vision as one of irreconcilable opposition. "Not as the world

119. Franziskus Stratmann, *The Church and War* (London: Sheed and Ward, 1928), 130.

giveth, give I unto you." We may add that often not as Christ seeth, but as the world I seeth, see we. Yet it remains true that the victory, which overcomes the world, is faith, our faith, the faith of Christ. For by faith, witness is borne to the sovereignty of God, from whom we are and to whom we go.

Chapter 10: Sons of God

In these words, the dignity of the members of the body of Christ is briefly epitomized. They are *filii in Filio*—sons in the Son.[120] It is a dignity theirs in the order of being. They *are* sons of God.

Thus, St. Paul in the Epistle to the Romans wrote:[121] "For those whom he foreknew, them he also foreordained to be conformed to the likeness of his Son."

Père Mersch, commenting on this passage, points out that we are to see in this adoption the work of the whole Godhead, and the fulfillment of the very incarnation of the Son. "For God," he says, "has given his Son, and he has given him so completely that the gift has entered into the substance of men, and they themselves are also become sons."[122] It is the filial character, which resides in the humanity of Christ in virtue of the hypostatic union,[123] that is communicated to his members. It is their privilege to enjoy a sonship in the Son.

Yet we are not to think of this privilege as a right that is ours, without any relation to the work of God in Christ. Though by the grace of adoption, men are here and now sons of God, yet that grace is given them solely in reference to their end, to what in the purpose of God they are to become. It points back to the accomplishment in isolation and pain of the obedience of the mortal flesh of Christ, and forward to the revelation of the Son of Man in glory. The former is its condition; the latter is its fulfillment. For then we shall see him as he is.[124] We do

120. See Mascall, *The God-Man*, 86; cf. Père Émile Mersch, SJ, "Filii in Filio," *Nouvelle Revue Théologique* 65, no. 5 (May 1938): 551–82.
121. Rom. 8:29.
122. Mersch, *Nouvelle Revue Théologique* (May 1938): 555.
123. See Mascall, *The God-Man*, 62.
124. 1 John 3:2.

well to remember these facts, as this book is brought to a conclusion with some remarks on the life of the individual Christian.

The church, the family of God and the body of Christ, supplies the context of the individual Christian's life. The Christian life is life within the church. It is this fact, which sets the individual in a proper relation at once to the Messiah and to his brethren. In the earlier chapters of this book we have been concerned with the former; our attention is now focused on the latter.

There is no room for an easy individualism in the Christian life; the energy of the individual Christian is set on the perfecting of the body of Christ rather than on his own salvation. He is conscious that he has been made a member of that body not for himself but that in all things God may be glorified. His adoption into the family of God, to which his baptism bears witness and brings about, is regarded as God's action upon the universe *outside himself*, the work of the whole Trinity. In the sonship of himself and his brethren in the Son of God, he sees the very fulfillment of the purpose of God for humankind. In the building up of the body of Christ is seen the end of the work of redemption, in which it can be truly said that "whence death arose, thence life also rose again."[125]

Moreover, the individual is conscious that, in so far as in him the victory of Christ that overcometh the world made manifest, he is himself contributing towards the fulfillment of these purposes of God. Yet the manifestation is no easy task. As was said above, in the church of Christ and in the individual members thereof, the dialectic of nature and grace is revealed in its sharpest form. There the tension of human life is at its highest, for there is reenacted the conflict of Messiah and the powers of darkness.

When the Catholic says that grace is the perfection of nature, he is sometimes, with justice, accused of ignoring how great the gulf is that separates man fallen from man created. But there is perhaps a sense in which the insight of this phrase draws our attention to the character of grace, as pointing towards the end of man, that too easily

125. *Missale Romanum*, Preface of the Cross.

escapes the critic. Nature is perfected by grace. In the life of grace, those fierce perplexities and questionings, that harass our natural life, do not disappear; they assume a new sharpness from the context in which they are now asked. For they are now posed in the place where the Christ is crucified. As Barth points out:

> His entering within the deepest darkness of human ambiguity and abiding within it is the faithfulness. . . . He takes his place where God can be present only in questionings about him. . . . He is not a hero or leader of men; he is neither poet nor thinker: *My God, my God, why hast thou forsaken me?* Nevertheless, precisely, in this negation, he is the fulfilment of every possibility of human progress, as the Prophets and the Law conceive of progress and evolution, because he sacrifices to the incomparably Greater and to the invisibly Other every claim to genius and every human heroic or aesthetic or psychic possibility, because there is no human possibility of which he did not rid himself. Herein he is recognised as the Christ.[126]

The questions that we ask are, in a measure, his questions. The fulfillment of his obedience, a task that devolves upon us in virtue of our sonship, is a fulfillment like unto his. The fierceness of the dialectic of nature and grace within us is a fruit of our participation in the sonship of Christ in the order of being. If we are sons of God, then we know that on our choices and decisions hinges not merely our natural future, but the building up of the body of Christ. It is our character as sons of God that, as it were, gives our decisions their ultimate quality. They are now set within the context of the obedience of the flesh of Jesus as that is fulfilled in the life of the people of God.

"Not as the world giveth, give I unto you." We are told often enough that the peace of Christ is not mere absence of conflict between nations. But we are sometimes led to suppose that it is an interior serenity of which we remain in possession throughout the changes and chances of this mortal life. Emphatically it is even less the latter than the former. The peace of Christ is the restless, onward movement of the obedience of his flesh. Its character as the unshaken possession of God is manifest only to faith and will be hidden until the last day. It is by faith that we confess ourselves sons of God. It is an act of faith, which

126. Karl Barth, *Epistle to the Romans*, trans. E. C. Hoskyns (London: Oxford University Press, 1933), 97.

the pull of the world requires us ceaselessly to renew. It is in itself the formal affirmation of that faith which overcomes the world.

Moreover, we are members one of another. It is in the light of this saying that we should approach the doctrine of the Communion of Saints. In the perplexity of the Christian life, we are not alone. There are those in whom already the victory of Christ is manifest, on whose prayers we rely. There are those in whom the good work begun on earth is being brought to completion. All alike are members of the one Head. All travel, or have travelled, the same *Way*.

"Christianity is Christ." So wireless preachers repeatedly inform us, and we cannot deny that they are right. The problem of the Christian life, the riddle of the church, and the puzzle of individual discipleship are intelligible when they are seen against the background of the cross. The theology of the cross is the theology of glory. For the very horror of Calvary is rooted in the dignity of the sufferer as Son of God. It is his glory that is manifested in the terrible isolation of that act of obedience. That is the gospel of God—the Way, the Truth, and the Life. Only thus does man ascend unto the Father. Only there is the whole mystery of life made plain and the secrets laid bare. And it is the eating of that mangled flesh and the drinking of that shed blood that is the very condition of eternal life. It is in the church of Christ that the word of the cross is spoken to a world perishing for the need of it.

Per ipsum et cum ipso et in ipso est tibi Deo Patri omnipotenti, in unitate Spiritus Sancti, omnis honor et gloria per omnia saecula saeculorum. Amen.

Part 2: The Stripping of the Altars

Part 2 Introduction: "That One Man Should Die for the People": Ecclesiological Fundamentalism, Kenosis and the Tragic

Scott A. Kirkland

Throughout the Signposts texts, MacKinnon often had occasion to speak of the church as the extension of the incarnation. Yet when he had spoken in this way, it had always been tensely related to a rather more Protestant proclivity—informed by Karl Barth, Emil Brunner and others—toward a more interrogative mood. If the church is the extension of the incarnation, it is only in its witness to the incarnate one who has entered into the precariousness of the wilderness. The texts in this particular volume, *The Stripping of the Altars,* are all, in one way or another, concerned with what MacKinnon names "ecclesiological fundamentalism"; that is, "a readiness to accept the historical experience of the Church as self-justifying."[1] The ecclesiological fundamentalist is one who has learned to "speak with the

1. See chap. 3 below, "Authority and Freedom in the Church," 211.

accent of Caiaphas," and so collude with political expediency for the sake of the maintenance of a privileged institutional structure. If there is continuity between these two sets of texts, then, it is in MacKinnon's intense moral, and thereby ontological, seriousness. For the church cannot be thought of as an extension of the incarnation if that means occupying a place at the table of Caesar. The table of Christ is the table of the poor, the oppressed, the vulnerable, and the marginalized. MacKinnon's irrepressible and restless sense of obligation to the particular, then, drives the church into a position of political vulnerability to the extent that the church finds itself unable to participate in the kind of judgements that would have one man die for the sake of the people.

Bishop George Bell (a name now shrouded in darkness) was fascinating for MacKinnon precisely because he formed an example of a refusal of political expediency that would turn international relations into a utilitarian calculus. Bell had publicly protested the practice of area bombing, had been an ally of the "Confessing Church" in Germany, and was a supporter of the resistance movement of which Dietrich Bonhoeffer was a part, and yet, he was also well at home in the halls of ecclesial and political power. MacKinnon saw in him someone who, while able to speak the language of power, "knew himself a citizen of another country, whose laws and demands were in increasingly sharp conflict with those of the province he knew."[2] Bell served as a point of contrast to "the weaker, more accommodating faith of lesser men."[3] And yet this is not necessarily because of the success of his political involvements; indeed, much like Bonhoeffer, he was condemned to failure. Here lies the concrete ambiguity of MacKinnon's ecclesiology, for success may indeed require the kind of compromise that would allow one man to die for the people. It may indeed be that the church need be open to the risk of failure, the failure that is crucifixion, and a failure that is not simply and glibly overridden by resurrection.

2. See chap. 6 below, "The Controversial Bishop Bell," 236.
3. Ibid.

MacKinnon saw the church's situation in the 1960s as one in which it had so clothed itself in the vestments of power that it was unable to perform precisely the kind of morally serious protest that is at the heart of its very being. Hence his turn to the tragic as a form of interrogation of ecclesial power. On the face of things, the oddest addition to this collection is the discussion of tragic drama's relation to theology, in the essay "Tragedy and Theology." However, by way of introduction to this collection, I want to suggest to the reader that coming to terms with this particular essay is critical to coming to terms with MacKinnon's overall strategy in this collection. For, as MacKinnon understands it, the banishment of the tragedians from Plato's *kallipolis* is performed again and again at each moment in which the *ekklesia* fails to take seriously the ambiguity of its decisions, and instead act after the manner of Caiaphas.

David Bentley Hart has condemned what he calls MacKinnon's "tragic theology,"[4] for the reason that Attic tragedy performs "a mystification of violence that sustains the sacred order of pagan society, the consecration of social violence as a restraint of cosmic violence, natural and divine."[5] At the heart of the Christian vision lies a primordial peacefulness, which the tragic defies, according to Hart, by locating heroic death on behalf of the *polis* at the very foundation of the political order.[6] Hence, Hart suggests that MacKinnon's appropriation of the tragic may have precisely the opposite intended effect in that the political order is simply reaffirmed by the sacrificial violence of tragic death. There are two things to be said here, not to rebuff Hart completely, but to open ways forward for the reader.

4. This designation is also assigned to Nicholas Lash. Hart acknowledges the differences between Lash and MacKinnon, but does not see as occasion for further qualification. David Bentley Hart, *The Beauty of the Infinite: The Aesthetics of Christian Truth* (Grand Rapids, MI: Eerdmans, 2003), 282–83.
5. Ibid., 284.
6. Ibid. "In the plays of Euripides someone often dies on behalf of the polis, heroically (which is also to say sacrificially); and it is just this gesture of exclusion, reappropriated by the polis under the form of a heroic *decision* that affirms the order of society, that is the very core of the tragic."

1. MacKinnon resists any simple classification of the "tragic" as indicative of a particular metaphysic. At the beginning of "Theology and Tragedy" (an essay Hart does not engage), MacKinnon argues that we cannot

> reflect a blind indifference to the multiple complexity of those works that we class together as tragedies. They are inherently complex and vary in emphasis; at best we can discern a family resemblance between them, and, in an essay like this, the author runs the risk not only of selecting examples tailor-made to his thesis, but also of imposing an appearance of similarity of conception where it is at least equally important to stress differences.[7]

Hedging himself this way, MacKinnon resists any simple categorization of the tragic and, consequently, provides himself with space for both theological appropriation and a proper reserve. There is no simple elision of tragic metaphysics and the gospel narratives, as Hart suggests, rather MacKinnon finds an instructive family resemblance; hence, MacKinnon is able to draw on a variety of resources exceeding Attic tragedy, such as Shakespeare, Conrad, and others. Further, MacKinnon makes immediate reference to the diverse work of figures such as Raymond Williams, George Steiner, and D. Daiches Raphael, almost in a gesture intended to point both to the elasticity of the category of the tragic as well as the diverse intersections of tragedy, metaphysics, and ethics in his contemporaries.

2. Hart fails to locate MacKinnon's use of the tragic within the context of his ecclesiological (and political) engagements.[8] Because of this, Hart does not articulate the way MacKinnon has wed his use of the tragic to the ability of the church to perform the sacred violence of the state. So, in "*Kenosis* and Establishment" MacKinnon's use of the dispute between Plato and the tragedians emerges precisely to chastise the ecclesiological fundamentalist, who "finds in the actual history of his church something of the security the *kallipolis* sought to

7. See chap. 2 below, 196.

8. Much could be said here about the relationship between MacKinnon's engagement with various issues in international relations and his work on the tragic. See, for instance, "Christian and Marxist Dialectic" in *Philosophy and the Burden of Theological Honesty: A Donald MacKinnon Reader*, ed. John C. McDowell (London: T&T Clark, 2011), 45–54.

offer."[9] While MacKinnon does not, in deference to Hart, acknowledge the cultic dimensions of Attic tragedy, MacKinnon's point is not to appropriate tragic metaphysics as such, but simply to suggest that the tragic functions as an "ultimate, irreducible form of representation of the relation of the transcendent to the familiar." Analogically, one might see then a relationship between the church and Christ, who, as the crucified forever outside the city gates, is unable to find shelter under its roof.

The other aspect of this collection that will benefit from some brief introductory remarks is MacKinnon's ecclesiological appropriation of the category *kenosis* in the Gore Memorial Lecture, "*Kenosis* and Establishment." A great deal of nineteenth- and early twentieth-century Christologies, both in Britain and in Germany, are concerned with the proper habilitation of the concept of *kenosis*. Lutheran kenotic theologians chiefly found themselves in a situation where the demands of the scholastic use of the *communicatio idiomatum* were such that kenosis came to be articulated in terms of the renunciation of potency on the part of Christ. Christ sets aside certain powers proper to divinity for the sake of inhabiting fleshly life, for were he to maintain impassibility, immutability, omniscience, etc., his humanity would be lost. Alongside this came the demands of historical criticism emerging in the late eighteenth century and gaining strength through the nineteenth century. This demanded attention to the historical reality of Jesus of Nazareth, as opposed to the apparent interpretative judgements made by the writers of the Gospels.

In Britain there was likewise an impulse toward an embrace of the concept of *kenosis*. Yet this came without the same kind of ontological pressures that accompanied the *communicatio idiomatum* of the Lutherans. In his Gore Memorial Lecture, MacKinnon explicitly locates himself in relation to P. T. Forsyth, Charles Gore, and Henry Scott Holland. Gore's doctrine of *kenosis* in *The Incarnation of the Son of God* (1891) and *Dissertation on Subjects Concerning the Incarnation* (1895) had stressed the abandonment of divine powers by Christ, yet did so with

9. See chap. 1 below, 194.

a reserve located in the Logos's eternal being. As Sarah Coakley notes, "Gore adopts what is now called a 'two centres of consciousness model', which denies any actual loss of 'divine and cosmic functions' during the incarnation."[10] The depotentiation in *kenosis* is an act of renunciation of some already existing divine power, as is illustrated in the imagery Gore employs.[11]

Forsyth, however, had articulated himself rather differently in *The Person and Place of Jesus Christ* (1909), which MacKinnon declares a "masterpiece."[12] Forsyth rejects the use of metaphysical categories in theology, what he calls "Chalcedonianism." He therefore presents us with a *kenosis* that is ethically ordered.

> And the history of Christ's growth is then a history of moral reintegration, the history of his recovery, by gradual moral conquest, of the mode of being from which, by a tremendous moral act, he came. It is reconquest. He learned the taste of an acquired divinity who had eternally known it as his possession. He won by duty what was his own by right.[13]

Christ's self-abnegation is accomplished "the holy way, by a moral act of love, not by a *tour de force*."[14] Forsyth's kenoticism, however, still suffers from the supposition that Sarah Coakley notes plagues the British formulations: *kenosis* is a renunciation from a position of already existing power, albeit moral, and so *power* itself is not of necessity recast in the kenotic act itself. We can see this in Forsyth when he states, "The self-reduction, or self-retraction, of God might be a better phrase than the self-emptying."[15] A certain kind of theological ontology (despite Forsyth's protestations) provides the conditions under which *kenosis* is conceptualized. Divine power is already thought before divine *kenosis*. The same problem is present in Gore, where the

10. Sarah Coakley, "*Kenōsis* and Subversion: On the Repression of 'Vulnerability' in Christian Feminist Writing" in *Powers and Submissions: Spirituality, Philosophy and Gender* (Oxford: Blackwell, 2002), 21.
11. Ibid., 20–21.
12. MacKinnon, introduction to *Engagement with God*, by Hans Urs von Balthasar, ed. E. L. Mascall, trans. J. Halliburton (London: SPCK, 1975), 16.
13. P. T. Forsyth, *The Person and Place of Jesus Christ* (Warwick: Hodder and Stoughton, 1909), 308.
14. Ibid., 313.
15. Ibid., 308.

imagery surrounding *kenosis* is of a powerful ruler condescending into a position of weakness.

In Henry Scott Holland, however, MacKinnon detects something rather different. As early as 1952, MacKinnon notes, "Holland's Christology is kenotic because he allows its full pressure to be felt by his doctrine of God."[16] Holland was attempting to begin his theological ontology with the notion of Christ's *kenosis*, though there is no technical Christological discussion in Holland's sermons. This was because Holland was a "theologian of revelation," and so demanded that the point at which we speak of Christ is in his historical particularity.[17] To allow the weight of *kenosis* to fall on one's doctrine of God is to ask the question of the relationship between humanity and divinity from the unified particularity of Jesus Christ—not from "below" as in historical criticism, or from "above" as in earlier kenoticisms.

Coakley's influential typology curiously doesn't make reference to MacKinnon. There are two reasons for this that we might surmise, which shall help us to elucidate more adequately what MacKinnon is doing. First, MacKinnon's reception of the concept of *kenosis* has much to do with his engagement with continental discussion, primarily through his engagement with Hans Urs von Balthasar and Karl Barth, although this is not immediately apparent in the Gore lecture. Second, MacKinnon's kenoticism is bound up with the rejection of certain regulative forms of power. He is not interested in rejecting power as such, but in theologically recasting power. This means he doesn't easily fall into the Coakley's typology, which attempts to trap kenoticists working either from "above" or from "below."

In 1969, MacKinnon published his first two papers on Balthasar. The Gore Lecture was delivered in 1968, and revisited before publication in 1969. It is, therefore, reasonable to assume that MacKinnon's engagement with Balthasar and the time he takes to think through *kenosis* are bound up together to a significant degree. Indeed,

16. MacKinnon, "Scott Holland and Contemporary Needs" in *Borderlands of Theology*, ed. George W. Roberts and Donovan E. Smucker (Eugene, OR: Wipf and Stock, 2011), 116.
17. Ibid.

MacKinnon had been engaging with Balthasar's thoughts, particularly in relation to Karl Barth, from at least 1952, when he read *Karl Barth: Darstellung und Deutung seiner Theologie* (1951). What is critical to MacKinnon's relating Balthasar and Barth is that it centers around the atonement and the problem of "old" and "new" Israel. Indeed, the *Shoah* looms large over the conversation. Balthasar„ he writes,

> has no use for a facile, theological optimism which forgets, for instance, the moment on the first Good Friday, when, according to the fourth Evangelist, the ecclesiastical statesmanship of Caiaphas had its victory, and those who spoke for the ancient people of God cried that they had no king but Caesar: which forgets the trauma inflicted upon Christ's Body in that moment, and the horrors which have been its consequences across the centuries even to this present.[18]

We can hear the Gore Lecture here, the church that tragically learns to speak in the accent of Caiaphas. Here we feel the heart of the tragic irony MacKinnon will locate in "Constantinianism"; the church, which supposes itself to be "Christ's Body," finds itself inhabiting the forms of "ecclesiastical statesmanship" that so easily elide divine and imperial authority. It is the church that finds itself tragically and ironically flogging Christ's body. So,

> if the memory of this climactic episode [Good Friday] and its appalling *sequelae* should silence the preachers of Christianity without tragedy, the recollection of this unstaunched wound may yet serve (if we will not seek to dodge its lesson) to win us deeper understanding of the abysses of divine love: that love of which the agony and dereliction of the cross is the only measure.[19]

MacKinnon notes elsewhere that one of the most pressing tasks in contemporary theology is "reconciling the use of the category of substance in the articulation of the Christological problem with the recognition that it is the notion of *kenosis* which more than any other single notion points to the deepest sense of the mystery of the incarnation."[20] Balthasar offers a mode of talking about the

18. MacKinnon, introduction to *Engagement with God*, 4.
19. Ibid.
20. MacKinnon, "'Substance' in Christology: A cross-bench view," in *Burden of Theological Honesty*, 251.

particularity of Christ, his revelation as the Son of God, that is bound up with the question of divine substance. That is, MacKinnon sees in Balthasar someone who takes seriously the attempt to reimagine reality itself in the light of the revelation of God in the *kenosis* of the Son of God. So, Balthasar "reckons that all attempts to escape the burden of a doctrine of the incarnation, with its inexorable demands on human thought, is an abandonment of the Christian reality."[21] It is reckoning with reality as such that is abandoned at the point at which we cease interrogating our thought with the real *kenosis* of the Son of God. It is "in the darkness of Golgotha itself that we plum most nearly the unfathomable secrets of the divine love."[22] Divine substance, that which gives "form" to reality as such, is kenotic in shape to the extent that we identify the crucified and resurrected Jesus with enactment of the life of God in our midst.

The coincidence of divine power and human weakness in the incarnation is scandalous. That God becomes a crucified human, and as this crucified human *is* God without change or diminution to his substance, requires that we fundamentally rethink what it means to say "God" and, therefore, the forms of *power* and *authority* that are bound up with our ecclesial life. In Balthasar, MacKinnon finds someone who takes this seriously. While he does not appear explicitly in the Gore Lecture, it would seem he is in the background to the reformulation of the concept of *kenosis* alongside MacKinnon's British precursors. This takes place in such a way that the particularity of Christ is taken seriously, as historical critics would have it. For there can be no evasion of the revelation of God in this particular human being. However, this is not to abandon the difficult task of metaphysics, of talking about divine substance, for it is precisely in the revelation of God in Jesus of Nazareth that talk about divine substance begins. Here is the paradox of the coincidence of opposites. The genius of MacKinnon's kenoticism, then, is that it seeks to take seriously the entirely orthodox demands of Chalcedon.

21. MacKinnon, introduction to *Engagement with God*, 7.
22. Ibid.

These essays represent MacKinnon at his sharpest, his most rhetorically poignant, and politically astute. Yet, they also represent someone with a deep concern for the inescapable burden of the presence of Christ. Truly, "there can be no way from man to God unless there has been first set in the wilderness a way from God to man."[23]

Scott A. Kirkland
University of Divinity,
March, 2016

23. See above Part 1, *God the Living and True*, chap. 1, 48.

The Stripping of the Altars

Donald M. MacKinnon

Introduction

The lecture that introduces this volume was delivered as the Gore Memorial Lecture in Westminster Abbey on November 5, 1968. The version spoken in the Abbey was somewhat shorter than the one that is now published.[1]

It may seem improper for one whose primary concern is the philosophy of religion to venture into the field of ecclesiology. But the crisis of belief through which we are living, and of which I am professionally aware literally every day, inevitably affects and is affected by the actual situation of the churches. Thus the weary archaism of the present establishment of the Church of England distorts and inhibits a properly existential realization of the actual, present *Sitz im Leben* of the Christian community, of its perils and its opportunities. But this is only one primary instance of the way in which those involved in ecclesiastical structures cling obstinately to

1. Originally published as D. M. MacKinnon, *The Stripping of the Altars: The Gore Memorial Lecture Delivered on 5 November 1968 in Westminster Abbey and Other Papers and Essays on Related Topics* (London: Fontana Library/Collins, 1969).

the fading memory of a position they once enjoyed, failing altogether to meet the realities of a post-Constantinian situation.

It is a common theme of these essays (for all their diversity) that the churches are in this present emerging from the age of Constantine, emerging from the tunnel of the experience, which began with that emperor's adherence to the Christian faith. To use a seeming pejorative such as tunnel is to suggest an almost philistine disregard for the achievements of Christendom in the domains of culture and of human civilization. Yet it remains a tragic fact that for those glories, a terrible price was paid. From Caesar, the church of Christ learned to speak with the accents of Caiaphas, learned how often it was expedient that one man should die for the people, how often it was a luxury to be indulged only by the irresponsible to leave the ninety and nine sheep in eager quest for the wayward stray.

Or if the church refrained from making those accents those of its own speech, it deliberately abdicated from the task of criticizing the methods adopted by allegedly responsible human authorities, finding in acceptance rather than in protest, in obedience rather than revolt, the discipline of a somewhat macabre *via crucis* for its members. Always there was the tacit assumption that the ways of government were the ways of God: because, by (presumably) the most damaging anthropomorphism of all Christian intellectual history, the creator and governor of the world had been invested with the quality of an absolute, human ruler, the savage exactions of Henry VIII (to take one extreme example) were received as parables of the Lordship of him who was among men as their servant.

We live in a radically democratic age, in which established sanctities are ceaselessly called in question, compelled to justify their claim by reference to the human values they promote. The temper of this protest is often crudely utilitarian, unaware of the serious criticisms to which a thoroughgoing utilitarianism in ethical theory is open (whether "rule utilitarianism" or "act utilitarianism" is in mind); but the demand which thus finds expression is the fundamentally healthy rejection of an order that certainly secures a measure of respect for certain traditional values, but only at the cost religiously of a profound deformation of the ultimately radical faith of the incarnation through its conversion into the underlying spiritual tradition of a supposedly supremely excellent civilization.

In such a situation, it is always tempting for the Christian to espouse the cause of conservatism, not in the narrowly political, but in the broadly cultural sense. The very weight of historical experience encourages on the part of the churches a collective bias in favour of their inherited securities. And of no church is this more true than the Church of England. That church certainly has its radicals; but sometimes (not always) they combine a tendency to treat questions relating to the historical foundations of their faith as irrelevant to its substance, with an obstinate, ecclesiological fundamentalism.[2] Jesus becomes virtually a variable to whom it is possible to assign as values whatever likeness a favored tradition of public and private devotional practice may crave. But this (to my mind intellectually intolerable) detachment from fundamental questions of belief is made possible and compensated by a deep, unyielding commitment to the historical forms of institutional, ecclesiastical existence. So one is told that for the faithful clergy and laity in an English diocese to choose their chief pastor could only lead to "chaos." But what is this chaos? Might it not be the chaos out of which a new, more objectively significant form of Christian presence to the modern world is fashioned? More profoundly, we have to ask ourselves whether by our conservatism we may not be seeking to quench the spirit of God, leading the churches towards a new birth, which must touch the most fundamental forms of their existence.

To emerge self-consciously, and in a spirit of acceptance (and I do not mean by this, endorsement of the standards of a so-called "permissive society"), into the light of the post-Constantinian age; to seek the forms of post-Constantinian existence, both in respect of inter-church relations and in respect of presence to the world; to purge

2. For instance, questions relating to the manner in which Jesus conceived his mission and approached his death. Cf., for example, the theology of John Knox.

out of the collective and private imaginations of Christian people the last vestiges of their eagerness to approach the believer *de haut en bas*; to welcome the many possibilities opened in a new situation; to radically rethink such ethical problems as those raised by the methods of modern warfare and by men's rapidly extending mastery over their environment; (most fundamentally) to liberate our basic theology from the inherited infection of centuries of acquiescence in an objectively false situation vis-à-vis public authority—these are the imperatives, and these the opportunities of the post-Constantinian world. We live in an age in which faith (and the institutional forms in which that faith is expressed) must be tested to destruction. It is tempting to seek to avoid that testing by numbing the sharpness of the challenge to faith, and expending every energy to conserve, as an archaic enclave in the modern world, the highly questionable structures in which Christian practice and belief were previously expressed. Let the structures go, and the confrontation becomes inexorable; yet that way is also the way of promise. It is as a contribution to various aspects of this crucial discussion that these essays are collected together.

One paper—that on "Theology and Tragedy," which appeared in *Religious Studies* in 1967—stands rather by itself. In the Gore Lecture, I refer to Plato's treatment of tragedy; I thought therefore that some readers might care to consult, in connection with this section of the lecture, an essay in which I endeavored to bring out the significance of that criticism, and the consequences of the unconscious readiness of Christian theological tradition to endorse it.

Inevitably some of these papers overlap; for, written, delivered or broadcast, they represent concern with the same problems. It is impressive that two of them, completed in November 1967 and in November 1968 respectively, pay tribute to Father Robert Adolfs's book *The Grave of God: Has the Church a Future?* I know I am not alone in finding in that small volume one of the truly prophetic works of recent years. If by my writing I can encourage Anglicans, especially those theologians who combine a *soi-disant* theological radicalism with an ecclesiological conservatism, and those who occupy positions of authority and decisive influence in the existing ecclesiastical structure, to apply its lessons to the evaluation of the alleged inheritance to which in various ways with various emphases they cling so resolutely, I shall not have written in vain. I would venture to hope also that those who already know Father Adolfs's book, and share my admiration and gratitude for it, may find the occasional valuable development, or even correction, of some of his themes in the pages that follow; I could imagine no greater tribute to this small book.

D. M. MACKINNON
Cambridge
December 21, 1968

Chapter 1: Kenosis and Establishment

> All this line of thought—all this way of conceiving of God's self-restraining power and wisdom—at least prepares our mind for that supreme act of respect and love for His creatures by which the Son of God took into Himself human nature to redeem it, and in taking it limited both His power and His knowledge so that He could verily live through all the stages of a perfectly human experience and restore our nature from within by a contact so gentle that it gave life to every faculty without paralysing or destroying any.[3]

These words occur towards the end of Charles Gore's most sustained study of the conception of *kenosis*, and I quote them at the outset of this memorial lecture in that it is with aspects of the notion of *kenosis* that I am mainly concerned. It is also appropriate to quote from this essay in particular in that it was written during the period in which its author was a residentiary canon of this Abbey Church. I wish, however, to follow the quotation from Gore's essay with another more extended quotation, this time from a remarkable book by a Dutch Augustinian prior, Father Robert Adolfs, entitled in the English translation *The Grave*

3. Charles Gore, MA, Canon of Westminster, Superior of the Community of the Resurrection, Radley, *Dissertations on Subjects Connected with the Incarnation* (London: John Murray, 1895), 224.

of God: Has the Church a Future?[4] The chapter from which I quote is significantly entitled "The Church and Kenosis":

> What we are now experiencing is the Church's coming of age, her maturity. She had to follow this "wrong way" in order to come to a better and deeper understanding of herself and her mission. The Church has not wasted time or trouble in following the wrong ways that I have referred to. She has not simply wandered aimlessly around. She has had to follow this way [of suffering] in order to achieve greater spiritual maturity.
>
> In the parable of the prodigal son, the father does not try to restrain his son when he wishes to set out on his journey. The son's road reaches a dead end, but he returns inwardly mature and with even greater love for his father, to the "origin" of his way, to the original parting of the ways. He will set out once more, but greatly enriched by all that he has experienced on the other way. He has not broken the link with his father. On the contrary, this link is greatly strengthened.
>
> In the same way, the Church has not lost the inheritance of Christ on her "wrong way". She has not broken the link with grace. She too can set out again, enriched by her experience and purified by suffering. Her new way must be a genuinely Christian way. Does it exist for the Church? I believe that it does, and I have called it the way of *kenosis*.

The whole chapter from which these words are a quotation merits the closest study and represents an extremely bold and encouraging extension of the concept of *kenosis* to the field of ecclesiology. Father Adolfs is of course a Roman Catholic, and he writes primarily for members of that communion; but the lessons, which he seeks to enforce both here and elsewhere in his book, are of nearly universal significance. The boldness of his argument is a most impressive example of the way in which, in the present ferment in the Roman Church, men and women are learning lessons of the greatest possible significance for the whole of Christendom. Father Adolfs applies the image of the prodigal's residence in the far country to characterize, in a single, comprehensive, devastating, and extremely illuminating picture, vast tracts of the church's history, from the conversion of Constantine until the present day. One is tempted to suppose that in his heart he more than half agrees with that friend of Charles Gore, Father

4. Robert Adolfs, *The Grave of God: Has the Church a Future?*, Compass Books, ed. and trans. D. N. Smith (London: Burns & Oates, 1967), 109.

R. M. Benson, the founder of the Society of St John the Evangelist, that the conversion of Constantine was the greatest single disaster ever to overtake the Christian church. Certainly, and here I can only express myself in heartfelt agreement with his underlying conviction, Adolfs regards the advent of the post-Constantinian age of the Christian church as a period of unexampled opportunity as well as of severe testing; unexampled opportunity in that it opens the doors wide to a new reformation in which the radical spirits in his own Church of Rome are among the foremost participants.

In the passage that I have quoted, he sketches the outline of a philosophy of church history, seeing the age which is ending as a necessary stage in the church's progress to maturity; many will agree with me that he puts too bland a construction on a long history of compromise and betrayal. But it is hard to have anything but the greatest admiration for the way in which he finds in the notion of *kenosis* one of the key ideas required for the renewal of the church's understanding of its mission. Historically, as the quotation from his dissertation "On the Consciousness of our Lord" well illustrates, the use of the notion of *kenosis* in the field of Christology will always be associated with Gore's memory, and it is therefore surely appropriate in 1968 to build a lecture intended to commemorate his work around the contemporary significance of that idea, even extending its scope to the sharp criticism of assumptions to which Gore remained in bondage throughout his life. If, however, I express myself in these terms in agreement with Father Adolfs, I know that I must scrutinize as strictly as I can assumptions by which I have myself often been guided.

What Father Adolfs is pleading for is, in the first instance, a renewal of understanding of the manner of the church's presence to the human societies in which its work is carried on; but he recognizes quite clearly that this touches also the nature of its self-understanding, and indeed the way in which it understands its mission and the faith by which its existence is defined. So he latches on to the idea of *kenosis* or self-emptying (a much criticized but, in my judgment, a crucially significant Christological concept) and urges its application in the field of ecclesiology at once in theory and in pastoral practice. Certainly the notion of *kenosis* as a Christological concept has been drastically criticized. Thus in his admirable Hulsean Lectures, *The Divinity of Jesus Christ*,[5] the late Professor J. M. Creed insisted that the conception of a depotentiated Logos, involved in the theory as he understood it, seemed to carry quasi-mythological suggestion of a very doubtful character. He did not see how it could be supposed that the Lord abandoned his cosmic functions for the period of the incarnation or even within the sphere of the incarnate life, withheld himself from their exercise. And there are other grave criticisms.

Such paradoxes in the theory are well known. Yet I would plead for it that it calls attention not only to what is suggested by Paul's words in Philippians 2 and elsewhere, but also to the unfaltering stress of the Fourth Gospel on the Son's dependence on the Father, on an authority affirmed because of and in the context of a supreme humility, an "infinite self-abnegation," in Dean Inge's phrase. If this authority is found intolerable, it is because of the indirection of its manifestation; we do not find it unbearable in the way in which we find unbearable the exercise of ecclesiastical authority either in the manner of the more intransigent officers of the Roman Church in the months following the publication of the papal encyclical *Humanae Vitae*, or in that characteristic of the kind of English bishop who graduates to the episcopal bench from the headmastership of an English public school. Further, the concept of *kenosis* advertises the relevance of the costliness of the incarnate life to the absolute. If one cares, so to speak, it raises again the issue of divine impassibility by asking what light, if any, the manner of the ministry and passion of Jesus throws upon the being of the divine in itself, and on the nature of its relation to the created world. We have already said that it puts a question mark against much of the manner and exercise of ecclesiastical authority. The career of the rabbi of Nazareth does not suggest that of a Roman curial cardinal, or that of the headmaster of an English public school.

The notion of *kenosis* dares to carry back into the initiating act of

5. Reprinted in the Fontana Library, 1964.

the whole incarnate life that which is qualitatively similar to what it manifested. "There was a Calvary above which was the mother of it all." It has, moreover, deep relevance to the articulation of the doctrine of an essential as distinct from an economic Trinity. Further, the extension of the concept to the field of ecclesiology enables us to achieve deeper perception concerning its primary Christological significance. When the concept is so extended, it is extended to a field in which acknowledgment of the unity of theory and practice becomes inescapable. It is arguable that at least some of the antinomies that we encounter in developing the concept Christologically are due to the extent to which our total understanding of the relation of God to man is obscured by the radically distorted image presented in and by the institution supposed to convey its sense to the world. When the significance of *kenosis* for ecclesiology is boldly grasped, when, for instance, such concepts as ministry and apostolate are thought through in accordance with its implications, its fundamental Christological sense may well receive drastic illumination.[6]

All this sounds excessively abstract; but one can bring it down to earth very sharply, even poignantly. Theological progress may be dependent on the criticism of the church's institutional experience, even the rejection of long tracts of that experience as fundamentally invalid. In such criticism may well lie the necessary condition of really fundamental theological progress. Yet the liberating dynamic of a purely theological idea may itself be among the initial conditions of such criticism. I say that it may be among those conditions; I am equally sure that they will also include precisely the sort of changes in the sociological position of the church that Father Adolfs indicates. He wrote with his own Roman Catholic Church in mind; I speak against the background of a very vivid sense of the decline in prestige and influence of the Anglican Communion, with my mind filled also by a sense of the presently precarious situation of Christian belief. I can only speak with any sort of authority if I admit that I speak as an

6. On the subject of kenosis in Christology, see my forthcoming Prideaux Lectures, delivered before the University of Exeter in 1966.

intellectual, as one who is professionally preoccupied with issues of validity, of truth, of verification. Yet these issues pressed most certainly on Gore's mind and the attempted magnum opus of his retirement, we recall with admiration, was entitled *The Reconstruction of Belief*. It may be judged a failure; but we must admire the temper of a man who saw the cruciality of the issues with which he sought to deal. If I am right, the idea of *kenosis* is precisely one of the potentially liberating theological ideas of the present, one of the ideas that may help towards a reconstruction, I will not say of belief, but of the presentation—I would myself like to say the "system of projection"—of the proximate object of belief.

I turn now, in the light of what I have set out in general terms, to comment critically on various types of fundamentalism that stand in the way of the sort of renewal the present not only demands but seems to make possible. I use the word fundamentalism advisedly; for it is most important that we should realize that the fundamentalist temper is by no means exclusively expressed in terms of an adherence to belief in the supposed verbal inspiration of the Scriptures. There are, indeed, many sorts of fundamentalism—ecclesiological and liturgical mention two at least as deadly in their way as the more familiar biblical variant.

It was remarked by the bishop of St. Andrews, Dunkeld and Dunblane,[7] in an article published in the October number of *Scan*, the monthly newspaper of the Episcopal Church in Scotland, that the Lambeth Conference of 1968 might be regarded as the swan song of traditional Anglo-Catholicism. The judgment was an interesting one, and the fact that it was made encourages me to continue the development of my theme by reference to the presence in that tradition of a temper that, if it cannot be condemned out of hand as imperialistic, none the less embodies in living and destructive form something of the spirit of apartheid.

When he became bishop of Worcester (according to the obituary

7. Dr. John Howe.

in the *Times*), Gore resigned from the English Church Union, the Confraternity of the Blessed Sacrament, etc.; this because he judged membership of such partisan societies incompatible with the obligations of the episcopal office. But throughout his subsequent career, for all his deep differences with the policy of the Anglo-Catholic party over such matters as the extraliturgical cultus of the Blessed Sacrament, he remained in the public mind identified with that attitude of rigorously exclusive superiority towards members of nonepiscopal churches, which has been perhaps the most sheerly destructive element in the Anglo-Catholic inheritance. It is worth recalling Gore's attitude in a lecture on the ecclesiological import of *kenosis*, inasmuch as it would be hard to conceive any attitude more totally alien to an attempted expression in institutional terms of *kenosis* as of the *esse* of the church, and as something supremely indicative of its apostolicity.

A future historian may well say that this evil temper (for so it must be characterized) was endemic in the Tractarian movement and the successive failures of Anglo-Catholicism, which succeeded it from the first. He may also say that it reached its cruelest expression in the venomous and obsessive campaign, coinciding to no small extent with the years of the last war, over the adherence to the projected Church of South India of the Indian dioceses in that country.

This episode still awaits detailed analysis by a historian, an analysis that must not shrink from anathematizing the curious mixture of imperial patronage and English parochialism that marked its underlying judgment on the developing pattern of Indian Christianity. It will also require something of the sensitivity of the tragic poet to portray the sad scandal of religious men and women bound by the traditional three-fold vows of the religious life, turning in a time of war and terror from the promotion of a spirit of peace to the sowing of seeds of bitter and destructive controversy. No one who is familiar (as I am) with the writings and spiritual teaching of such men as the late Father W. B. O'Brien, SSJE, the superior of the Cowley Fathers at that time, or of the late Dom Gregory Dix, will question the great services that these men did not only to the church but also to many individuals; they were men of the greatest spiritual depth. One must therefore call it tragic that they so bent their energies at that time to the service of the harshest and most intransigent bigotry. It is also unfortunately true that they received a large measure of backing from the most distinguished theologian on the episcopal bench at that time, Dr. Kenneth Escott Kirk, bishop of Oxford, whose Bampton Lecture, *The Vision of God*, is one of the greatest works of Anglican theology in this century. If one says that these men did great damage, one does no more than point out what is involved in seeing something genuinely tragic in their behaviour. It is no answer to say that great principles were at stake. Issues of truth are obscured by the weapons men and women use to fight them. Of the spirit manifested in that episode one's verdict must be that it bore no mark at all of that manner of concern for ultimate truth on which, in the Christian's understanding of the church's Lord, the Father has set his seal: I mean that witness to the truth that no more relies on the compulsive power of the superior that leaves the issue open, and is receptive, expectant, always seeking to fulfill the law of self-emptying, of *kenosis*. The word I would emphasize in that last sentence is the word "receptive." An authentic Christian fidelity to tradition is always receptive, ready to learn, open to promise.

Yet what was seen written in large letters in the bitter agitation over the Church of South India was a temper, which had already, by its arrogance, inflicted damage in untold cases at a more personal level. I am not thinking, as those who hear or see these words may suppose, simply of the way in which individual priests have resisted any and every suggestion and resolution of the Convocations or the recommendations of successive Lambeth Conferences to admit to Communion non-Anglicans who have not received episcopal confirmation; such episodes are indeed deplorable. But I refer to the attitude of mind, which has continually queried the authenticity of the ministry of the non-episcopally ordained, and in particular of their sacramental practice. It is not the "fencing in" of the Anglican altar that I have in mind; rather it is the refusal to develop a concept of the authentically Christian (I am trying to avoid such overworked terms as orthodoxy and validity) that will encourage, without sacrifice of that which is supposed to be precious truth, a readiness to permit the way in which that truth has been received to win enlargement from those who stand within a seemingly alien tradition. There is an issue here, ultimately, of spirituality; but it is also one that touches what to an intellectual must lie near the heart of the matter, namely the manner of receiving and understanding the mysteries of faith. There is offense in the older attitude, not only against the claims of charity but also against those of truth.

But how may a man receive that which seems to contradict what he believes? What is the paradigm and model of enlargement with which we must work? Is it one that allows the fragmentariness of our perceptions to stand in need of correction, or is it one that is unselfconsciously committed to the assumption that the Incarnate was, in simple sense, omniscient and endowed his apostles with a comparable infallibility of insight? We must reject the latter assumption categorically on Christological grounds. For surely the manner of Christ's ministry imposes on us the need to reconstruct altogether the concept of the divinity predicated of Christ, and our concepts of the attributes whereby we suppose the unity of that divine nature anatomised. Some such demand was made admittedly by kenoticists of different schools; and here I include Peter Taylor Forsyth, as well as the Charles Gore whose essay I quoted at the outset of this lecture, his friend Henry Scott Holland, and their successor in the development of the kenotic idea, Frank Weston, bishop of Zanzibar. We need to continue their work and find in it the source of ethical illumination that, in the essay quoted from his *Dissertations*, Gore clearly thought we might find. It is indeed as a contribution to the extended use of the concept in the field of ecclesiology that this lecture is offered.

A little while ago, I referred to the many varieties of fundamentalism. In the volume *The Apostolic Ministry*,[8] which has recently been reprinted in a new edition, we have a nearly classical case of the spirit of ecclesiological fundamentalism. But the proper corrective to all fundamentalism lies in a more profound theology, and where theology is concerned, Christology is for the Christian its key.

"He that hath seen me hath seen the Father," Jesus said, according to St John, who also said in the same Gospel, "I and the Father are one [thing]," and further, "my Father is greater than I." These sayings, set in the mouth of the Lord by one of his most profound interpreters, put to the theologian the task of reconstructing the concept of identity involved in the second logion so as to avoid its apparent contradiction with the third. To pose the question in terms of the logical compatibility of two propositions, and the avoidance of the counterintuitive consequences of asserting both of them, has a very old-fashioned ring. Yet the demand made is one that, if we seek to fulfill it, involves us sooner or later in the most radical criticism of all our fundamentalisms. Indeed, such a criticism is a condition of successful reconstruction. We seek a certain internal consistency in our concepts, and if we achieve it, then our logical analysis precipitates us into criticism of any attempt to establish a security for ourselves by allowing as unauthenticated other roads for which surely room must be found on a proper map of the way of faith. It is not the exaltation of autonomy in the abstract that brings down our most treasured idol; it is learning that receptivity belongs to God as he is in himself. And we must say that receptivity does belong to God as he is in himself, if we deny that Christ is a mere simulacrum of the divine but rather insist that in him we have "God's presence and his very self and essence all divine." His invitation to the outcast is not adequately seen as a mere parable of the divine invitation, but rather as its actuality become event.

One notices today a tendency in Christological discussion to quote with admiration the remark of Professor John Knox: "The divinity of Jesus was the deed of God. The uniqueness of Jesus was the absolute uniqueness of what God did in him." The confusion of categories

8. K. E. Kirk, ed., *The Apostolic Ministry* (London: Hodder & Stoughton, 1946).

wantonly made in Knox's first proposition offends me as a philosopher. What is even more disquieting is the extent to which his vaguely disguised adoptionism is commended as a valuable contribution to the development of the doctrine of Christ's person. In the statements made in this section of the lecture, it will be seen that I am committed Christologically to complete acceptance of the *homoousion*. It is indeed in the strength of this commitment that I am urging the sort of resolute reformation of ecclesiological assumptions I believe to be implied by recognition that in the rabbi of Nazareth we discern the ways of God as he is in himself.

The sort of radical reformation of ecclesiastical styles for which I am pleading in this lecture is immensely easier for us in that we have entered the post-Constantinian age. The deadly evils that characterized the Anglo-Catholicism of the early forties that I have mentioned (and they were deadly evils and are such still where they remain) are of course part of the built-in inheritance of the Constantinian Church, the church whose status is guaranteed and that allows the manner of that guarantee (the exercise by the civil power of a measure of external compulsive authority) to invade the substance of its life. The temper of exclusion encourages men to think of membership of Christ's body after the manner of the claim *civis Romanus sum*. In Anglo-Catholicism, it was a claim that by such membership men stood at the heart and center of history and thus, after the likeness of a sharply exclusive citizenship, were the superiors of all lesser breeds without the law. In the complexities of Anglican history, we know also that such attitudes have had, where relations with the Free Churches are concerned, a certain continuing confirmation through the social position of the Church of England. Too often, establishment has been a ground for boasting rather than an opportunity for presence; a status ensuring a counterfeit security rather than a way of assuring that there shall be no withdrawal from the actualities of human life.

May I turn to another related but more general topic? "The end justifies the means": so Caiaphas, when he gave counsel, that it was expedient that one man should die for the people, "that the whole nation perish not." It is not enough to dismiss his argument as that of a hard *Realpolitiker* governed by *raison d'état*, eager to preserve the theocracy. The danger he foresaw was real enough, the threat to place and nation, for example. Less than forty years later, what was left? There were the martyrs of Masada; but the splendour of their devotion hardly in itself compensates for the destruction that laid Jerusalem almost to the ground. The statesman must always seek to preserve the ordinary man and woman from demands too great for them to bear; an elite can make a Masada possible, but what of lesser men? The presence of Jesus and the Lazarus whom he allegedly brought back from the tomb was a deeply disturbing factor, and such must be eliminated.

Moreover, it is not only the ecclesiastical statesman who speaks with the clear, realistic accents of Caiaphas. The Socratic principle—the principle of following the argument whithersoever it leads—demands that we turn a bright light on the extent to which we indulge in the ways in which we seek to commend the faith—a kind of dishonest sophistry—and on our related readiness to ignore the extent to which it may be that the ardour and skill that an individual displays in apologetics frequently ministers to his own self-importance. For in such corruption the apologist is too often encouraged by the churchly institution he claims to serve. Apologists are valuable; their skills are taken too often at their face value, receiving the endorsement of the institution they serve, which finds in their expertise a weapon too valuable lightly to be criticized. "That one man should die for the people": the casualties in the decision of which I am now speaking are truth, integrity, openness of mind—but the apologist himself is among them. He is not seen as a human being with human responsibilities and human frailties; he is seen as a tool, a *ζῶον ὄργανον* (Aristotle's phrase for a slave, in *Politics*), of the institution.

These last remarks may seem loosely connected with what has gone before, and indeed almost peripheral to my central theme. The young Christian in the academic world, and I have lived and worked in that world now for thirty-two years as a teacher and four years before that as a student, can easily be blind to the sort of abuse of genuine talent encouraged by ecclesiastical and quasi-ecclesiastical institutions. Men and women are taken from their proper, fundamental, professional work and the resources of their gifts mercilessly exploited by pressures of various kinds, including (and here I speak from experience) the powerful tools of spiritual blackmail on the one side and flattery on the other. There is a characteristically Christian philistine disdain here for disinterested concern with the truth for its own sake. There is also an almost certainly deliberate encouragement of dishonesty in that university teachers receive incentives to neglect the work for which they are paid (usually out of public funds) in order to undertake the apologetic task. There is a graver pastoral irresponsibility in that the lasting spiritual damage that is done to individuals in this way is often completely overlooked until it is too late.

Perhaps these words will suffice to show why I regard both the exclusiveness that expresses itself in a cruel bigotry and the blindness that refuses to query means that serve that institution's supposedly observable welfare as aspects of the same kind of idolatry of the institution seen as the embodiment of an ultimate security. During the Spanish Civil War, an Anglican apologist for the cause of General Franco urged the claims of his forces on the grounds that their victory would at least ensure the preservation of the external life of the church. The situation was extreme, but the question sowed in my mind more than thirty years ago a deep scepticism concerning the value to be assigned in this present to preserving the external life of the church, at least in forms easily recognizable as continuous with those that we know and take for granted. It is no accident that these questions are being asked radically and with greatest effect in the Church of Rome; but they are questions that we must face in our own situation and in the essentially Anglican setting of Westminster Abbey and in commemoration of Charles Gore. It is worthwhile that we should ask what for the life of the Anglican Communion, and especially the Church of England, is implied by the radical application of the law of *kenosis* to the evaluation of its present institutional life. Hitherto I have spoken primarily with a vivid memory of the failure of the Anglo-Catholic tradition. But I am now going to discuss the issues against a less restricted background.

At the heart of the Christian story we may see the opposition of Christ and Caiaphas: of the one who asked as a rhetorical question what shepherd, if he lost one sheep, would not leave the ninety and nine to seek it out; and the one who gave counsel that it was expedient that one man should die for the people. Whatever may survive the demythologization of the highly questionable myth of apostolic succession, empirical study of church history reveals how often and at what depth of commitment the way of the church has been that of Caiaphas rather than Christ. In the situation of radical unbelief with which we are confronted, we are offered, if we are prepared to be bold enough and to allow the liberating power of such ideas as *kenosis* to have their way with us, a chance that may not come again for centuries. This is the chance to lay aside the burden of the past, to begin our recovery from the disaster that, according to Father Benson, overtook the Christian Church with Constantine's conversion. But it will not be easy, and as the rest of this lecture will seek to suggest, while there will most certainly be immeasurable gains, we shall also have to be prepared to lose much that some of us cherish (myself, for the record, less than many I know), whose loss will certainly issue us into a world that we are bound to find strange, and that will be for all of us at some points uncongenial.

The word "establishment" suggests inevitably, and particularly in the setting of Westminster Abbey, the constitutional position of the Church of England. Yet, although such a position is clearly incompatible with post-Constantinian realities and is widely recognized as being so, it is not of establishment narrowly conceived that I wish primarily to speak. There are, however, two matters to which I wish to refer.

1. We hear very much today on all hands of demand for participation

in decision-making processes. The term "alienation" is freely used—in senses only loosely related to its relatively precisely defined employment in the early deprivation presently experienced by those who clamor for a greater say in the shaping of their destinies, whether in the field of national and regional government, in industry, in the world of the universities, or in the ecclesiastical world, especially in the Church of Rome. But, what of the Church of England?

In the life of that church, it is a little less than eight years since the day on which Lord Fisher's announcement of his impending resignation of the primacy of all England was followed immediately by the announcement that he was to be succeeded at Canterbury by the then archbishop of York, and that the vacancy so created in the Northern Province was to be filled by the translation from Bradford of Dr. Donald Coggan. So the expected presence at Canterbury of one generally regarded as an Anglo-Catholic was to be offset by the appointment to York of one equally conspicuously associated with the Evangelical tradition. No Sunday on which the *plebs sancta Dei* (the holy common people of God) assembled for worship might invoke the guidance of the Holy Spirit for those charged with the appointment of Lord Fisher's successor was allowed to intervene. The matter was judged, in the corridors of power, too important (or perhaps too insignificant) to wait on an interlude of prayer.

It would be hard to conceive a more radical denial of the most elementary right of Christian people to participate in the choice of their chief pastors, or a more contemptuous public dismissal of the claims of prayer. No one has yet suggested in so many words that the Patronage Secretary has replaced the Holy Ghost in the Church of England's understanding of the proper method for choosing its chief pastors, but its practice encourages the belief that such a substitution has taken place, or that we shall soon hear that the passages in the Fourth Gospel relating to the "Other Advocate" are to be demythologized in terms of the gift of such a functionary. But such advertised contempt for the claims of prayer inevitably and properly breeds an answering contempt for those who make themselves a party to it. This sort of bland dismissal of the assembled, common prayer of the faithful as a thing of no account is inevitably met by an answering mistrust of the men who without scruple accept appointment under such a system, and spring eagerly to its defence when it is met with challenge from the standpoint either of theology or ethics. It is my opinion (it is also, I admit, my fervent hope) that we may see radical change in this matter soon. Certainly, as a teacher concerned with Christian ethics, I regard it as my duty to do what I can to promote such a change and to point out that no church that adheres to such methods in the choice of its chief pastors, and defends continued adherence to it on grounds of the admittedly searching consequences of substituting a more earthly, democratic procedure, has the right to speak of the ethical value of participation in other decision-making processes.

If we believe that in democracy, for all its cumbrous inconvenience on occasion, we have still the most effective method on the political plane for making power accountable to those in whose name it is exercised, we must surely be impatient to rid our church life of the surviving remnants of structures that first took their shape in a dark age of royal absolutism.

Increasingly one sees, however, how much growth to spiritual maturity (a genuine "coming of age") is bound up with the withdrawal of the kind of external framework that, for centuries, ecclesiastical authorities have taken for granted as the context of their activities. The growth of a real public contempt for accepted styles of ecclesiastical behaviour, and the dissemination of this contempt through, for instance, the satirical programs of BBC television, is something to be positively welcomed. A study of the Fourth Gospel suggests (and the lesson is continuous with the teaching of the synoptists) that Christ's subtlest foes were those who would make him king, imprisoning him so completely in the structures they would claim to erect on the foundation of their devotion that his work of being lifted up from the earth to draw all men to himself was put in jeopardy by their anxious zeal.

2. Although it is late, even desperately late in the day, one may hope

that in the post-Constantinian age the churches will be able to turn their energies again to serious engagement with the ethical problems raised by war. None would dispute that in the centuries-long story of the churches' failure, few chapters are darker than that relating to war. Where England is concerned, the passing of establishment as we have known it would surely lead to a day in which episcopal lawn sleeves would cease to flutter in the breeze as their wearer bestowed the diocesan benediction upon the latest Polaris submarine. Here we should find sheer gain without any loss at all. Yet, at a deeper and more pervasive level, the readiness of any church to face the implication of Father Adolfs's challenge to us all concerning the whole Constantinian era of ecclesiastical history would surely make possible a radical rethinking of the assumptions on which so much Christian debate concerning the ethical problems of war is usually conducted.

But it is not these problems so much as the ultimate sense of the concept of establishment that I want to discuss in this lecture. Yet one word first (and here I may seem to substitute association of ideas for argument). We are told that we must choose between establishment and the "existence of the ghetto." I would ask, what of the Warsaw ghetto? That was a place of suffering, certainly, but one surely nearer the center than the periphery of the world's travail. Sometimes I admit to disliking intensely the use by Christians of the term "ghetto" in such contexts as the one I have illustrated. What indeed were, what indeed are ghettos, other than standing monuments to Christian failure across the Constantinian ages to engage with the problem of the old Israel, to seek the healing of the schism created on the first Good Friday, the first and perhaps the most horrible rent in Christ's body. And ought we to be so sure that we should not find something in ghetto existence profoundly to be welcomed? Perhaps I stand too much here on a phrase; perhaps I am being overly sensitive linguistically; but the problem, or rather the mystery, of the old Israel should ever be with the new. And in the matter to which I have referred, we have to reckon with a supreme historical failure on the part of Christendom.

If this lecture has a unifying theme, however, it is this. What is cushioned is likely to be invalid. What encourages us to defend the security allegedly bestowed by our traditions puts our Christian understanding in peril. That understanding is imperilled also, of course, by the cult of the alleged autonomy of faith, according to which faith is creative of its own objects. Here too there is flight to a security, albeit an inward security, a withdrawal from accepting the peril and the promise of the incarnation. It is, I repeat, not with establishment in the narrower sense that I am concerned in this lecture, but with the cultivation of the status of invulnerability, issuing in a devotion to the structures that preserve it. This is a condition we may seek in the domain of ideas; we may also seek it on the plane of institutions, of inherited structures. The ablest contemporary apologists for the continuance of establishment in the narrow sense have often urged the extent to which its continuance makes possible a Christian presence to the forces which direct and shape the life of our society. Their critics, on the other hand, find such presence too much a make-believe, too much a source of the illusion that we are actually exposed to the stresses and strains of the conflict between faith and unbelief, when all the time we are providing ourselves with some sort of ready-made assurance that these conflicts are resolved in a providential order that governs our comings and goings and makes all things work together for good. And it is with the critic that I myself agree.

To speak in these terms may seem a deliberate flirtation with obscurity, when what is needed is definite and clear presentation of choices to be made. But the issue of *kenosis* and establishment is, in the end, an issue of spirituality. To live as a Christian in the world today is necessarily to live an exposed life; it is to be stripped of the kind of security that tradition, whether ecclesiological or institutional, easily bestows. We deceive ourselves if we suppose that we do not seek to hide ourselves away from the kind of exposure to which I am referring. To do so might quite properly be thought the besetting sin of the characteristically Anglican ethos, a cultivated avoidance of extremes. And whether we like it or not, today we do live in an extreme situation. For myself, I know that while I accept this at one level, at another I long for the sort of protection against the sharp pressure of ultimate questions that various forms of make-believe offer. I would be false to my experience if I did not include among those forms of make-believe that which is often offered as participation in church work actively directed towards the Christian penetration of the supposed key positions in our society.

I mentioned a while back the BBC's satirical programs. A few years ago (according to information given to me; I did not myself see the program in question), an episode occurred that may be thought to pinpoint the lessons of this entire lecture. In a program (not, I think, specifically satirical), a vicar was invited to speak on the significance of Christmas, only to have his words completely drowned by a clamor of eager and somewhat raucous humanist voices. Immediately, the spokesman of official Christianity raised the cry of free speech, insisting on the vicar's right to be heard, etc.

Yet, profounder reflection would suggest that this "happening" was an acted parable of the Christian situation in the contemporary world, a situation in which *omnia abeunt in silentium*. We simply have not "got the answer" to radical unbelief (whatever the state of affairs indicated by the tendentious and misleading phrase "having the answer" may be). "What we cannot speak about that we must assign to silence" (Wittgenstein). Such silence is itself a kind of indirect communication, the ultimate *μαρτρία τλ ἁληθεία*.

To speak in these terms is not to be guilty of irrationalism. It is to express the conviction, which at some level we all share, that in Christian belief we reach the frontiers of the intelligible, the mysterious actuality of the divine self-emptying. Certainly the writ of logic runs in the field of theology. But we cannot always trace the precise way in which it does. Thus we know (and this I have insisted in this lecture) that we must, as far as we can, eliminate self-contradiction and every other counterintuitive element from our concepts. Yet still we may, rather we must, admit a final and inescapable failure to represent the manner of God's presence to the world in Christ, the quality of the transcendent decisively disclosed in him. And in this situation we do well to consider silence as a "system of projection" of the ineffable. But it must be a silence expressed in action: not simply an unwillingly accepted aphasia. One could regard it indeed as a generalized form of the silence to which, in the great scene of Rolf Hochhuth's *Soldiers*, Bishop Bell is reduced by Churchill: a silence that bears witness to the fact that we have reached beyond argument to a place in which all that is left us is to affirm not ourselves but that to which, however haltingly, we are bound to witness.

The vicar's situation in that televised scene is a paradigm as well as a parable of the church's acceptance of the law of *kenosis* vis-à-vis the world in which it is set. It is not to be received as an argument in favor of a cult of powerlessness or failure, recalling the well-known, deeply unhealthy cult of despair as the only *praeambula fidei*, which was fashionable in the forties. It is, rather, a defeat that is not a defeat, because it is eloquent of hope as well as of failure; it is suffused by a sense of promise of that which is not yet, but which is even now coming to be, which is indeed coming to be as the church begins to realize existentially as well as theoretically the law of *kenosis*, the law of the incarnation, by which the manner of its own fidelity is bound.

Because I am an intellectual, I am continually aware of the vulnerability of every form of apologetic, and the absence of any kind of intellectual security in believing today. Yet I know that I find these things frightening partly because I am too much the heir of a deeply false tradition of conventional apologetic, which looked for public confirmation of Christ's victory, won in the darkness and manifested to his own by the strange, unparalleled light of Easter, in the stabilities of a so-called Christian order. There is no deeper misunderstanding of the *mysterium Christi* than that which insists, against all the evidence, in construing the resurrection as a descent from the cross, publicly and unambiguously visible to all standing around, but made the more overwhelmingly effective by a thirty-six-hour postponement. We all of us in different ways, in different situations, have to learn the extent to which we are prisoners of utterly misleading imagery concerning the nature of Christ's victory over the world and the manner of its manifestation.

So the imperative is clear to go forward, not clinging to external protection but embracing insecurity, and to go forward in hope. It is indeed on a note of hope that I would draw towards my conclusion; for I do myself regard the coming of the post-Constantinian age as occasion for the renewal of hope: this, even though I find much that frightens and distresses me because, like everyone else, I have clung and continue to cling to my own securities. (Hence indeed the detailed references to the Anglo-Catholic experience with which this lecture began.) Moreover, this hope, as we have seen, is one that ranges over a wide field, including the territory of interchurch relations, the relation of the church to the world in which it is set, theology and the life of the intellect, the deepest levels of spiritual awareness, etc. It is a hope big with the promise of a more inclusive, if much costlier, charity, and I would insist that, for myself, I see the future as likely to bring more gain than loss, provided we are bold enough and sufficiently freed from bondage to the false imagery of the past, to rise to the extent of its opportunity.

But my last word of all must be rather different. We hear much today of the supposed damage inflicted on Christianity by Plato and the tradition springing from him and claiming in a measure his authority. In my judgment, a great deal of such polemic is both ill-informed and irrelevant. Thus it often fails to do justice to the deepest damage that Plato's authority inflicted on Christian tradition. I refer to the extent to which that tradition took over Plato's flight from the tragic as an ultimate, irreducible form of representation of the relation of the transcendent to the familiar. In the argument of *The Republic*, this criticism is a prolegomenon to its author's attempt in the καλλιπόλις to establish a world without ambiguity, a world from which the kind of darkness that Sophocles, for instance, had profoundly understood was expelled. For Plato, it was demonstrably blasphemous to query the certainty of "a happy ending." Yet his own dream of the καλλιπόλις was itself instinct with that tragic quality whose irreducible presence anywhere in the scheme of things he had so rigorously sought to deny.

The ecclesiological fundamentalist of every school, whether he admits it or not, finds in the actual history of his church something of the security the καλλιπόλις is sought to offer. He may find this security realized in the form of the ecclesiastical structure; or he may find it through imposing on the questionable contingencies of his church's history vis-à-vis civil society, an interpretation that makes bold use of the category of the providential. He finds in the contemplation of that history the sort of drug that he needs to still the interrogative temper, and the obstinate determination to ask awkward questions and to go on asking them; he uses the study of that history as a kind of tranquilizer whereby he can lull himself into supposing the unknown somehow known, the unfathomable somehow plumbed to its depths. The ragged edges are made to disappear; the terrible reality of human waste, to which the churches have added so much by the ways in which they have dealt with men and women, is pushed out of sight. In God's world, all must surely be for the best; how otherwise can it be his world? Yet Christ experienced dereliction, and although in faith we proclaim him raised from the dead, that resurrection did not annul the previous experience, which was its dark condition.

We are on the threshold of an age in which we are going to be able to learn these lessons anew, as we are sometimes gradually, sometimes with shocking rapidity, divested of the burdens laid on our backs by the sorry patterns of past ages. Yet we must not suppose that we shall ourselves escape the reality of the tragic in our novel situation, even if our experience makes it possible (as it has not always been in the past) for us to recognize that such reality belongs to the very stuff of the church's existence and the church's presence to the world.

We cannot forecast the form of the experience which awaits us; we will certainly be disappointed of many of those fears with which we anticipate the advent of the new insecurity as well as of the hopes with which we greet its coming. Loss of security will not be as frightening a thing in actuality as it is to many in prospect; exclusion from a traditionally accepted place in the ancient structure of our society is likely to prove a means of presence rather than withdrawal. Yet we will not find the καλλιπόλις, let alone the ultimate reality of the kingdom of God, in our future experience; we can only hope that, because a false dream has yielded or begun to yield to a temper more deeply perceptive of the mystery of *kenosis*, we will be a little better prepared to recognize our frailty, and that it is in weakness that our strength is made perfect: in genuine weakness, not the simulated powerlessness of the spiritual poseur.

These last remarks are obscure; but prophecy is always hazardous, and we are on the threshold of an unprecedented experience. Our first duty is to free our imaginations of the kind of hesitation that comes from our archaism and our unyielding confinement within the categories and imagery of past ages. But though I believe we are about to learn deeper lessons concerning the laws of Christian existence than have been possible for centuries, these laws are still laws of Christian existence—that is, laws of existence in dependence on the one whose essence lay in his dependence on the Father. If the lessons therefore bite deep they will teach us not to seek deliverance from the tragic in our future, but the presence of the ground that alone makes possible the endurance of its burden. I almost said the significant endurance of its burden; yet to speak in such terms would be to contradict the substance of this lecture, in that it belongs to the heart of the idea of *kenosis* that ultimate significance shall be received, not imposed.

Gore Memorial Lecture delivered in Westminster Abbey on November 5, 1968

Chapter 2: Theology and Tragedy

It is now some years since Professor D. Daiches Raphael published his interesting book *The Paradox of Tragedy*, which represented one of the first serious attempts made by a British philosopher to assess the significance of tragic drama for ethical, and indeed metaphysical theory. Since then we have had a variety of books touching on related topics: for instance, Dr. George Steiner's *Death of Tragedy* and Mr. Raymond Williams's most recent, elusive, and interesting essay, *Modern Tragedy*. To entitle an essay "Theology and Tragedy" might be thought to invite needless trouble for oneself; to indulge to a dangerous degree the human intellectual obsession (so thoroughly castigated by Wittgenstein) of supposing that "the meaning of a word is an object." After all, if one confines one's regard to the Greeks, one has to recognize that between the treatments of their common theme of *Electra*, Sophocles and Euripides are in fact doing very different things. There is no gainsaying the significance for Euripides of the postponement of the murder of Clytemnestra until after that of Aegisthus, still less of his introduction into his play of the morally upright peasant, who has had the banished Electra in his keeping and whose simple integrity contrasts both with the corruption of the obsessive preoccupation with a dreadful, supposed duty of brother and sister. The element of propaganda is unmistakable, while in Sophocles's *Electra* it is altogether absent—although Dr. Victor Ehrenberg in his very interesting monograph on *Sophocles and Pericles* has argued strongly for an element of subtle political commentary in the treatment of Oedipus in *Oedipus Tyrannus*, and of Creon in *Antigone*. These remarks may serve to show that the title does not express a blind indifference to the multiple complexity of those works that we class together as tragedies. They are inherently complex and vary in emphasis; at best we can discern a family resemblance between them, and, in an essay like this, the author runs the risk not only of selecting examples tailor-made to his thesis, but also of imposing an appearance of similarity of conception where it is at least equally important to stress differences.

"The poets knew it all already." So said Sigmund Freud, and the reader at once thinks of the remarkable fact that the theme of Oedipus's guilt is presented by Sophocles as the drama of an interrogation (it has been mentioned by historians of detective fiction as one of the first ventures in that genre on the stage), which becomes progressively the drama of a man's self-scrutiny, culminating in a moment, simultaneously of ἀναγνώρισις and of περιπετεία, in which he learns a truth about himself so terrible that he can no longer bear to look upon his world, and blinds himself that he may no longer see with his eyes the bearers of relationships it seems to violate the frontiers of discourse to attempt to characterize. Again in his study of *Hamlet and Oedipus*, Dr. Ernest Jones, Freud's biographer, suggests that some of the complexities of the prince's behaviour become intelligible if we admit the poet's awareness of the traumatic elements in a son's relation to his mother, and to his father and his mother's lover, and indeed finds the significance of the writing of the play in the poet's biography as a "working out" of just such conflicts in his own life.

Yet when a philosopher recalls Freud's words, he is inclined by reason of his professional commitment to suggest that the poets "knew it all" only in the sense of a vague, intuitive perception which must yield place to effective articulation in terms of general concepts. True enough, neither *Oedipus Tyrannus* nor *Hamlet* can be regarded as works of psychological theory. Yet the philosopher, in the condescension towards the poets that marks his reception of Freud's words, is of course more than he may realize the heir of the ancient quarrel between the poets and the metaphysicians. If all Western philosophy is "a series of footnotes to Plato," as Alfred North Whitehead suggested, those who contribute to those footnotes may (even if they repudiate, for instance, their master's attachment to fundamental falsehood in political theory, viz. the thesis that a final solution of the problems of human order and culture can be achieved by the concentration of unfettered legislative and executive power in the hands of a carefully selected and minutely trained elite) remain, here in spite of Aristotle's sharply perceptive criticisms, blindly attached to other perilous assumptions imposed by his authority.

Plato's quarrel with the tragedians would seem to have three separable roots (I am thinking here of *The Republic*):

1. He found in them a theology he regarded as inadmissible (viz. one that represented the gods as indifferently the authors of good and evil). One thinks here of the concluding passages of Sophocles's

Trachiniae, laying responsibility for the terrible events of that play—by turns fantastic, horrifying, shocking, humanly outrageous, and expressive of a kind of religious devotion (I refer to the manner of Heracles's cremation)—fairly and squarely on the shoulders of heaven. This, it is implied, is the way the world is; thus the hero—who has laid all Hellas in his debt by the range and extent of his labors, after he first degenerates into a drunkard who will make war upon a city to recompense an insult or to gratify a lust—comes to his end; thus his wife, Deianira, a woman caught up in a monstrous world of demigods, patient, in a genuine way capable of more than a measure of compassion in her treatment of Iole (commentators have contrasted it with Clytemnestra's attitude to Cassandra), eager to regain her husband's love, and guilty, in her pursuit of that end, of nothing worse than folly in her use of the shirt of Nessus, encompasses both the death of her husband and her own death, unforgiven to the last by the hero to whom she had remained loyal; so it is that Iole, the object of Heracles's desire, becomes the wife of Hyllus, his son. This is the way things are. We can represent these events; we can even, in the deeply tragic figure of Deianira, suggest the extent to which men and women are trapped less by their weakness than by what is accounted virtue in them. (In Deianira's case, it is her tenderness that betrays her. A more formidable woman would have pursued a grimmer stratagem with a less destructive result.) This theology Plato repudiates, stating quite dogmatically that the gods are the authors only of that which is good; the origin of evil remains opaque, but we cannot attribute it to heaven. There is, of course, later in *The Republic* with the development of the notion of to τὸ μὴ ὂν, the ontological correlate of ἀγνωσία, more than a suggestion of the later, developed, ontological characterization of evil as "not being," in the sense of privation: (a view of which I will only here say that it has only to be stated clearly, and worked out in terms of concrete examples, to be shown to be totally inadequate as an analysis either of moral or of physical evil. Of this doctrine, I would echo words often used by the late Professor H. A. Prichard: "Whatever is true, that can't be!"). But in book 2, when establishing canons of theological censorship and developing, in the context thereof, criteria of the theoretically admissible in theology, Plato contents himself with insisting that even as we know *a priori* that the concept of divine metamorphosis is internally self-contradictory, so we know *a priori* that the theologoumena with which the *Trachiniae* ends are likewise inadmissible. Even as the notion of the construction of the regular heptagon is mathematically impossible (I use an example employed in other connections by Wittgenstein), so the notion of a god who is the author of the evils that overtook Heracles and Deianira is the notion of an *Unding*.

2. Closely connected with the above is the falsehood that Plato discerned, or thought that he discerned, in the suggestion that the virtuous man or woman could be overtaken by catastrophe, which touched the very substance of his or her life, leaving him or her the helpless prey of evil men or of natural adversity, or else disintegrated within and destroyed. Plato's preoccupation in his ethical writings with the consequences in terms of reward of doing good must be seen in this context. If he writes sometimes almost as a utilitarian, for whom personal morality may be recommended on prudential grounds, and at others (for instance in his portrait of the tyrant in book 9 of *The Republic*) as one who would present virtue as its own reward by a revelation of successful evildoing as its own punishment, he does so because he is deeply at war with the suggestion, undoubtedly present in some tragedies, that there is evidence for the ontological irrelevance of moral goodness in the manifest discrepancy between, for example, gentleness (in Deianira), or fidelity to justice and truth (in Sophocles's portrayal of Electra), and the outward rewards and inward recompense achieved through the exercise of these virtues by those who have thus schooled themselves in them.

3. Finally, attention to tragedy encouraged the attitude of the φιλοθέαμων, and substituted for the movement from the many to the one (as fundamental to Plato's map of the *itinerarium mentis ad Bonum* as to his ontology, and as Aristotle saw, one of the most damaging, uncriticized assumptions of his thought) the review of a whole series

of examples of human experience. Agamemnon and Clytemnestra, Orestes, Pylades, Electra, Chrysothemis, Ajax, Medea, Hecuba, Andromache, Priam, Heracles, Prometheus—we pass them in review; we look at their predicament, now from one perspective, now from another. We enlarge our sympathies maybe, but this we do at the cost of forgetting that there is a pearl of great price to be won if we concentrate our energies and our attention upon the one that stands over against the many, from which the many derive, and which in its transcendent dignity will establish our flickering resolve by revealing the way of life of the saint as the surest intimation of the ultimate.

Even those who disregard Plato's theory of forms, except as a splendid example of revisionary metaphysics, criticized and even discarded by its own author when in the *Parmenides* he brought out the sheerly unintelligible uses to which he had bent the notions of *παροῦσια*, *μεθέξις*, and *μιμήσις* in its exposition, and in the *Sophist* and *Theaetetus* turned instead to fundamental questions in the philosophy of logic—even they unconsciously adhere to his relegation of tragedy to a very secondary role in the enlargement of our understanding of the world around us. At best it may provide us with exemplary material; but serious exposition of the nature of what is will be left to more general, and more subtly organized statement. What is sometimes forgotten, however, is the extent to which Plato might in fact have found, in the central theme of *The Republic*, the subject presented unforgettably in the long, complementary requests made of Socrates by Glaucon and Adeimantus—two young men revealing, in the style of their scepticism, the sort of urgent restlessness vis-à-vis the "Idea of the Good" of which he speaks in book 6, the stuff of tragedy. The passage in which the theme of *The Republic* is set is one of the great passages of moral philosophy; hardly anywhere else is the issue of the ontological import of moral excellence more clearly or more unflinchingly presented. Its architecture is admirable, and the manner in which the two young men complement each other is perfectly designed to the purpose of the whole. Thus Adeimantus buttresses the theoretical queries of Glaucon with recollection of what he has gleaned in the way of moral education, not from the self-conscious arguments of a Thrasymachus or a Callicles, but from the scale of priorities he has discerned to operate in the casual appraisals he has heard passed on the lives of those around him. But the central opposition is that of the perfectly just and the perfectly unjust man, with the portrait of the latter filled in by the detail of the myth of Gyges, reminding the reader that supreme effectiveness in human life is only achieved when disregard of the sanctions of traditional morality is made possible by the acquisition, whether by effort, by inheritance, by good fortune, by opportunity, or by a mixture of all alike, of unchallengeable predominance on the plane of power. Which of the two has the root of the human matter in him—the historical Socrates or Pericles? The latter is represented by Thucydides as a supreme political realist, admitting the element of tyranny in the Athenian ἀῤχη, but justifying it by reference to the enormous human superiority of the Athenian system over against the Spartan, ready to use without hesitation the resources put at her disposal by Athens's allies in the Delian confederacy, and continuing to do so for purposes that he believed at once Athenian and, in a measure, universal, even if the peace of Callias had terminated open hostilities with Persia and thus apparently brought to an end the raison d'être of the confederacy. And if we are honest, we must admit that Pericles had a case against the historical Socrates, as Plato saw him, against the man whose image we catch in *Euthyphro, Apology, Crito, Phaedo*, and in whose school Alcibiades was partly formed, whose scrupulosity inhibited action, and the inconclusiveness of whose positive doctrine encouraged a scepticism more ultimately corrosive than any suggested by the most destructive sophistic teaching. Further, we must remember, in spite of Plato, that we can see a sample of the moral insight the Sophists enabled men to gain, in, for instance, the treatment by Euripides of the vengeance of Electra and Orestes to which we have already referred.

Thus what for Plato is the *point de départ* of an essay in revisionary metaphysics is also the stuff of which tragedy is made. To say this is not to subscribe to a Hegelian conception of tragic conflict as the conflict of two opposing systems of right. In his judgment on *Antigone*, Hegel is wrong inasmuch as Antigone, for all the obsessive quality of her preoccupation with Polynices and the Amazonian temper she displays towards Ismene, is a nobler human being, serving a higher cause than Creon, identifying, as he does, the security of the πόλις with his own personal dignity. Had Plato used tragic drama as his "system of projection" for engaging with the problems presented by Glaucon and Adeimantus, he would not of course have been Plato. He might incidentally have avoided some of his most disastrous mistakes in political theory, but we do not see the theory of forms as an essay in revisionary metaphysics aright unless we see that it is offered in part as an alternative way of dealing with one of the issues that, across the centuries, those who have written tragedies have sought to explore.

So Shakespeare in *Julius Caesar* (the only work in the English language on the subject of political obligation that engages with the problems facing the German conspirators against Hitler in July 1944, as R. H. S. Crossman rightly pointed out) reveals Brutus betrayed into make-believe, a kind of sad self-deception concerning the bloody details of the purpose to which he has lent himself, and then by his continuing scruple, into the sort of *fainéantise* that dooms his enterprise to disaster (I am thinking of his insistence that Antony be spared), but still remaining a man of nobler stuff than the other figures in the play. No one can doubt this who sets over against each other Brutus's scrupulosity and the quick, resolute ruthlessness of the Triumvirs (including the very young Octavius) in the short scene of the proscription. The evil that Caesar did lives after him: "O, Julius Caesar, thou art mighty yet." Brutus is the victim of Caesar's ambition as well as of his own folly and unwillingness to face to the full the moral issues of assassination, preferring to see in a murder a ritual act whereby the city is purified, as it were, by a "holy and unbloody sacrifice." Yet this unwillingness is born of his nobility, of the scrupulosity that makes him so ill-adjusted to the more effective Cassius, and which reveals him as a human being of better stuff than the Triumvirs, in whose cold and detached listing of their victims, the evil that Caesar did is revealed as triumphantly alive.

But what have these considerations to do with theology? We are often told (this is Professor Raphael's view, although he admits a partial exception in the Jansenist Racine) that there is no place for tragedy in the Judaeo-Christian worldview. But is this in fact true of the gospels as we have them? If we recall the "open-textured quality" (the *Porosität*) of the concept of tragedy, can we be quite sure that it does not apply in full measure, *mutatis omnibus mutandis*, to the Christian story, especially, for instance, if we allow our imaginations to include, within the compass of that story, such terrible *sequelae* as the intrusion of a theologically founded anti-Semitism into the public prayer and private imaginations of generations of Christians, even conceivably into the text of the New Testament itself, in, for instance, the Gospel according to St Matthew and the Acts of the Apostles, and even the Gospel according to St John? Whatever may be true of Judaism, there is a sense in which Christianity demands to be presented as the tragedy of Jesus, of the one who, for intentions that the believer must judge of supreme significance, abdicated any responsibility that his influence might have conferred on him to arrest the movement of his people towards the final catastrophe of 70 CE. The Christian believes that in Christ's passion he finds at once the judgment and the redemption of the world; it is a desperately human occasion fraught not with a great, but with an ultimate, significance. But it is also failure, not in the language of devotion, but in that of literal fact. It is in the figure of Judas Iscariot that the failure of Jesus is focused, and the tragic quality of his mission becomes plain, "Good were it for this man if he had not been born." Yet through his agency, the Son of Man goes his appointed way, and of his own choice; for in a few hours' time, he will say: "Thy will, not mine, be done." There is no solution here of the problem of the moral evil; there is nothing moreover that the Easter faith somehow obliterates. For it is to his own, and not to the world, that the risen Christ shows himself; and even those who accept the record of the empty tomb as factual admit that in itself that emptiness is no more than a sign pointing.

We need, perhaps, to explore with very great care the sense in which the term "tragic" may significantly be predicated of the gospel records. Such an exploration may throw more light than we expect on the question of the "system of projection" appropriate to the Christian reality; but it is also bound to raise, within the context of Christian theology, questions analogous to those that Plato regarded as so serious that he tried to discredit altogether the claim of tragic drama to represent the notion of what is—and that on theological grounds.

Religious Studies, 1961

Chapter 3: Authority and Freedom in the Church

No one concerned with questions of religious truth today can long escape the problem of freedom and authority. The issue has recently been pinpointed by the decision of the Roman Catholic theologian, Charles Davis, to leave his church, both because he rejects certain doctrines and because he repudiates the method by which his church as an institution constrains its members, both clerical and lay, not only to adhere to formally defined dogmas, but to submit to the deliverances of its ordinary magisterium and even the day-to-day policies and decisions of its executive authority. Charles Davis's action expressed not only an intellectual but also a moral revolt. He was making a costly protest against an institution, which in its workings seemed to set obstacles in the way of Christian living rather than help to promote its growth.

If we begin by distinguishing these two elements in Davis's protest, we soon see that the moral aspect of his protest is also of profound theological significance, for he is raising the theological problem of the church as an institution; of the manner in which, as an institution, it exercises authority over its members. By implication, he is raising the whole theological question of the forms in which the church's allegedly apostolic mission is carried on.

Davis's action is admittedly a response to the extreme situation that he has encountered in the most authoritarian of all the churches, the Church of Rome. Inevitably it seems a comment on a whole number of episodes, some publicly known and many more not, in the recent history of that church. For instance, one thinks of the intellectual damage unquestionably done to the visionary Pierre Teilhard de Chardin by the decision to inhibit publication of his writings during his lifetime, and to prevent him from taking up the kind of academic post in France that would have made it possible for him to submit his ideas to the kind of criticism that they badly needed. The history of his development reveals how he was driven in upon himself, and in consequence was encouraged by isolation to adopt eccentric and unbalanced attitudes. (To say this, of course, is not to deny his genius; it is only to remind ourselves of his tragedy.)

But Davis's action is something of wider significance; it has lessons to teach men who have not been exposed to the sorts of pressure that clearly he has known, but who are nonetheless dimly aware that they must face the theological and ethical problems raised by churches as institutions.

My own experience is Anglican; and it is almost commonplace to remark that in practice the Anglican Communion, and especially the Church of England, is the least authoritarian of the churches. Yet the ecclesiastical temper encourages its leaders, encourages also those who undertake the spiritual direction of its members, to allow the end to justify the means. "It is expedient that one man should die for the people": in these words of Caiaphas, we catch an indelible impression of the attitude of mind of the responsible ecclesiastic. They express the major premise of a great many practical syllogisms whose conclusion is always the same; that the individual shall be broken, or that his or her claims shall be disregarded.

I am mainly concerned with the problem of intellectual freedom, with the question of the attitude of authority towards searching inquiry touching the very foundations of faith, with the posture that the inquirer himself may properly adopt in the face of that authority;

but I want to set the question in the context of a theological, even a Christological, exploration of the nature of humility, the humility in particular demanded of those who exercise authority in the church of Christ. To approach the matter in this way, however, reveals that the principles with which we are concerned have a wider relevance and require application in many other connections, if the ministry of the church is to reflect the image of the servant-God.

"To follow the argument withersoever it leads." This Socratic injunction is supposedly a categorical imperative for anyone who would philosophize, however much he may fail in practice to fulfill its precepts. But can anyone who is in some sense committed to Christian faith allow himself, or be allowed by authority, a comparable freedom? The question that I have heard most searchingly put—did not the church spoil so-and-so as a philosopher?—is one that can have a number of senses. For instance, it may refer to a deflection of intellectual energies imposed by external authority, but it may also advertise a subtler, interior willingness to turn aside from the queries that reach to the very foundations. This is a turning aside that ecclesiastical authority encourages by the use not only of psychological deterrents but also of more insidious incentives.

One may, however, use the language of this question—did not the church spoil so-and-so as a philosopher?—to ask whether it is logically possible for a man to acknowledge a divine self-disclosure and an ultimately significant divine action in a particular set of historical events, and remain open at all levels to expanding intellectual horizons and to the necessity of enlarging, deepening, and revising his moral perceptions. Even if one allows that an affirmative answer to this question about openness is logically possible, one has still to concede the extent to which the pressures of ecclesiastical authority and institutional convention combine to sap the interrogative, unaccommodating temper of the inquirer and substitute for his restless eagerness the more submissive and conformist temper of the apologist.

Such submission is frequently counselled in the name of humility, of humility at once towards God and towards one's fellows. It is certainly, as we shall see, near to the heart of the Christian revelation that humility is a fundamental attribute of the divine as disclosed in Christ, and therefore, inasmuch as Christ is consubstantial with the Father who sent him and no mere simulacrum of the one whom he characterizes as greater than himself, an attribute of the divine as it is in itself. But humility is more often than not presented as a kind of submissive obedience to the church's traditions, to its institutional and organizational development, irrespective of the historical and social factors that may have shaped it, and the built-in consequences of the past decisions of its leaders.

Much less is said of the extent to which those who exercise such authority must display humility in their turn; much less too of the extent to which the styles of triumphalism in, say, the Roman Catholic Church, or (again I speak as an Anglican) the elaborate ceremonial masquerade of establishment distort not only the manner but the substance of an apostolic presence to the world.

In the last analysis, it is with the manner of such presence that we are concerned, with the manner, too, of the church's witness to the truth. This emerged very clearly in the affair of the French worker-priests in the early 1950s. It was not simply the deep political involvement of many individuals that prompted brutal intervention by Rome, it was the worker-priests' obvious preference for a method of getting alongside people where they are to one suggesting the declaration of a truth delivered from on high, which offended authority.

The apostle is able to teach only so far as he is also learning, learning all the time. This is the way of presence. The ecclesiastic fears it because it robs him of the security that he finds for his own status and mission, as long as he can continue to address both his inferiors and his prospective converts as it were *de haut en bas*, as a Christ descended from the pinnacle of the temple, silencing questions by a manifestation of power, but by that action, withdrawing himself from the common way of men and women, from both the constant and the transient conditions of their lives.

You may well ask at this point whether this kind of approach does not argue for a complete abrogation of authority in matters of religious belief, or at least suggest that those in whom such authority is vested be required to abdicate their proper responsibilities. It may indeed be said that the temper of the approach is more that of John Stuart Mill's essay *On Liberty* than, let us say, that of Paul's Second Letter to the Corinthians. We must concede a responsibility to ecclesiastical authority for safeguarding what is sometimes called, in a rather misleading phrase, the "deposit of faith"; but such authority must also acknowledge the cutting edge of the question: *quis custodiet ipsos custodes?*—who will guard the guardians? What is at issue is not the need of mitigating the impact of irresponsible and random speculation and experiment, but the manner in which such direction is imposed, and also the limitations of its scope.

This, I argue, is a theological question. Of course, "we have this treasure in earthen vessels": and these earthen vessels include historical institutions. But those who help to maintain and operate them must always remember just how much these institutions are the products less of divine providence than of the grisly complexities and accidents of human history. To serve them, no doubt, is a psychologically satisfying role for those called to exercise office and administration in them; it may indeed become so satisfying a role that it inhibits all power to criticize, all power to recognize the need for radical renewal, even for that kind of transformation that can only be described in terms of death and resurrection.

There is a passage towards the end of Whitehead's *Process and Reality*, which is very illuminating here:

> When the Western world accepted Christianity, Caesar conquered; and the received text of Christian theology was edited by his lawyers. The code of Justinian and the theology of Justinian are two volumes expressing one movement of the human spirit. The brief Galilean vision of humility flickered through the ages, uncertainly. In the official formulation of the religion it has assumed the trivial form of the mere attribution to the Jews

> that they cherished a misconception about their Messiah. But the deeper idolatry, of the fashioning of God in the image of the Egyptian, Persian and Roman imperial rulers, was retained. The Church gave unto God the attributes which belonged exclusively to Caesar.[9]

One can hardly overpraise the insight of this passage, especially the unerring diagnostic precision with which it shows how Christendom has succeeded across the ages in ignoring the overwhelming Christological implications of such a saying as "I am amongst you as he that serves" by externalizing its catastrophic theological import in terms of an alleged Jewish refusal to see how (or that) Jesus fulfilled the messianic role.

Whitehead is inaccurate in his choice of the word "Galilean" to convey the heart of the matter on which he has laid his finger; what he so characterizes by a geographical expression is as much of Jerusalem, synagogue, temple courts, upper room, praetorium, and place of execution as it is of lakeside, hillside, Capernaum, Tiberias; but he is utterly right to fasten on the extent to which the fusion of the faith of the incarnation with a cultural whole, including Hebraic, Greek, and Roman elements, has issued in a disastrous subordination of the mysteries of the self-revealing, the self-giving, the serving God, to a highly wrought complex of ideas, ultimately hardly compatible with what has been disclosed.

Rightly, Whitehead fastens first on the Roman ingredient, the extrapolation of the concept of executive imperial *gubernaculum*, to convey the idea of a supremely authoritative providence, delegating his powers to those whom he has bidden in his stead to guide and rule his people. This spirit is not only manifested in the Church of Rome, we see it wherever institutional Christianity, when called to answer the question of the nature of its authority, does so in terms of direction in accordance with laws more or less clearly formulated, or (here I am thinking of the Church of England, as by law established) by reference to a position constitutionally assured.

There is no doubt in my mind that the Anglican appeal to the alleged

9. Alfred North Whitehead, *Process and Reality* (New York: Free Press, 1979), 520.

position of the Church of England in the life of this country as an unalterable constant does often play a disastrous role in stifling the spread of intellectually and ecclesiologically radical ideas. The appeal rests, of course, on a falsification of the facts of history; one has only to remember the seventeenth century to see this. But, worse, it encourages the kind of intellectually frivolous pragmatism that today we simply cannot afford, and it also ministers to a most offensive kind of spiritual pride.

If we are to pursue more than a make-believe theological radicalism, we must find in what Whitehead calls the "brief Galilean vision of humility" the sources of a deep renewal of Christological, indeed of essential Trinitarian understanding. But this renewal will come only if we set our theological imaginations in a hard light and acknowledge the corrupting effects of history upon them, being ready to criticize sharply and to resist any tendency to represent the ways of God with men in terms of a particular cultural and political stabilization of human forces. Whether our ecclesiastical leaders recognize it or not, we confront the unlimited opportunities, as well as perils, of a post-Constantinian age.

There is something almost pathetic (if it were not also so coldly cruel in its manifestations) about the ways in which ecclesiastical authority seeks to retain the styles of a past age. In the Church of Rome, we have had since the Modernist movement repeated instances of authority seeking to coerce or break the individual, without any sense of that authority being itself a kind of partner to a dialogue that must, I will not say go on, but rather be set in motion to further the cause of apostolic presence in the world. I will mention two recent examples within the Church of England. In 1966, we saw prelatical authority intervene to apparently destructive effect in the affairs of the Sheffield Industrial Mission, while blandly refusing any explanation for an action that many still regard as scandalous. Justice may have been done, but it certainly does not seem to have been done. And many would say the same over the appointment to the deanery of Guildford in 1961.

It would be unfair, in this general context, not to notice the way in which some who are called radical in parts of their theology—in their approach to the New Testament, for instance—combine a nearly complete skepticism concerning the historical life of Jesus of Nazareth with what I can only call an ecclesiological fundamentalism. By an "ecclesiological fundamentalism," I mean a readiness to accept the historical experience of the church as self-justifying. Such men are happy to find that any external norm by which its development may be judged is unattainable.

It is easy to see how such a theology (which it is ironic to recall was that of the more extreme Catholic Modernists) issues in an admiring apologetic for actual ecclesiastical institutions. At bottom, of course, it is anti-intellectual. It is also profoundly conservative, in the end identifying what is with what ought to be, and therefore of course it has its peculiar appeal for Anglicans. All the roughness, untidiness, the perplexed, even tormented self-interrogation that belong to Christian belief in this century are subtly blurred, softened, and made to vanish away. We are a long way from the deep spiritual perception of those Spanish Catholics, mentioned by the late Albert Camus in his study of revolt in human life, whose faith in the sacraments remained undimmed while they refused to receive them in prison in protest against their church's endorsement of the methods and styles of the regime that supposedly had saved and preserved its external life. Their action is almost self-contradictory, but it is profoundly, even passionately, Christian in inspiration.

It may seem that in what I have been saying, I have moved a long way from the simpler, less harrowing issues of intellectual freedom. But the enormities of which the intellectual is made aware belong to the same family. He is asked to prostitute his gifts in the cause, not of inquiry, but of the service and defence of an institution, some of whose historically acquired habits must surely repel him. He must not, of course, ask for power without responsibility, but he is right to see in his situation a parable of the need of all the churches to renew in this day and age their understanding of the manner of their apostolic presence to the world. And that renewal demands a contemporary recovery of the sense and inwardness of Christ's own apostolate. If we are told that the state of the evidence makes such recovery impossible, and that we are left with the institution or nothing, then some of us, if we are honest, will say that we must content ourselves with that nothing and admit that faith, always precarious, is no longer a way that we can follow.

To say these things openly is not to court the easy rewards of a masquerade boldness, but rather to suggest that authority in the present is only effectively exercised in a setting of acknowledged doubt—a doubt to which it may be we are commanded by the imperative of faith itself.

BBC Third Program, March 1967

Chapter 4: Intercommunion: A Comment

The "Open Letter" to which reference is made in the following article, was presented to the archbishops of Canterbury and York in the autumn of 1961, and released to the press on November 2 of that year. It was signed by a number of Anglicans, mainly, though not exclusively, concerned with the teaching and cognate subjects, and urged the necessity of an immediate readiness on the part of the Anglican Communion to acknowledge the authenticity of the sacramental ministry of those churches that had rejected the historic episcopate, and whose ministers had, in consequence, not received episcopal ordination. This attitude should express itself in a readiness on the part of Anglicans (in appropriate circumstances) to avail themselves of such sacramental ministrations and to admit, without let or hindrance, to Communion at Anglican altars all persons who (although not episcopally confirmed) were recognized as full members of their own churches, and who desired to receive the holy sacrament at an Anglican celebration of the Eucharist.

In short, the letter advocated mutual acceptance here and now of their sacramental ministries of churches formally each separated one from another. It pressed the importance of such a step on Anglicans in particular, as, in their recent history, they had become popularly identified with a rigorously exclusive attitude, over the admission to Communion of those not confirmed by a bishop, and over the receiving of the sacrament of the Lord's body and blood from the hands of a minister who had not received episcopal ordination. It was thought that for

Anglicans to make such gestures at once of welcome and of acceptance in the situation of 1961 might help to release resources of mutual understanding, and indeed of charity, desperately needed if the hopes of healing the rents in Christ's body were not to perish from long disappointment.

As one who had been more actively identified with the Anglo-Catholic tradition than any of the other signatories of the "Open Letter," I hesitated a great deal longer than they did before signing. Yet in the end, I became convinced that their cause was that not only of charity but of truth, and I added my signature almost at the last moment. Some weeks later, I wrote the following article to clear my own mind, and to defend my action to those who had been surprised and even shocked by it. This article was published in *Theology* for February 1962, and as its argument coheres with that of the other pieces in this volume, it is included with them.

December 1968

The recent publication of an "Open Letter" to the archbishops of Canterbury and York on the subject of intercommunion was a controversial act. Although the signatories could plead that their intention was to urge a reconsideration of present policies and attitudes rather than to provoke controversy, their action was inevitably controversial in consequence. The criticisms immediately called forth have been of two kinds. To some, the letter has seemed an intolerable intrusion on the part of so-called theologians into matters that must inevitably seem quite different and much more difficult when viewed from the standpoint of the parish priest; moreover, the manner of the letter's publication was thought by many of these critics to display a wanton disregard of the convocations. To others, however, the letter has seemed the work of irresponsible and impatient men, swayed by their hearts rather than by their heads, deceiving themselves into believing that they could pursue charity at the expense of truth.

Thus the letter has been criticized both as the expression of academic, theological arrogance, and as the work of impatient men, carried away by the force of overwhelming emotion. If therefore its publication is to be justified, it must be shown as the action of men who were both intellectually aware of what they were doing, and also conscious of the limitations both of their insight and of their viewpoint. In this short article, the present writer is speaking only for himself, but he is tolerably sure that for those who designed the letter, and for those who for various reasons found themselves compelled to sign it, its preparation and publication represented only a stage in a continuing action. That action, moreover, is one that must be continued, though not in the preparation of manifestos with the issues raised. For the issues are ones that come up most acutely at the level of ordinary human life in the world. Thus critics of the letter, who urge theologians and academics to recall how artificial and privileged their situation is, are saying something very important. It is hard not to be irritated by those who continually refer to the traumatic experience someone has undergone at a "youth conference" somewhere or other. Few people spend more than a very limited period of their lives at youth conferences, and the experience gained at such gatherings is artificial and restricted, although no doubt valuable. Where these islands are concerned (and the Scottish situation is very different from the English), these issues have got to be *schematized* (if a philosopher of religion may borrow Kant's language) in terms of the sorts of situation that arise in quite ordinary towns and villages.

But what are the issues, and what of the manner in which they are to be faced? Look at the term—*intercommunion*. We are all of us familiar with the kind of controversial positions that men assume as soon as they hear the word. We have all of us assumed them in our time. A. says, "Before all else we must remember that the Lord's Table is the Lord's, not ours"; B. replies, "Intercommunion is the goal of our effort to be brought to unity in the truth; it cannot be the means." And then, as an apologetic rider, B. reminds his antagonist that in England the Free Churches, which have long practiced intercommunion, are not apparently all that nearer to organic unity. Is it not worth inquiring whether this kind of argument, valuable no doubt in its time, is not now become sterile through much repetition, even as discussion of related questions of ministry has become sterile through exclusive concentration on such notions as validity? Thus, should we not quite properly ask much more closely about those persons whose joining together in Holy Communion is under discussion, and what it is that they are being invited to do?

No one whose experience is confined to Western Europe and largely to these islands can fail, if he is honest, to be impressed by the demand that he consider objectively the situation of the Christian minorities in Asia, in India, in the emergent African nations, and that he make the effort to see with their eyes, and to feel with their hearts, the burdens we lay upon them by bidding them accept the consequences of our dark and terrible religious history as a necessary constituent of the "good news" of Christ. We all pay lip-service to the importance of a sense of historical relativity; we need to practice that awareness in our lives, and not dignify a tragicomic spiritual imperialism with the name of fidelity to the traditions that we have received. Yet the same principles that bid us concede a genuine autonomy to the so-called "younger churches" and accept their fruits must guide us in our more intimate relations here at home.

"We have all sinned and come short of the glory of God." In concrete terms, in the sphere of interchurch relations, that means that we are all of us the spiritual heirs of men and women who were ready to persecute or to acquiesce in persecution. It is impossible here to underestimate the importance of the issues raised by Professor C. H. Dodd in his "open letter" on "non-theological factors" promoting disunity, which was written as part of the preparatory material for the Lund Conference on Faith and Order in 1952. By reminding the English, Scottish, and Irish delegates of the wrongs to which their ancestors had been severally parties in the seventeenth century, he brought discussion down to earth. "The blood of the martyrs is the seed of the Church." Yet if the martyrs of the sixteenth and seventeenth centuries were "united in the strife that divided them," from the manner in which their witness was exacted from them there sprang, not simply that which belongs in some sense to the church of Christ, but traditions of life and culture estranged in all sorts of ways one from another. Professor Dodd spoke of the factors to which he called attention as "non-theological"; and there, in my submission, he was wrong in paying lip service to a tradition that artificially restricts the reference of the term "theological." What he advertised touches the substance of Christian life as it is received and lived, and the deep analysis of its origin, fruit, and consequence belongs, if anything, to theology.

But what has this to do with "intercommunion"? A great deal, inasmuch as we are now turning our attention towards the communicants who are actual men and women, sustained and illuminated, irritated and sometimes infuriated by particular traditions of Christian life and thought. Where the sacrament of the Lord's Supper is concerned, we must not neglect the actualities of concrete traditions and received (and deeply cherished) insights. Here again we seek a way through the sterility of debate between those who pretend a (nonexistent) general agreement in Eucharistic doctrine, and those who insist that there can be no intercommunion between those who understand the rite as differently as an Anglo-Catholic and a Zwinglian. "It is better to give than to receive." How wise the man who, commenting on this text, remarked that he was relieved, because to give was usually much easier than to receive. "Giving and receiving"—I want to suggest most seriously that we (and here I address Anglicans) approach the difficult question of intercommunion by way of a consideration of what is involved in concrete terms in giving and receiving. We must not pretend to a unity of understanding that we have not attained. If we do that, we deceive ourselves, and although we may profess and call ourselves liberals, we know that we are guilty of a kind of make-believe, and therefore we are at war with ourselves. Let us admit that a tendency to hold on to what we have inherited or made our own is a powerful factor in our behaviour; let us admit that such fidelity is a protection against the kind of indifferentism that may often seek to masquerade as open-mindedness or even courage; let us admit, moreover, that such receptivity on our part can be a parable of a true response to God's grace (although it can also be something very different). But having said this, let us go on to ask to learn to receive from other traditions, at as deep a level as we can, that is at the level of Sacramental Communion.

In fact, of course, we Anglicans in England have already received, in other ways, very much from those from whom we are separated, whose ancestors, in fact, we persecuted; and this not only in the relatively restricted spheres of religion and theology in the conventional sense, but in much that pertains most intimately to the health of our national life, for which as members of an established church, we are supposed to have a special responsibility. Few of us in our serious moments would dare claim that the Christian tradition of England could dispense as easily with the strength of "nonconformist conscience" as it could for instance with the highly questionable, class-distorted religion of the largely Anglican so-called "public schools."

To write in these terms is not to be guilty of theological irresponsibility. Rather, it may be justifiably suggested that the writer is laying upon ordinary men and women the burden of a very hard task. But the healing of our unhappy divisions must surely be just such a work. It is indeed this to which those who counsel patience are bearing witness. Only, like others in other matters, they are inclined to take the sheer difficulty, the costliness of the enterprise, as an argument that we should do nothing at all but wait. It is significant that in the almost obsessive preoccupation with episcopacy that characterizes so much ecumenical discussion today, little or no time seems to be left for a grave meditation of the inwardness of Christ's words concerning the mission of the Holy Ghost—"I have many things to say unto you; but ye cannot bear them now. Howbeit when he, the Spirit of Truth is come," etc. Of course, this is but one manifestation of a pervasive distortion of theological activity, and dissipation of theological energy, to which we must return in the concluding section of this article; but it is a manifestation of peculiarly poignant import for the article's first preoccupation.

For it is indeed to the working within us of the Holy Spirit that we all of us must turn, if we are to make the effort to overcome our divisions. It must be said without qualification that if a blindness towards what

Professor Dodd indicated by the term "non-theological factors" characterizes the traditionally devout, it is also displayed continually in the behaviour of the good "conference men and women" of the ecumenical movement. The present writer has been spared the kind of traumatic experience that many claim to have had at youth conferences, but he recalls having had on two occasions to protest vehemently when invited to take part in highly select consultations on Anglican-(Scottish) Presbyterian relations to be held in the depths of Sussex. Simple economic facts would ensure that such meetings could only be utterly unrepresentative and their discussions correspondingly trivial. It would be hard to estimate too highly the damage done to serious efforts to grow into unity by this sort of unself-critical ecumenical sectarianism. The critics of the "Open Letter" are abundantly justified in their insistence that, where England is concerned, the issues must be seen in terms of their presence in the concrete life of the parishes. Where they are wrong is in their refusal to accept the abundant life of Christian traditions other than their own as inescapable spiritual facts. In the artificial, enclosed life of Anglo-Catholic Oxford, the present writer, although frequently at that time in demand as a speaker at ecumenical gatherings, could remain insulated from the inward effect of Christian division. In Scotland, this was impossible. There, as one whose attachment to the minority Anglicanism of that land was and is incomparably deeper than ever it could be or can be to the institutional reality of the Church of England, the pressure could only be felt much more severely—not because of the majesty of the Church of Scotland, a national church today in a sense in which the Church of England is not, but rather because of that church's readiness, on the whole, to accept and to try to learn. To write in these terms must not be accounted disloyal. The heart and center of this article, where interchurch relations are concerned, lies in its serious attempt to raise the problem of giving and receiving, and to raise the further question of the way in which that problem must be faced in terms of actual, local worshipping Christian Churches.

Where the theology of the Eucharist is concerned, what is here advocated as an approach to intercommunion clearly implies an attitude at first sight paradoxical. No effort must be made to slur over the realities of disagreement or the depths and seriousness of estrangement in respect of Eucharistic understanding. We must all of us, with a new profundity and a new simplicity, learn at once to revere what we have received, and by going to the traditions of others to learn of them, to set what we cherish under the judgment of Christ. I almost said: "of justification by faith," but I suspect that to use such phrase (however surely understood) might for some at least conceal rather than reveal the searching that I have in mind. If what is implied is paradoxical, I submit that it is paradoxical not as outraging understanding, but as suggesting at once the nearness and the difficulty of the insight that can surely overtake us if we open our minds to receive it.

In conclusion, however, a rather different issue must be raised. If this article has any single underlying thread, it is a plea for concreteness against abstraction in approach to Christian unity. It would indeed seek to bring the bigoted denominationalist and the "conference ecumenical" under the same judgment. But this plea for concreteness demands that we go further. I have already referred to the almost fantastic distortion of contemporary theological activity, which the present sterile debate on episcopacy has occasioned. (It would be a moot point whether there is not discernible here a greater *trahison des clercs* than we can see even in the equally obsessive preoccupation of official Anglicanism with canon law revision.) Anyone reading reports of the discussions of episcopacy, ministerial validity, and the rest, which go on unremittingly, might suppose that in these matters lie the central concerns of the faith in this day and generation. What evidence is there, in an age of radical unbelief and of profound searching of the foundations, of comparable energies being directed towards fundamental questions of faith and conduct? Or have we honestly so far retired from the concrete that we suppose, for instance, the existence and nature of God, the person of Christ, the possibility of faith, matters secondary in importance to the precise minutiae of the constitution of the Church of South India? Or are we in our heart of hearts so frightened of the tremendous intellectual and moral efforts involved in seeing, or trying to see, what becomes of Christian belief as a way of life in 1962 that we turn, almost in relief, to the parlor games we can play with our denominational abstractions? Such a question may seem unfair, but at least some of the terms in which it is cast have surely the unfairness of caricature, which advertises, by throwing into relief, some features of its subject. To those who are professionally aware of the truly searching questions that are being asked of Christians, of the utter precariousness of the structure of belief by which in some sense they live, there is something frightening here, compelling even those aware of the limitations of their own theological perceptions and knowledge, to prophesy.

We need urgently, all of us, whether Anglicans or non-Anglicans, new beginnings—I say deliberately beginnings. It is as an element in such new beginnings that, in my view, the "Open Letter" must be judged (it was indeed because I regarded it as such an element that I signed it). Its justification lies, in fact, in the future, and it is for those who signed to ensure that by the way they go from there they further and do not hinder that validation.

Theology, February 1962

Chapter 5: Is Ecumenism a Power Game?

Professor Ian Henderson's book[10] demands to be read, and to be read particularly by Anglicans—whether they be of the establishment south of the border, or of the fifty-six thousand Scottish Episcopalians north of it. They will not enjoy it, they will be tempted to score off it, or to reject it disdainfully as the attempt of the Glasgow Divinity Faculty to make an honest woman out of the *Scottish Daily Express*. But if they resist such temptations, its appearance could well mark a milestone in the history of interchurch relations in these islands. I am myself

10. Ian Henderson, *Power Without Glory* (London: Hutchinson, 1967).

a Scottish Episcopalian, and this may explain where I stand. Yet I understand something of what moved Professor Henderson to write as he did, and I want to ensure that his book is taken seriously. Twenty years ago, when the news that I was going to the Regius Chair of Moral Philosophy in Aberdeen became known in Oxford, an Anglo-Catholic priest—incidentally a theologian and an exponent of Christian existentialism, not one of the parish clergy—remarked to my wife: "I hear that Donald is going to keep the light of the faith burning in darkest Scotland." This remark, admittedly, is too extreme in its arrogance to need any comment. But I should add that my wife is, and was, a Scottish Presbyterian. There is much to be said on behalf of the Anglican Communion, but there is nothing at all to be said for the attitude illustrated, except to ask whether it is spiritual pride born of ignorance or ignorance itself born of spiritual pride. Henderson only glances at the kind of bigotry I have illustrated. The targets of his argument are to be found among the ecclesiastical statesmen and manipulators, one might say among the Annases and Caiaphases rather than among the Pharisees. One of the things that really moves him to fury is the extent to which the manipulators of ecclesiastical influence and power have been able to present Christian division in these islands as something that can be healed by a cunningly devised scheme of integration, which turns aside from the frightening depths at which issues of culture as well as of belief have to be acknowledged as pulling men and women apart.

Certainly Henderson underestimates the spontaneous passion for unity that lies behind such gestures as the Nottingham Declaration. But this is partly because, in his book, he is in fact breaking the strange silence that has prevented the whole issue of Anglican arrogance from being faced openly at all levels—theological, ethical, social, cultural. The example I quoted is only one among very many I could give from a lifetime spent between the two countries of England and Scotland. Such things are part of the built-in inheritance of divisions that are much more than merely theological, and they must be brought right into the open if union is to be more than something that, fairly or unfairly, a great many will deeply resent as a cunningly contrived surrender of weaker to stronger, and which in consequence must serve to prevent rather than further that complete mutual acceptance in faith and charity of which it should be the expression.

The time has come when men must stand up and be counted. As one illustration of the sort of arrogance that he seeks to unmask, Henderson mentions in his eighteenth chapter the Tirrell case. This is a matter of fairly recent history in which a young American Episcopalian priest named Tirrell, who was pursuing advanced studies at Edinburgh University and would have exercised a full sacramental ministry as an ordained assistant in St. Giles Cathedral, Edinburgh, was frustrated by the action of the bishop of the Scottish Episcopal diocese of Edinburgh. Clearly, opinion on the wisdom of the minister's invitation to this young man to assume the position of assistant in the High Kirk of Edinburgh was divided among his Presbyterian brethren. But no one can doubt that the strong opposition to the proposal on the part of Bishop Carey, the bishop of Edinburgh, played a decisive part in wrecking it. Had he taken a different line, the whole matter would have had a different outcome. Of course, the circumstances were complex and confused; in human life they very often are. Yet I believe that Bishop Carey should have taken the risk of giving the young American Tirrell the green light. Whatever the situation, such an action on his part could only have had in the end a deeply healing effect. Certainly Henderson would agree that if Tirrell—still, I presume, researching at Edinburgh[11]—were now regularly celebrating the Lord's Supper in St. Giles, he would have had to write a very different book. I say that, had Bishop Carey acted otherwise, his action would have had a deeply healing effect; I say this because there is an enormous amount that simply calls for healing—a long history of superciliously arrogant insults, of contemptuous disregard of the claims of devoted men to exercise a true ministry of the gospel, which Anglicans have to try to blot out, and which they can only begin to blot out by concrete action such as the *encouragement*, not merely the *permission*, to Tirrell

11. He has now left that city. (Author's note, February, 1969.)

to celebrate in St. Giles. Henderson repeatedly points out the pathetic arrogance that would query the validity of the orders of a Bonhoeffer or a Berggrav. By his choice of names, he almost makes his readers forget the hurt, borne, I repeat, in strange silence, so often done to lesser men not called upon, as these two were, to face extreme situations, but still never lacking in an ultimate fidelity to the calling by which they believed themselves called.

Henderson, as I say, does not fasten so much on the outrages committed by Anglican bigots, as he does on the pertinacious subtlety of their neighbours—so often, in his view, the superiors in ecclesiastical diplomacy of the men of the Kirk. His book betrays a deep preoccupation with the actualities of power in the ecumenical situation. In his introductory note, he admits a debt not only to Gadamer and Jaspers, but also to E. H. Carr, Reinhold Niebuhr, and Sir Halford Mackinder. It is these last, he claims, who have helped him to his awareness of the "power game" that he thinks is being played. And here his analysis, which of course is open to challenge on many points of detail, does suffer from his failure to sympathize sufficiently with the real passion for unity, for the healing of our unhappy divisions, which in the end has undoubtedly inspired the ecumenical movement on the continent of Europe as well as in this country. It was this passion that expressed itself in the Nottingham Declaration ("unity by 1980")—an episode that, I suspect, embarrassed not a few ecclesiastical statesmen. Certainly, Henderson is aware how closely the growth of a decent religious toleration has depended on the acceptance of denominational loyalties as expressive of genuinely conscientious religious disagreements. He has much that is salutary to say on the readiness of ecumenical zealots to identify the goal of their negotiations with the "will of God," *tout court*. But the impact of his argument would have been sharper had he shown the extent to which the attitudes and policy he detests have drawn their strength from the spontaneous eagerness of ordinary men and women, and not least the young, to have done with "far off, unhappy things," and find for themselves a newer and more perfect way. Their optimism may be naïve—even slightly pathetic—in its disregard of historical and cultural actualities. But one should hesitate before quenching such a spirit. A Europe that came to know Adolf Hitler had its moments of nostalgia for the hour of Woodrow Wilson.

To say this is not to deny, but rather to emphasize, the importance of Henderson's urgent demand that the ecumenical spends more time in self-knowledge, in getting as far as possible a full purchase hold on what he, the ecumenical, is up to, on his unacknowledged motives and intentions.

"All power tends to corrupt." And this goes not only for the more familiar forms of ecclesiastical power, but for the power exercised by the negotiator, by the member of the small elite at the handpicked conference, suddenly intoxicated by the belief that he is helping under a special guidance of the Holy Spirit to shape the future form of the church. Moreover, as Henderson repeatedly points out, these things are not done in a cultural vacuum. In the end, it is with the faith and Christian practice of simple men and women that these negotiators are playing. In the end, we have to reckon here—and I repeat that I speak as an Anglican—with a deeply searching book with hard lessons to teach us, for all its alternating moods of irony, suppressed passion and sheer rambunctiousness.

The detail of its analysis is, I have said, often open to challenge. Henderson is a man of strong individual convictions, and few, if any, are likely to agree with his every judgment. He is a Scottish Presbyterian, professedly more in sympathy with the "moderates"—with whom, in the eighteenth century, David Hume established something more than a mere *modus vivendi*—than with the "high-flyers," qualifying his admiration for the great Dr. Thomas Chalmers with some perceptive criticism. It is enormously to his credit that in these and other controversial matters—for instance, the attitude of the Scottish missionaries in Malawi—he trails his coat openly. His book may distress, irritate, and infuriate, but it has a harsh honesty, and it is theologically a deeply serious work. I say "theologically" advisedly, for throughout it is written as a plea not only for charity but for theology, for the kind of theology that demands of the theologian a very hard thing—namely, the continued struggle for a deeper self-knowledge, for the kind of theological debate (even with himself) that the ecclesiastical statesman seems too often to mute.

Henderson brings against the Anglican Communion the grave charge of attempting a new-style ecclesiastical imperialism, a takeover bid disguised as a zealous pursuit of Christian unity, but related, of course, to the eclipse of Great Britain—of that Britain often simply described as England—as a great power, and also to the manifestly declining strength of the Church of England. These charges, as he makes them, need to be qualified. But they are not groundless (and, I repeat, in this respect, I suspect that for a great many Anglicans, north as well as south of the border, the Tirrell affair of which I spoke earlier was a moment of truth, a moment when they had to ask themselves where their church really stood, how far its public face corresponded with its private secret heart). What needs, I think, to be stressed is the extent to which the Anglican approach to these issues today, on the official level, not only expresses a bland forgetfulness of the insults of the past but also shows itself almost incurably intellectually pragmatic, hopelessly in bondage to the illusion that it is by the method of some sort of institutional arrangement that the moral and spiritual hurt of the people will find, if not healing, at least a kind of temporary and possibly permanent anesthesia. But, as the Professor of Systematic Theology in the University of Glasgow well knows, the age of pragmatism is past. We live in the midst of an overwhelming crisis of belief, and if he is partly justified in emphasizing the insularity and nationalism of Anglican theologians, illustrated sadly by the bishop of Woolwich's judgment on the work of that magnificently contemporary theological figure, Helmut Gollwitzer, he is also right if he stigmatizes as frivolous the belief that a contrived coming together will somehow solve the testing problems of the possibility of faith.

Henderson says, interestingly enough, very little about the undoubted renewal today of party conflict in the Church of England. Yet one has only to turn to the texts of discussions in Convocation and

Church Assembly on prayer book revision to be made aware that the Church of England, and indeed the Anglican Communion, is a deeply divided church. The term "comprehensiveness" may be used sometimes not to advertise a source of strength but to disguise and conceal deep undercurrents of profound, even passionate, disagreement. Initially, within the Church of England, this comprehensiveness was secured by the Elizabethan Settlement, which sought through the intervention of the executive to secure a real conformity at the level of religious practice, coupled with a measure of genuine freedom at the level of intellectual opinion. Always at some point, the Anglican Communion reveals itself even today as still in bondage to the belief that some such imposed settlement can contain and subdue, through enforced adoption of agreed forms of worship (including here the so-called inauguration services of uniting churches), the stresses and strains or deeply opposed theological convictions. In the days of Anglo-Saxon industrial and political predominance, with the prestige accruing therefrom to characteristically English institutions, there was some possibility of a part of that prestige endowing with its authority the English "folk-church" (using the word in Troeltsch's sense). But today we live in a situation in which it is mere dishonesty to pretend that the crisis of characteristically English institutions does not infect, and is not in turn infected by, the obvious crisis in the existence of the Anglican Communion. It is tempting to turn aside from these realities to the seemingly hopeful world of reunion negotiations. It is tempting, and, as I have said, it is in a measure made possible by the eager passion for unity that Henderson takes too lightly; but it is escape nonetheless into a world of make-believe—a world in which good men incline too easily to think that they have fulfilled the will of God by ignoring the realities of history.

In two passages in his book, Henderson touches on the important topic of the relations between the Church of Scotland and the tiny, fiercely traditionalist Free Church of Scotland, standing over against the Kirk in the Highland area. He makes it very plain that part of the reason for the continuing strength of that Free Church in that area must be sought in the terrible story of the Highland Clearances. There are those who will write this book off as the mere expression of Scottish nationalist sentiment. But how many, one wonders, of those who attended the Holland House Conference could tell of the trial of Patrick Sellar, to which Professor Henderson refers, and could dare to suggest—as he does in a very interesting passage towards the end of the book—that even at this midnight hour for the Highlands, the Church of Scotland and Free Church might find a new road to friendship in a resolute common effort to face the whole issue of the Highland economy. If Anglicans are to speak with men of the Church of Scotland, they should be reminded of these things and respect the man who does ask just how they suppose a contrived reunion will serve the cause of flesh and blood humanity in the Highlands and in the Western Isles. There is an earthy quality in this book, an obstinate, attractive awareness of complexities. It will be the greatest pity if its rollicking, slangy method of presentation is allowed to obscure its underlying importance. I admit I find some of it uncongenial, and I should like to express my deep regret that in the pen picture of the late Professor James Pitt-Watson in the chapter on the Coronation, which mentions his romantic attachment to royalty and his ecumenical ardour, no mention is made of the great courage which he displayed in the autumn of 1956 at the time of the Suez Crisis. In debate in the General Assembly in 1954, he had defended the "just war" tradition against the pacifists. When he believed that tradition violated by Anglo-French armed intervention in October 1956, in defence of their alleged rights over the Suez Canal, he said so openly in a way that was certainly costing to one who was temperamentally conservative. While many Christians have used the tradition of the just war as a way of making respectable their adherence to the amoralism of "my country, right or wrong," Pitt-Watson was not of their number. And though he may have been a little starry-eyed when he went to Westminster Abbey for the Coronation in June 1953, in the harsher hour of 1956, he showed a steadfastness for which many hold his name in reverence. One gathers he did not meet with entire sympathy in the presbytery of Glasgow at that time.

However, I know that, by and large, I must take Henderson's book seriously because it is a call to deeper self-knowledge, a call to honesty, even to repentance. He asks for an intermission to all Anglican-Presbyterian conversations in these islands for a quarter of a century; here he is not likely to have his way—and he knows it. But it would be very sad if the grounds of his plea are dismissed as little more than an outburst of bad temper. Perhaps a period of silence would be a good thing, even a period of prayer and a truce to conference. We do not need the bustle of contriving ecclesiastics so much as the recollected silence of men and women seeking to remove from their hearts what stands in the way of complete mutual acceptance.

Ave crux, spes unica. I want to suggest that in the field of interchurch relations, the fruit of this very simple, very fundamental confession of faith should be found in a readiness to sit down and learn—not to contrive, but to give oneself to learning: to learning of the flesh and blood Christian experience of those within a different tradition from one's own, gladly accepting the opportunity to receive the sacrament of the Lord's body and blood from their ministers. We must bear with them as they are, and their antagonism to our own ethos is something that we must train ourselves fully to understand. We must not suggest that, out of contrivance on the part of ingenious and skillful men, devoted to their role but inevitably identifying themselves with it, what may only be won through a discipline of acceptance, through admission of pride and eagerness for power can, by less costing methods, be achieved almost in a few hours. "It is better to give than to receive." Who was the wit who said he was glad, as it was certainly so much easier? Can Anglicans learn to receive, not insights simply, but Christian men and women as their teachers of the complexity of the world upon which Christ set the mark of his sovereignty, when alone among the sons of men, himself the Son of Man, he laid all power aside and, at once the man for God and the man for men, on his cross established that place where past bitternesses are not forgotten—no, not forgotten, nor overlooked—but made new, which is very different?

BBC Third Program, June 1967

Chapter 6: The Controversial Bishop Bell

It was to George Bell that, in 1946, Dietrich Bonhoeffer's parents gave the copy of the *Imitatio Christi* that had been with him in captivity, in the Nazi prison where the famous *Letters from Prison* were written.[12] A few months before Bell had learned that he was not—as very many outside as well as within the Church of England had hoped—to succeed William Temple as Primate of All England. On July 16, 1928, a little more than four years after Bell had become Dean of Canterbury, William Ralph Inge had written of him: "George Bell is a wonderful man. If I were Baldwin, I would pass over all the old bishops and send him to Lambeth. Everyone except Cosmo would be delighted."

Yet thirty years later, when he died, the man whom Inge had thus regarded as already suitable to succeed his former friend and master in the primacy had been for twenty-nine years bishop of Chichester; the same man who received from Bonhoeffer's family a precious relic of the devotional life of one of the men most surely regarded as formative of the Christian mind of the present age. If Christian faith survives in the twenty-first century, Bonhoeffer, by his writings and by his faithfulness unto death, may well be judged one of the men who made its survival possible. Among his mentors, and his closest friends, was George Bell—a man called to serve as chaplain at Lambeth in the

12. It should be added that at the time the script was written, the author had not obtained a copy of Dr. Eberhard Bethge's great *Life of Dietrich Bonhoeffer*, published in 1967 in Germany and to appear in due course in English translation; this work contains much extremely interesting material on a Bonhoeffer's relation with Bell. While none of this material seems to demand a correction of statements made in judgments passed in the text, it remains true that no one reading Bethge's work can fail to have his sense of Bonhoeffer's great indebtedness to Bell enlarged and deepened. In it, we learn also of the extent to which the prisoner whose *Letters from Prison* are now so widely influential was, in the years during which they were written, constantly in the bishop's prayers; more constantly, one suspects, in his mind than in that of any other single person, except the member of Bonhoeoffer's own family and those engaged with him in various ways in the struggle in Germany, to which he returned in the late summer of 1939 and in which in the end he met his death.

months immediately before the First World War. He was called to serve at a Lambeth, whose style and manner he has superbly captured in his own great biography of Randall Davidson, a place utterly different from the Stockholm where he saw Bonhoeffer in 1942, and still more from the Flossenburg where his German friend faced his last ordeal. If you like, Bell bridges the gulf between those two worlds. But he does very much, more than supply a formal link between them, establish a sort of ritual continuity between past and present. In his own way, in his own circumstances, he endured the cost of the transition between the two. It was for this reason, we may say, that Davidson's former chaplain understood Bonhoeffer in some ways much more profoundly than the self-confident avant-garde "nonreligious" of today who claim too lightly to be his disciples.

The irony is further deepened when we remember that one of the places in which this depth of understanding was supremely demonstrated in action was the House of Lords. For it was in that setting that Bell delivered his speeches in criticism of the policy of strategic bombing—in that setting where indeed, even in the circumstances of 1943 and 1944, they were bound to have a far profounder impact than, for instance, they would have had they been made at the Chichester Diocesan Conference. As his biographer, Canon R. C. D. Jasper suggests these speeches marked a watershed in Bell's career. So much prepared the way for their delivery: the years of ecumenical activity, his parochial and diocesan experience, his long and complex involvement in the German Church struggle, even his sense of the establishment of the Church of England as providing a context within which it might exercise a genuinely prophetic responsibility towards the national life. And after the speeches had been given, nothing could ever be the same for the speaker again. The return to Lambeth as primate was simply out. But much more than that—the speaker decisively showed himself as the man who had proclaimed the way of the post-Constantinian Church of the future in a setting curiously eloquent of the hopes that first flooded the Christian mind in the remote fourth century. If you like, he tested the moral significance of the establishment to destruction. Yet, of course, Bell knew that he was in his action continuing, in a changed context, the witness that Archbishop Davidson had very courageously borne in the same House of Lords in the matter of reprisals for the zeppelin raids of the First World War. Here is a most significant element in historical continuity that one may easily overlook. When all was said and done, Randall Davidson was a great man, with a truly great man's capacity for growth. No one knew this better than his biographer, and perhaps he saw himself at first as doing no more than continuing into the Second World War the tradition his master had established in the First.

But it is with Bell, the man himself, that I am concerned in this talk—even with the deeper cost to himself, because he was the sort of man he was, of the witness he tried to bear. At first sight, there is sheer contradiction between his unwillingness to endorse the methods adopted in a supreme emergency to defeat an implacable and monstrous foe and his early awareness of the depth of evil embodied in the Nazis. Again, in his meeting with Bonhoeffer at Stockholm, he learned of the beginnings of a conspiracy, which on July 20, 1944 revealed itself to all the world as committed to an act, or indeed to acts, of political assassination. It is not for nothing that R. H. S. Crossman remarked that the only work in the English language really to engage with the moral issues of that plot was Shakespeare's *Julius Caesar*, a work that plumbs to the depths the real ambiguities of political assassination. But Bell had not shrunk, more than two years earlier, from commending this conspiracy at the highest level. Yet deeply aware though he was, before very many in these islands, of the moral and spiritual enormity of Hitlerism, he wrote to the *Times* in the anxious days in 1938, between Godesberg and Munich, pleading the cause of settlement rather than justice, emphasizing the small difference between what Chamberlain had accepted in principle at Berchtesgaden and what was demanded the following week on the Rhine. The champion of the German Confessional Church appeared among the advocates of appeasement, at a time when Temple urged Christians to pray for justice rather than peace.

Oh yes! There is contradiction all right. His biographer is right to mention the favorable impression the subsequently convicted murderer Joachim von Ribbentrop made on him at their first meeting on November 6, 1934 in the Athenaeum. He was not always, by any means, a good judge of men, and he displayed on occasion just a little of what Halifax's biographer, Lord Birkenhead, has recently characterized as one of Halifax's besetting weaknesses, an unwillingness to recognize the naked reality of evil. But Dr. Ulrich Simon dedicated his somber, yet profound *Theology of Auschwitz* to the memories of George Bell and Victor Gollancz. Although Canon Jasper seems to shrink in his biography from presenting Bell "warts and all," his work is sufficiently minute in detailed information to enable the reader to perceive some of his subject's flaws. We are, after all, dealing with a human being: one certainly, in my judgment, to be regarded as an authentic apostle, but, as such, condemned to know the one abiding law of an authentic, as distinct from a merely formalized, apostolicity—the law summarized by Paul when he spoke of those who were "deceivers and yet true" and of himself as "one whose strength was made perfect in weakness."

Bell saw very clearly the problem of the means—saw the problem with the clarity that only comes to the man who does not simply look on a problem from afar, but who acts in respect of it. Where his judgment on strategic bombing was concerned, he had formidable support in letters from one of the most percipient authorities on strategy and armament in the United Kingdom—Sir Basil Liddell Hart, a man with a rather frightening capacity for being technically right in his judgments in these fields. Bell did not show himself as simply an ecclesiastical jackass intruding on a layman's preserve of which he knew nothing; he showed himself possibly endowed with that kind of intuitive perception that, in a democracy, is constantly and rightly regarded as a necessary check on the tendency of the experts to assume a kind of moral sovereignty over the man in the street—over those whom Bell called in the doggerel verses he wrote about his career, the "Nobodies."

Yet even if the deep encouragement of Liddell Hart's letters had not been forthcoming, Bell would have gone on—doggedly, obstinately, with that kind of certainty, at once interrogative and persistent, that is one mark of what may be judged *prima facie* to be authentically apostolic. So in 1943, the Dean of Chichester—A. S. Duncan-Jones, who had in 1938 published with Gollancz a valuable account of the German Church struggle—had to tell Bell that he would not make a suitable preacher for "Battle of Britain" Sunday in Chichester Cathedral. And of course there were other weightier consequences.

Canon Jasper's biography is very valuable in that it shows clearly the detail of the life of his subject. If someone goes back to his book after reading or seeing the memorable scene in Hochhuth's play *Soldiers*[13] in which the author brings Bell into Churchill's presence to argue the moral issues of the strategic bombing policy, he will feel himself plunged into the world of characteristically Anglican diocesan administration. Of course, the European historian will find highly significant material relating to the German Church struggle, but Hochhuth's drama belongs to a different world from, let us say, the problems of ecclesiastical discipline in Brighton in the years following the rejection of the Deposited Book, the height of the Anglo-Catholic demand for a developed extra-liturgical cultus of the Reserved Sacrament, even from Bishop Bell's later involvement with N. P. Williams over projects of reform in the relations of church and state in England. These references indeed evoke the atmosphere of the narrower, more specialized, more peculiarly clerical styles of ecclesiastical controversy and excitement. Yet this was part, and an important part, of Bell's world. In a way, indeed, the deep student of his life can trace the continuity between his disciplinary policy where "Devotions" was concerned, his concern for a measured autonomy for the established Church of England, and the sort of spirituality—I use the word advisedly—expressed and caught in this imagined, yet at the same time deeply informative, confrontation with Churchill.

13. The German text of Rolf Hochhuth's play *Soldaten* is published by Rowohlt; English translation published by Andre Deutsch, 1968. See also Appendix, 236-38.

As I say, Jasper's greatest virtue is in his capacity for relating detailed information. In terms of personal appraisal, his writing has a curiously hollow quality. For instance, his treatment of Bell's marriage and obviously very happy home life, although it is not perfunctory, remains almost conventional. Perhaps where matters so intimate are concerned, this was inevitable. Yet all the time, one has the feeling that here is the material for a great biography rather than that biography itself. If you read it, as I did, before reading Hochhuth's scene—and I am talking about this scene in the play, not, I insist, the play as a whole—and then read that scene, you will, I think, be deeply disturbed by the latter, but you will also be electrified. For suddenly in this man, often out-argued, aware of the contradictions in his position, you see someone who, out of the assured ambience of the Church of England at its most self-consciously influential, came to belong with Dietrich Bonhoeffer—more fittingly laureate with the gift of that surely precious *Imitatio* than with the primatial dignity.

You will be disturbed because Hochhuth makes you feel the ambiguities of Bell's position—its ambivalences, its contradictions; here was this man spared the bitterest experiences of the war, whose objectives certainly included the survival of elementary human decencies, daring to criticize military enterprises costlier than any other in the toll they exacted of precious human lives. The laity rates in Bomber Command were higher in proportion to the total number of men engaged in its work than that of any other branch of the services. What earthly right had a man living as Bell lived to seem to criticize the men who died as they did? I say "to seem to criticize" for he pleads part of the time that he is criticizing not them, but the policies they are implementing, the calculated indifference to the lives of noncombatant men, women and children—noncombatant in the sense in which the aged, the disabled, the six-months pregnant and the unweaned must surely be judged such. And he argues on—stumbling, hesitant, and almost regretful. He is nearly defeated in the argument; one senses that he comes to think he has no leg to stand on. It is in his very compassion that he is undermined, by the suggestion that that compassion is born of his relative security from the fearful experience that was the frequent lot of the men who did the actual work in the Hamburg fire raid of 1943 or the later bombing of Dresden. What right had he to speak of a problem of means? Only the right belonging to a strength made perfect in weakness.

To speak in these terms is not to indulge in a recent, perhaps still fashionable cult of failure or despair. A man's actions are in one respect μιμησεις. Imitations and intimations of his own reality—a reality that is a matter of social inheritance and environment as well as of personal endowment. They are such intimations, and such reflections, even as they also, because they are actions, sometimes profoundly affect the reality from which they spring. So with the witness of George Bell. It was essentially an English, an Anglican, fidelity, and it has a great deal of the ambiguity that irritates the more direct Christian spirits about the characteristically Anglican thing. Jasper gives his readers an account of the setting that made Bell's witness what it was: Hochhuth reveals in his fiction something of the cost to the witness, a cost he had to pay in his own Anglican spiritual currency. He did pay it in full, and therefore we call him beyond dispute of apostolic stamp. And of the authenticity of that payment, the gift of Bonhoeffer's *Imitatio* was surely the sign.

But actions do not leave the world as it was, and this, of course, goes for patronage secretaries *et hoc genus omne* as well as for lesser and for greater men. For the Church of England, Bell's life is most surely a sign of things already coming upon it. Within the framework of the establishment—in which for most, though not, I have good reason for saying, all of his life he believed—he heralded, indeed he lived out existentially, the approach of post-Constantinian Christianity. The Dutch Augustinian Father Robert Adolfs has suggested that the church that is coming to be is one that will view the whole history of the Christian Church from the fourth century as a kind of collective experience of the far country in which the prodigal spent his inheritance with harlots.[14] Where the Church of England is concerned,

14. Adolfs, *The Grave of God*, 109.

the feel of its peculiar far country may be caught in the Athenaeum rather than in the very different clubs associated with the name of Soho, but the former club is province of that same delightful, and in the end spiritually destructive land. Although Bell was in a sense always quite at home in that province—he had grown up in it and, to a large extent, he accepted it as relatively excellent—he also knew himself a citizen of another country, whose laws and demands were in increasingly sharp conflict with those of the province he knew. The laws and demands were in conflict with the familiar routine—yes—but the content of these laws and demands is far from clear. So he stumbled, even lapsing into the sad silence of a man defeated in argument. Yet in his apostolate, he both achieved for himself a painful self-knowledge and also, by the very sharpness with which he expressed the contradictions of his way, he brought the future nearer. It is for this reason that he is one of the most significant figures in the history of the Anglican Communion in this century; it is for this reason also—and this in the end is much more important—that like Bonhoeffer himself, by his witness he confirmed the weaker, more accommodating faith of lesser men. And if we find him in the end silent, even evasive, are we wrong to hear across the centuries the echo of another interrogation—"Answerest thou nothing? Knowest thou not that I have power to release thee and power to crucify thee?" What we cannot speak about, that we must assign to silence (to quote Wittgenstein). Yet silence is the most eloquent witness of all.

BBC Third Program, November 1967

Appendix

On Thursday, December 12, 1968, a very effectively abridged English version of Hochhuth's play commenced a run at the New Theatre in London. Those who have seen this version and who have been able to avert their attention, even temporarily, from the author's unfortunate obsession with his (in my view) extremely implausible solution of the mystery of General Sikorski's death, will recall that in Bell's long and extremely complex argument with Churchill in the third act, the bishop is finally defeated as a result of his petulant and grossly unfair comparison of a bomber pilot responsible for the death of young children in the Hamburg "fire storm" raid of 1943 with a pathological rapist who violates a girl of seven in a public park and afterwards murders her in an effort to conceal his identity. Earlier in the act, Churchill had shown himself as a man weighed down by the multitude of decisions facing him as supreme executive in Britain's war effort, and oppressed by his sense of the menace of the future. Indeed, he had come to the verge of inviting the bishop's counsel and pastoral help in his genuinely anguished perplexity. But Churchill—knowing the extraordinary courage of the airmen thus criticized, who face a terrible death night after night in the line of combatant duty—is quite properly outraged by Bell's words and asks him immediately to leave. So the bishop goes, defeated by his weakness, his mission unaccomplished, even the pastoral ministry Churchill almost invited him to offer in his own deep uncertainties, unfulfilled. It is tragic failure on Bell's part; the flaw in his equipment, namely his inability to effectively sustain an argument in a way at once assimilable by his opponent and profoundly challenging to that opponent's assumptions, is disastrously proved. He is thus thrust back on the υαρτυρία of a powerless silence at a deeper level undefeated, having indeed defined by his protest more poignantly than ever his great opponent's own tragedy. Yet by his acceptance of that failure (an acceptance that acknowledges his own defeat, not that of his cause), he points beyond himself to the sense that, for Christian faith, is ultimately to be found (in a manner unfathomable to human ratiocination) in the stuff of human tragedy through the finally tragic failure of its passion. "Answerest thou nothing?" Whatever ones verdict on Hochhuth's technical skill as a dramatist, or on the obsession with the Sikorski affair, which obscures his very probing of Churchill's involvement in the bitter dilemma that faced him over Poland, this third act of the English version of his play is ethically and theologically highly significant. It is a comment, achieved through an imagined dialogue between two great antagonists who never thus faced each other, that highlights at once their personal significance and (for the Christian) the deepest lessons to be gleaned from the history of George Bell's apostolate, and that, at the same time, draws our perception down to the unacknowledged, tragic depths of human existence, where the standards of ordinary moral judgment are not abrogated, but rather turned now one way, now another as the metaphysical import of the issues that engage men and women, and of the men and women engaged by those issues, are partly laid bare. We are deprived of the facile consolation of any sort of "happy ending" (though we are given practical lessons for the future), but we are enabled to pierce the screen of human history towards the place where its extremities are focused in a cry for redemption. A cry that is answered not by the advent of a deus ex machina but by the coming among men of one "whom they know not"; who indeed, when they partly know, they will contrive to destroy, thus not only revealing the lie in their own souls, but ensuring irretrievable disaster for Christ's mission. Yet in this irretrievable disaster is our peace.

December 20, 1968

Select Bibliography of MacKinnon's Works

"Vexilla Regis: Some Reflections for Passiontide, 1939." *Theology* 38 (Apr. 1939): 254–59.

"Surveys: Christian Social Thought." *Theology* 38 (May 1939): 378–82.

"No Way Back: Some First Principles of Catholic Social Judgment Restated." *Christendom* 9 (Sept. 1939): 292–98.

God the Living and the True. London: Dacre Press, 1940.

"Flesh and Blood Have Not Revealed It Unto Thee." *Theology* 40 (June 1940): 426–31.

The Church of God. London: Dacre Press, 1940.

"What is a Metaphysical Statement?" *Proceedings of the Aristotelian Society* 41 (1940–41): 1–26.

"The Nature of a Christian Sociology." *The Student Movement* (May 1941).

"Christianity and Justice." *Theology* 42 (June 1941): 348–54.

"Survey of Devotional Books." *Theology* 45 (Aug. 1942): 107–10.

"Where Do We Go From Here?" *Blackfriars* 23 (Sept. 1942): 353–58.

"Some Questions for Anglicans." *Christendom* 13 (June 1943): 108–11.

"Some Reflections on Democracy." *Christendom* 13 (June 1944): 175–77.

"The Moral Significance of the Atomic Bomb." *Humanitas* 2 (Autumn 1948): 26–29.

"The Nature of the Christian Hope." *Ecumenical Review* 4 (Apr. 1952): 293–95.

"Christian Optimism: Scott Holland and Contemporary Needs." *Theology* 55 (Nov. 1952): 407-12.

Christian Faith and Communist Faith: A Series of Studies by Members of the Anglican Communion. (editor) London: MacMillan, 1953.

A Study in Ethical Theory, London. A&C Black, 1957.

"Some Notes on 'Philosophy of History' and the Problems of Human Society." In *The Logic of Personal Knowledge: Essays Presented to Michael Polanyi on his Seventieth Birthday*, 171–78. London: Routledge and Kegan Paul, 1961.

"Teilhard de Chardin: A Comment on his Context and Significance." *The Modern Churchman* 5 (1962): 195–99.

"God and the Theologians 2: Grammar and Theologic." *Encounter* (Oct. 21, 1963): 60–61.

Preface to *The Divinity of Jesus Christ*, by J. M. Creed, 7–11. London: Collins, 1964.

"Teilhard's Vision." *Frontier* 8 (1965): 169–71.

"Aristotle's Conception of Substance." In *New Essays on Plato and Aristotle*, edited by R. Bambrough, 97–119. London: Routledge & Kegan Paul, 1965.

The Resurrection: A Dialogue Arising from Broadcasts, with G. W. H. Lampe. Edited by W. Purcell. London: A. R. Mowbray, 1966.

"Can a Divinity Professor be Honest?" *The Cambridge Review* 89 (Nov. 12, 1966): 94–96.

"What Sort of Radicalism?" *Frontier* 11 (1968): 116–17.

Borderlands of Theology and Other Essays, edited by G. W. Roberts and D. E. Smucker. London: Lutterworth Press, 1968.

The Problem of Metaphysics. Cambridge: Cambridge University Press, 1974.

Introduction to *Engagement with God*, by Hans Urs von Balthasar, 1–16. Edited by E. L. Mascall, translated by J. Halliburton. London: SPCK, 1975.

"The Relation of the Doctrines of the Incarnation and the Trinity." In *Creation, Christ and Culture: Studies in Honour of T. F. Torrance*, edited by R. W. A. McKinney, 92–107. Edinburgh: T&T Clark, 1976.

Explorations in Theology 5. London: SCM, 1979.

"Reflections on Mortality." *The Scottish Journal of Religious Studies* 1.1 (Spring 1980): 40–44.

Creon and Antigone: Ethical Problems of Nuclear Warfare. The Boutwood Lectures for 1981. London: The Menard Press, 1982.

"Prolegomena to Christology." *Journal of Theological Studies* 33 (Apr. 1982): 146–60.

"The Spanish Civil War 1936–9: Catholicism's Minority Voice." *New Blackfriars* (Nov. 1986): 494–98.

"Eternal Loss." *New Blackfriars* (Nov. 1988): 472–78.

"On Comprehending the Threat." In *The Nuclear Weapons Debate: Theological and Ethical Issues*, edited by R. J. Bauckham and R. J. Elford, 6–15. London: SCM, 1989.

"Aspects of Kant's Influence on British Theology." In *Kant and His Influence*, edited by G. M. Ross and T. McWalter, 348–66. Bristol: Thoemmes Antiquarian Publishing, 1990.

"Intellect and Imagination." In *The Weight of Glory: A Vision and Practice for Christian Faith. The Future of Liberal Theology. Essays for Peter Baelz*, edited by D. W. Hardy and P. H. Sedgwick, 29–35. Edinburgh: T&T Clark, 1991.

"Collingwood on the Philosophy of Religion." *The Scottish Journal of Religious Studies* 13 (1992): 73–83.

"Reflections on Donald Baillie's Treatment of the Atonement." In *Christ, Church and Society: Essays on John Baillie and Donald Baillie*, edited by D. Fergusson, 115–21. Edinburgh: T&T Clark, 1993.

Themes in Theology. Edinburgh: T&T Clark, 1996.

Philosophy and the Burden of Theological Honesty, edited by John C. McDowell, with the assistance of Scott A. Kirkland. London: T&T Clark, 2011.

Index

9 781451 49628
Printed at Repro India Ltd.